The Philosophy  *of*
Dr. Amartya S... *...phy*

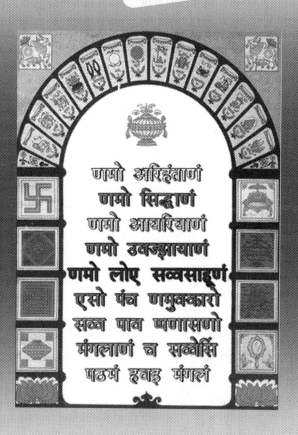

णमो अरिहंताणं
णमो सिद्धाणं
णमो आयरियाणं
णमो उवज्झायाणं
णमो लोए सव्वसाहूणं
एसो पंच णमुक्कारो
सव्व पाव प्पणासणो
मंगलाणं च सव्वेसिं
पढमं हवइ मंगलं

Dr K R Shah

The Philosophy of welfare economics of Dr.Amartya Sen and Jain Philosophy

Author: - Dr. K R Shah

ISBN: 978-1-4269-5023-0 (sc)
ISBN: 978-1-4269-5024-7 (e)

Trafford rev. 01/20/2011

 www.trafford.com

North America & international
toll-free: 1 888 232 4444 (USA & Canada)
phone: 250 383 6864 ♦ fax: 812 355 4082

This work is dedicated to

> ➤ My wife, *HARSUTA*, who is a persistent brook of encouragement throughout my life in general and particularly for my Ph.D. thesis.

> ➤ My son *VIKAS*, helping me in my all work as a good friend and adviser.

CONTENTS

PREFACE

The researcher is Jain by birth and lived with Jain surrounding in the state of Gujarat and in the state of Maharashtra in India. The researcher has deep rooted Jain culture in his blood. The Jain philosophy was taught to him at the age of five and received his preliminary and intermediate knowledge reaching the age of twelve. The higher education, marriage and family responsibility had kept him away from religious study and activity during major period of his life span. Researcher studied the courses in Jain philosophy from university of Mumbai. Researcher took intensive interest in Jain philosophy for more than three years after completing his diploma course in Jainology. The keen inquisitive nature and to make use of educational qualification of master degree in economics and study in management courses resulted in idea of research work. The welfare of human in material term and spiritual term is the supreme priority today in this miserable world. Dr.Amartya Sen gave a new presentation to economic fabric by weaving the new idea of welfare in it. Earlier the economics was considered as science. This thinking has changed after incorporating philosophical approach in it. It is understood that a HUMAN has to get change himself, rather than changing the laws of science. This was the most challenging task for the researcher to highlight the welfare term in economics and welfare term in Jain religion.

Researcher selected four concepts from four books of Dr.Amartya Sen which are most concerned for the welfare of human. The first concept of choice and welfare is the basic thing regarding how the human makes a choice in economics. The right and wrong notion about choice and ultimately the benefit of choice to human with the help of agency in his well being and welfare by way of planning and policy in governing system with the help of elected representatives at all level.

The second concept is regarding capability and development as freedom. Here Dr.Amartya Sen has considered the development of capability of person is the sole welfare for human and its development is the freedom. Ultimately every human being wants the freedom and not slavery. Development in terms of freedom is the true welfare of human.

The existence of disparity in world is the root cause of unhappiness in the masses. The heterodoxy in the society, high and low class in the society, cast and creed, power in terms of politics, economics and deep-seated idea of superiority and inferiority are the hurdles in the way of welfare for human in this world. The inequality is the perfect point to discuss and find out the solution. Dr.Amartya Sen had discussed the subject very elaborately and given the remedies for the same.

Dr.Amartya Sen was moved by the very scene of communal conflict, where a labourer had gone for daily wage earning, was stabbed in riot. The poverty and hunger is present in this world from the beginning and no one is able to eradicate it from this world due to various reasons. The poverty and famine are related to each other in different sense. Poverty is the result of lack of entitlement and famine is the natural calamities. Entitlement can be arranged and famine can be prevented with advance information and timely measure for prevention of it. In both the cases, poor is the sufferer. The governing agency has to decide proper policy and implement it whole heartedly in benefit of people, who are below poverty line. The welfare of these people is the concern of economics. Dr.Amartya Sen has studied the causes and effects of famine in light of six great famines of world which had accrued at different time.

I have selected four concepts of Jain religion, which are the most appropriate and relevant for the welfare of human in material as well as in spiritual term.

AHIMSA PARMO DHARMA- Researcher believes that dharma means to follow the right thing in life. Non-killing is the supreme religion. Jain religion believes in this principle. This is the mother of all virtues. Non-killing is the centre from where all the threads of good things start and weave a nice fabric. Non-killing is the main blessing for human to get control on all his psychological activities and all physical activities. The karma existence will be negligible. No karma or negligible karmas become rapid course of action for emancipation. Human is having lot of benefits by adopting the vow of non-killing. Lord Mahavir practised non-killing throughout his life and preached his followers to follow the same. Non-killing will bring peace in the world, makes human to understand the situation better, creates brotherhood. Non-killing gives birth to non-stealing, not to speak lie, observe celibacy and not to hoard more than necessacity things required for life.

The second concept is related to karma. All the activities of body and mind attract the karma as per Jain philosophy. You have to experience the effect of karma as you are the doer of it. Karma gives you pleasure and pain. The karma is the main cause of transmigration for living beings. The good karmas can give you an opportunity to have birth as Tirthankar. The auspicious karmas will result in the form of birth as 1) celestial body, as 2) human and 3) infernal and 4) Tiriyanch body due to inauspicious karmas. You can emancipate your soul only in human birth. You can stop karmas coming to the soul and burned them too. You have to get rid of all eight types of karma for emancipation of your soul as per Jain philosophy. Emancipation will give eternal bliss and no rebirth.

The third concept is of non-possessiveness. Possessiveness is the root cause of all quarrels. Possessiveness is the root cause of inequality. Possessiveness is the root cause of degradation of environment. This bad habit gets converted into greed. Person does all sorts of wrong things due to greed. Human does not acknowledge the existence of other human. The universe turns into hell. Peace will be nowhere in this world. Human has no limit for his desire. The Moral and ethics are kept at distance. This spoils the entire atmosphere of spirituality.

The fourth concept is of Anekantvada-many-sidedness. This is a part of logic and a part of pramana in knowledge. Here lord Mahavir has given a magical formula to human, how to respect others' view and cultivate the habit of seeing negative and positive points in the same thing. This is very useful in today's atmosphere of conflicting world. This will give a key to human to avoid the situation of conflict and to create a peaceful atmosphere. This has many other benefits as you transform it in to a predication form. The many-sidedness works at all level in big as well as small enterprises, institutions and departments. This works in industry as well in service sector. This works in government as well as in private sector. It has literary application in which you can travel from general nature of a thing to particular nature of a thing by way of application of nayas.

All four concepts are the pillars of Jain philosophy and logically explain the religion to human. The world can experience peace and prosperity. The Jain religion talks about present, past and future birth of a person. Jain religion gives satisfactory explanation about everything including the birth, death through karma theory. Jain religion shows the way to get out of the cycle of birth and death, one who desires. Jain religion shows the way for emancipation of soul as ultimate goal of human.

I have made a few changes in some of the chapters and have edited my thesis for this print version.

I am highly gratified for the great generosity of Dr.Amartya Sen, who has kindly allowed me to use his four books as chapters in my thesis and further make use of them for the print version.

I would like to express my appreciation for the general guidance which I received while discussing the structure of the thesis as well as the valuable, important suggestions on each and every chapter from my beloved guide Prof. Nitin J.Vyas. I acknowledge with deep gratitude the constant assistance and co-operation that I have received from Dr. (Kumari) Utpla Mody. She has also read the final version of the manuscript and corrected me where necessary.   I have been very fortunate for the comments and suggestions made by my friends. I am thankful to Federation of Jain Association in North America known as JAINA of U.S.A., Jain Academy, Shri Kunthunath Swami Jain Foundation, and Shree Vardhman Sthanakwasi Yuvak Mandal Charitable Trust, all from Mumbai for helping me morally and financially to complete my thesis in three years time. I could not complete this work without the help and continuous encouragement from my beloved wife Harsuta and my enthusiastic younger son Vikas at London. They have given me full support, co-operation and mental peace to finish my work.

The style of writing can be considered as that of research work but my guide wants it to be on the map of the world as a critical study book. I hope that my work will be well received by the circle of intelligent and critical study groups within the society.

K.R.SHAH

1 Introduction of the Thesis

1.1 Introduction-Philosophy

Every philosophical thought of school has two branches, ethics and metaphysics. Ethics relates to the code of conduct, metaphysics refers to the mode of thinking. As person becomes perfect in ethical value, life grows on the foundation of a deeper insight, which proves to be wisdom and not error, because it is workable.

When you look at the history of philosophy, you can make out that Plato and Aristotle took help of politics and ethics, in Middle age, the philosophers took help of theology and in 19th century Newton and Bacon took help of history, politics and science. Indian philosophy had not taken any thought from any of the above sciences but developed on account of bounty of nature and predominantly land protected by Himalayan Range in North, East; in West and South by sea. Indian philosophy is spiritual in nature. Indian philosophy developed by intuitions of sagas.

The curious mind is more of an imitation of something natural where as scientific mind is more of reasons. The result of science is visible. The philosophical thoughts are abstract. Scientific disputes do seem resolvable, many moral disputes do not. Aristotle likes to point out that first of all, our morality is an essential feature of our circumstances as human being.[1]

Darsana is the nearest equivalent meaning of philosophy in Indian tradition. It is however important to note that Darsana is the most popularly

---

[1]   Martha Nussbaum Book: - Moral disagreements classic and contemporary reading Edited by Christopher W. Gowans. Page no. 178

accepted "equivalent" to philosophy in India.[2] Kanada in Vaisesika Sutra used the 'Darsana' as philosophical knowledge. Haribhadra, A Jain saint and writer of various books on Jain philosophy had used this word in 6th century in his book titled "SAD DARSAN-SAMUCCAYA".[3] Eight centuries latter, a renowned Vedantin Madhavacarya summarized fifteen schools of philosophy in a work called "SARVA DARSAN SAMGRAH".[4] The book "sarvasiddhantasarasamgraha" of SAMKARA and book "prasthananabheda" by Madhusudana Sarasvati had written on different philosophies.[5] Dr.S.Radhakrishnan says "For the Hindus a system of philosophy is an insight, darsana. It is the vision of truth and not a matter of logical argument and proof." [6]

"The Buddhist tripitakas (400B.C.), Called the heretical opinions ditthi (dṛsti in Sanskrit from the same root "Drs" from which darsana is formed)" "The Jain thinkers had fixed the meaning of darsana as a system of philosophical thought".[7] Here 'Seeing' is in sense of receiving visual sensation, followed by the mind working on them and converting them into perception. Dr.S.Radhakrishnan puts it that "the perception includes within its scope, conceptual knowledge and intuitional experience".[8]

1.2   The philosophy of welfare economics of Dr. Amartya Sen

Ethics teach man "HOW" he should be rather than "WHAT" he should be. The ethic is in Economics, Sociology, and Psychology. The ethics is a code of conduct. Now a days "WELFARE" in   economics is an ethical aspect. it is necessary to find out right meaning of the welfare, In the light of philosophical approach to economics.

---

2   Translated by K.Satischandra Murty, Book; - English Translation of 'SADDARSAN   SAMUCCAY' by Haribhadra.

3   K.Satischandra Murty, Book: - 'philosophy of India' page no. 3-7

4   English translations by E.B.Gowell and A.I.Gousg 'Sarva darsan samgrah of Madhvacharya' Edited by K.L. Joshi

5   S Radhakrishnan, Book: - An idealist view of man, page no. 122

6   ibid, page no. 100

7   Nathmal Tatia book: - Studies in Jain philosophy, PhD .Thesis year 1951. page no.149.

8   S. Radhakrishnan Book- Indian Philosophy vol.1, page no. 43

A dictionary meaning -The term welfare in economics is the health, happiness and fortune of person or group, organized efforts designated to promote the basic well being of people in need. One has to analyze this in subjective as well as in objective manner. The welfare of human is most important task for economists. "The economist, like everyone else, must concern himself with the ultimate aims of man"—Alfred Marshall. Earlier it was thought that individual and society will have maximum benefit in market regulated economy. Welfare economics think on the line of maximizing the human happiness without making others to suffer.

Jeremy Bentham born in 1748 and died in 1808 considered as RADICAL philosopher. His philosophy divided in to two. (1) Association principle and (2) Greatest-happiness principle.[11] We can define this as "VIRTUES". Ethics is necessary because men's desire and conflict is a cause of egoism.

Pareto was an Italian economist. First he thought for welfare of man. He took the welfare in individual term. He thought in terms of "OPTIMAL" which was a goal. The Pareto formula is as follows.[9]

- If everyone in the society is indifferent between two alternative social situations X and Y, then the society should be indifferent too;

- If at least one individual strictly prefers X to Y, and every other individual regards X to be at least as good as Y, then the society should prefer X to Y.

- The Pareto optimality is "in a given choice situation, consider the set of alternatives X from which choice should have to be made. An alternative X belonging to that set will be described as Pareto optimal if there is no other alternative in the set which is Pareto-wise better than X."[10]

Marshal agreed for MORALITY. Prostitution is not a productive activity as per Marshal, but an immoral activity. Hare, Rawel, Harsanyi and Kenneth Arrow were distinguished economists to think in term of welfare. Rawls' variation of the approach leads to principles of justice, which give a particularly high priority to the least well-off group in society. Kenneth

---

[9]   Amartya Sen, Book: - collective choice and social welfare, Page No.21
[10]   Ibid, Page no.21.

Arrow was most accepted economist in this area. His "impossible theorem" was a landmark in welfare economics.

EDWARD J. GREEN: - [11] The Malthusian population Theory is in confrontation with the rapid transfer of technology to third world societies in the past several decades. This transfer indicates that groups of people who have traditionally enjoyed a low level of material welfare are willing and able to change their way of life radically in order to raise that level.

Survivors of serious famines have the power to acquire food - to grow it (production based entitlement), to buy it (trade based entitlements), by selling their labour for cash or food (own labour entitlement), by being given food by others (inheritance and transfer entitlement), or through access as "looting" are the terms as per Dr.Amartya Sen.

STEVEN STARATWICK: - In their 1944 work, Theory of games and Economic behaviour, VON NEUMANN and MORGEN STERN showed individual choices were among uncertain prospects and satisfy weak consistency postulates of rationality. [12]

HARSANYI: - Harsanyi showed that these postulates would, when coupled with a weak ethical postulate, logically entail that social welfare was an additive function of individual utilities. [13]

A sophisticated account of this view has recently been developed by RAWLS in his "A THEORY OF JUSTICE"[14] which argues among other things, on the different principle, a maxim like principle of social justice which tells us to maximize the prospect of the worst–off class in society as opposed to the sum of individual utilities.

E.F.MCCLENNEN:- The well-known Arrow impossibility theorem for social welfare function is a negative result.[15]

In recent years, however, there have been a number of significant developments which appears to promise a way out for the Arrow impasse.

---

[11]   Editor: - Joseph C. Piti, Book- Philosophy in economics, Page no.11.
[12]   Ibid Essay by Steven Staratwick, Page.no.63
[13]   Ibid Essay by Steven Staratwick, Page.no.63
[14]   Ibid Essay by Steven Staratwick, Page.no.63
[15]   Ibid Essay by E.E.Mcclennen, page.no.93

By enriching the information available, concerning individual ordering in such a manner as to permit some form other of interpersonal comparison. The original ARROW impasse is avoidable and constructive results are obtained.

LOUISL WILDE[16] - The focus of welfare economics began to shift from comparing allocations in a given economic environment to comparing system of economic organization, which might operate within entire classes of economic environment. Indeed the entire "PUBLIC CHOICE" approach to welfare economics is a manifestation of this shift in emphasis. This is a theoretical welfare economics.

The question of "MORAL and JUSTIC" came in to picture. Dr. Amartya Sen said very properly that "OUGHT TO BE" of Socrates was very important. Aristotle considered problems of ethics in connection with the social life of the people. Aristotle regarded ethics as the doctrine about the moral of man as a social creature, as a political animal. Dr. Amartya Sen said in his book rationality and freedom that "Every one's utility goes up '. This is not required in 'interpersonal comparison". Pareto condition is sufficient. [17]

The philosophical aspect is important in economics for the concept of Welfare. The world had experienced the capitalist economy. The laissez-faire policy was most important in 18th century. The industrial revolution and Keynes theory of multiplier effect was not able to give proper remedy to the weaker section of society. The socialist theory of China, Russia, East European countries, Cuba or Dictatorship in Italy, Germany, recently north Korea, Idi Amin of Uganda and Mobuto of Congo and Pakistan could not eradicate the difference of "Haves" and "Haves not" in the society. The democracy spread over the world. Democracy had broken the boundaries of static thoughts and discovered the new area.

Economists were forced to think in terms of man due to gigantic progress all around the world. There were lots of inequality in society and no proper distribution of gross national product. The old utilitarian theory along with libertarian theory ultimately progressed towards the development, freedom, social justice and capability approach in the name of welfare economics.

---

16   Ibid, Essay by Louis L.Wilde,page no.137

17   Amartya Sen, Rationality and Freedom

DR. Amartya Sen quoted Henry Wallace saying that "The century on which we are entering can be and must be century of common man." in his book "Development thinking at the beginning of 21st century."[18]

Dr. Amartya Sen suggests the radical changes in development thinking. According to Dr. .Amartya Sen the reasons for development of world are as follows.[19]

Development experience

1. Post war construction of Japan and Germany.
2. Growth in Europe and North America due to high employment.
3. Welfare state from Europe and financial burden.
4. Astonishing economic growth of Asia.
5. Fast economic expansion of Latin America.
6. Economic crosses and reform in Russian and East Europe.
7. Rapid economic transformation of China.
8. Elimination of food dependency in third world and South Asia.
9. Famine improvement in Sub Saharan Africa, India and China.
10. Increase in international trade.
11. Longevity improvement in world.

China and India and many developed countries have conquered the world market by exporting their product. India is the number one exporter of intellectual goods known as "Information Technology" in the world. Now government is paying attention to the welfare of people. The consumption concept has improved the standard of living of the people at lowest level. In India, girl child matter is taken on top priority at central as well as state level for birth, education and medical attention.

Dr. Amartya Sen put forward the thought of collective choice theory, development as freedom, inequality, and Poverty and hunger eradication by way of development of capability as the concepts of welfare economics. Dr. Amartya Sen talks about Human values, Human rights, Human dignity and Human happiness. This thought has been further developed as Human well-being. Economists are looking into the future especially

---

[18]   Amartya Sen, Development thinking at the beginning of 21st century, Page no.1

[19]   ibid

for conversation of natural resources, protection of ozone layer. They are especially looking into well-being of man.

Dr. Amartya Sen noted the contrast of "non-ethical" character of modern economics and the historical evaluation of it is an offshoot of ethics. Dr. Amartya Sen is of the opinion that philosophy does play an important role in any field. The thought of Dr. Amartya Sen on welfare in the field of economics made him the right choice for NOBLE prize. Dr. Amartya Sen awarded noble prize in Economics in the year 1998.

1.3   The Philosophy of welfare in Jain religion

The Indian philosophies are divided in to two distinct sections (1) Non-Sraman tradition – Brahmanical. Six traditions were known as brahmanical tradition, having faith in god and (2) Sraman tradition.

> (1) Non-Sraman tradition–Brahmanical. Brahmin started the Yagna and YAG, a religious activity as rituals. They sacrificed the animals in this yagna. They were using SOM RAS-wine as part of rituals. The Brahmins were full of greed for wealth. "My son this means money to us, a great deal of money for sacrifice." [20] This was easy way to maintain themselves and enjoy the luxuries.

Manu divided the society in four categories (1) Brahman (2) Kshtriya (3) Vaisya (4) Sudra. Vaisyas were on lower level compare to Brahman and Kshtriya. They were harassed by Brahman and Kshtriya. Sudras were not allowed to stay in city limits. They had to serve compulsorily the rest of the three communities. They were not getting enough remuneration for services which they rendered. Sudras were exploited in all respects by the society. They were explained that this is due to their karmas in past life. The social volcano erupted. The killing and injustice were the main causes. People were ready to get out of this type of exploitative social situation and living conditions. They waited for new opportunity.

> (2) Sraman tradition – non-brahmanical. Three systems known as Jain, Buddhist and Ajivaka were known as sraman tradition. They did not believe in god. Jain have a firm conviction that world is eternal and there is no creator or destroyer. In Jain religion, Tirthankar

---

[20]   Srigala jataka, page no.142, 496

was the authority. Tirthankar was the human but with keval jnana. Tirthankar was preaching the religion. Tirthankar was known as omniscient. The meaning of omniscient is -The knowledge of soul is in full capacity and able to know quality and modes of all living and non-living things in the universe through past, present and future in sense of time.

The killing and injustice in society gave a birth to revolution. Their leader was lord Mahavir and latter on Lord Buddha. Lord Mahavir had opposed vehemently the sacrifice of animals in the name of rituals. Lord Mahavir had propagated the principle of NON-KILLING - Ahimsa. This was liked by majority of people (population) of the society and especially women. Women opposed to cook and to eat the meat. They preferred to remain vegetarian. Lord Mahavir introduced number of eye-catching changes in the society. Lord Mahavir put brotherhood in society. Lord Mahavir emphasized the moral life in place of ceremonial life. Lord Mahavir pleaded for the concept of perfect saga in place of god. The Sutrakrtanga denounces the pride of birth as a one of the eight kinds of pride by which man commits sin. Jain religion did not favour the caste system. Lord Mahavir believed in equality. People are allowed to follow Jain religion, provided they are able to practice the laid down instructions of Jain religion.

Jain philosophy contains many useful thoughts for man to achieve his material, as well as spiritual goal. Material prosperity is connected with Vyavahar naya and emancipation of soul is connected with Nischya naya. Vyavahar naya teaches householder how to live the life with material prosperity through religious practice. Nischya naya teaches how the ascetics and house holders should lead their life and to follow religion for final goal of emancipation of soul. Jain religion is a perfect combination of Vyavahar naya and Nischya naya.

The jiva is conscious and material is inanimate. The relation of jiva and pudgal-material is eternal. Jain religion categorically states that jiva can have freedom from the association of pudgal and attain the position of pure consciousness. The ethical ways and means make soul free from the association of pudgal. One can have evolution from material level to spiritual level which is welfare in final term. Keval jnana is the position of the soul. The consciousness will turn into pure knowledge-keval jnana and non-physical existence will release from the cycle of birth and death.

The main principles of Jain religion are non-killing-ahimsa, truth-Satya, non-stealing-Achurya, celibacy-Brahmacarya and non-hoarding-Aparigraha. The application of these principles will result as likely equality; man will be less egoistic due to the virtue of love, humbleness, develop tolerance, subsidise kasaya-passion, ready to help helpless people and create brotherhood. The Jain religious principles will advise you regarding the process of being from becoming. The being concept in Jain religion is for individuals. Jain religion gives importance to karma. Annihilation of all karmas is necessary to obtain liberation of soul.

The glorious Jain religion is more than 3000 to 3500 years old. The historical evidences are available. The historical and archaeological proof of lord Adinath is there. He was known as "KESHI" having long hair and in standing posture known as in KAYOTSARGA position. The naked statue was found during excavation. It is recorded in history that King Kharavela of Kalinga invaded Magadha in 161 B.C. second time. He brought back the idol of AGRAJINA, of the first Jina (Rsabhadeva) which had been carried away from Kalinga three centuries earlier by king Nanda 1(first) around 423B.C.[21]

The Yajurveda mentioned the names of three Tirthankar (1) Rsabha – 1st Tirthankar, (2) Ajitnatha – 2nd Tirthankar, and (3) Aristanemi-18th Tirthankar. Lord Neminatha was 22nd Tirthankar and predecessor of lord Parsvanatha. He was the cousin of the lord Krishna of the famous epic MAHABHARATA. Lord Neminatha's father and lord Krishna's father were brothers. The 23rd Tirthankar lord Parsvanatha was from 872 B.C. to 776 B.C.

The 24th Tirthankar, Lord Mahavir was born in 599 B.C. and died in 527 B.C. Vardhman was his real name. He was second son of a Kshtriya chieftain in Magadha. Lord Mahavir enjoyed all royal comforts in his life for first 30 years. When saints visited the royal palace and saw young Vardhman, they impressed by his serenity, equanimity and named him as Sanmati. Vardhman entered in to ascetic life at the age of thirty. He led the life of ascetic for twelve years and six months. This long and strict self mortification qualified Vardhman to attain kevaliship. Thereafter he was recognized Omniscient and known as Mahavir. Lord Mahavir taught the religion for thirty years and organized the system of ascetic and householder. This is known as Chaturvidh Sangh – four fold communities.

---

[21]   N.P.Jain,Ahimsha,Ultimate winner, page no.210

Lord Mahavir propagated the religion of "JINA". Lord Mahavir known as "NIGRANTH NATHPUTA" therefore it known as nigranth religion. Lord Mahavir was also known as Sakyamuni. [22]

During Lord Mahavir era, People were mostly engaged in agriculture and dairy industries. The small portion of population was engaged in trade, commerce, small-scale manufacturing, mining, forestry and day-to-day service provider besides warrior. Disciple of Lord Mahavir, Sraman ANAND, [23] had made a limit of his wealth up to 12 crores gold coins. Sraman Anand was having limit of four gokuls as animals. One gokul means 10,000 cows. Sraman Anand made a limit of agriculture land. Sraman Anand was having limit of 500 HALE measured land. The one NIVARTAN is measuring 200 X 200 square hands land. One hundred Nivartana is equal to one HALE. One hale is measuring 4,00,00,00 square hands land. [24] His main profession was agriculture and dairy industry. Another Sraman named MAHASATAK, [25] a disciple of Lord Mahavir, was having a limit of 24 crores gold coins filled in nickel vessels. There was a female potter named HALAHALA, a disciple of Lord Mahavir,. She was having 500 shops to sale pottery in capital and in state. Ladies were free to live their lives. Ladies were bringing dowry from their parental house and keeping it with them. Ladies were using cosmetics and perfumes. They were wearing colourful dresses made out of cotton; plant fibre, silk and wool.[26]People were celebrating the festivals. People were observing social customs. The food habit and day-to-day life was comfortable. People were taking Ayurvedic medicines for cure of disease and care for physical condition. Robber and thug were in existence in those days. Vices like drinking of Wine, gambling and prostitution were in existence in those days. There is a famous story of dancer AMRAPALI in literature. The story of ANGULIMALA, robber is famous in Buddhist literature. The princess CHANDAN BALA, a female disciple of Lord Mahavir, was sold as slave due to circumstances.

---

22 Ibid, page no.36
23 Chief Editor- Shri Mishrimalji Maharaj, (Hindi) Book:- Upasakdasang Sutra, page no.27
24 Ibid, page no.27
25 Ibid, page no.167 to 170
26 Kailas Chand Jain, book;- Lord Mahavir and his times, Chapter no.7,page no.237-275

Agamas are having the full description of Jain religion. Agama literature is considered as an authority on Jain philosophy. The vani or the sermon of lord Mahavir called "APTAVACHANA" which is known as agama literature. Earlier, it was in the form of SRUT JNANA-to hear and remember. Later on, it converted into canonical literature. The forth council met under the leadership of Devarddhigani in the year 454 A.D. at Vallabhi.[27] Lord Mahavir sermons were arranged, classified and codified in the form of canonicals literature in the council. They are known as ANUYOGAS. The canonical literatures divided in to four parts.

1) Prathmanuyog – Details of religious stories. Here the stories regarding life of sixty three shalaka purush are narrated. They were Tirthankars, Chakravartis, Vasudevas and baldevas as per historical records.

2) Karananuyoga – Day to day activities of house holder and ascetics. The duties and religious practices have to follow as Karan Charan.

3) Carnanuyoga - Arithmetic calculations. This is in term of time, length, breadth and distance as well as area of continents and seas. The measurement of cosmos is given there.

4) Dravyanuyoga – Details related to dravyas. The six eternal substances, the real and the nine tatvas are described in various ways.

A learned ascetic, named Shri UMASVATIJI translated the essence of agamas in Sanskrit language for the benefit of other religious scholars and gave them a opportunity to understand the Jain religion. Shri Umasvati's book named "TATTVARTHADHIGAMASUTRA" is enjoying the support of both the sects, Swetambaras and Digambaras. Various learned monk wrote the literature piece by piece and express their thought regarding, logic, epistemology, Anekantvada, Six Dravyas, nine tatvas, emancipation of soul, karma, ascetic and householder rules and regulation and many more things over a period of time.

---

[27]   Ph.D. Thesis of Hirabai Boradiya, "Jain dharma ni mukhya sadhvio ane mahilao" page no.101

Jain philosophy is humanitarian. Jain religious system is known as "CHATURVIDH SANGH" = fourfold community. They are as follows (1) Ascetic–Male=Sadhu (2) Ascetics-Female=Sadhvi (3) House Holder-male=Shravaka (4) House Holder-female=Shravika. A householder status is lower than ascetic status. The religion followed by a householder is known as "VYAVAHAR DHARMA" and followed by an ascetic is known as "NISCHAY DHARMA".

When renowned Vedic scholar, Brahmin Indrabhuti Gautam became Lord Mahavir's principal ganadhar along with ten others than the Sangh got off to a tremendous start. Each one of them brought 500 pupils with them in Jain religion. Chandana was the head of the nun order. Sankha Sataka as the head of house holder men and Sulasa and Revati as the two heads of house holder women as their number were larger. In the sixth century B.C., The chaturvidhsangh grew to a large number with 14000 monks, 36000 nuns, 159000 laymen and 318000 laywomen followers, during Lord Mahavir lifetime. [28]

The community welfare programmes are as follows.

Education: - (1) Scholarship for bright Jain students (2) hostel and college facility for students.

Health: - (1) to run Hospitals and clinics (2) Guest house in major cities for visitors and patient's relatives.

Welfare: - (1) Community welfare funds (2) Community organizations (3) Panjrapole for Animal and bird shelters (4) old people homes.

Places of pilgrimage: - (1) Guest houses at all places of pilgrimage. (2) Upasharyas, temples and residential place for monks, nuns and meditation centre for lay people.

The elected members of Sangha do various activities. They maintain the Sangha property and keep proper account of income and expenditure.

Jain Sangha and Ahimsa:-They run hospitals for people. These hospitals are open for all. The other communities are taking benefit of Jain sangh hospitals. Jains are always with open heart and not to restrict the humanitarian benefit for their community. They run "PANJRAPOLE"- a

---

[28]   N.P.Jain, Ahimsha-ultimate winner, page no.39

house for sick or physically unfit animals (cows, buffalos and oxen). The main purpose of Jain religion-AHIMSA is served here. They run hospital for animals & birds. They work for causes preventing the animal and bird's cruelty. They work for saving the healthy animals meant for slaughterhouse. These activities are a part of AHIMSA programme. These activities give tremendous boost to donate for the benefit of society.

1.4   Object of the Study

This thesis itself is the philosophy of welfare in both ways. It is a humble attempt at correlating the religion and economics in human life and to show how to have peace, happiness and wellbeing in the life. The aim of writing this thesis is to combine the better aspects of the ancient and the modern welfare approach. My efforts are to find out the welfare aspects in each concept taken as chapter. The findings regarding welfare aspects will narrate at the end of chapter.

The religion is a most inseparable part in the life of man. The economics is a day-to-day force to live the life. It was a question how to correlate the thing in right prospects. Both the subjects are carrying the main theme of welfare for man. Man has certain good qualities. Basically man follows religious thought in his life. Humanist admits the spiritual view of the universe.

The subject matter is very vast. One has to become aware of a limit. My thesis is a selection of few topics for welfare in the vast writing of Dr. Amartya Sen. Dr. Amartya Sen wrote on many subjects. Dr. Amartya Sen's favourite subject is Welfare. The four books are selected as four concepts. I have selected the following Books of Dr. Amartya Sen. They are (1) Collective choice and social welfare (2) Development as freedom (3) Inequality Re-examined (4) Poverty and famine.

Jain philosophy relates the man and his welfare in many ways. Lord Mahavir had thought for six types of living beings on earth. Jain religion is highly devotional and logical. Jainism emphasizes on ethics. The material prosperity is there in Jain community. Jain religion considers donation as virtue. They do use money as per religious guidelines. Jain community has given attention towards the welfare of man and nature (Total eco system). Jain Philosophy is humanitarian in nature of perfect bliss and perfect happiness for man. There is a process to gain the perfect bliss and perfect happiness. In this process, one has to follow three spiritual steps. These three steps show the way for emancipation of soul. They are known as "Samyag jnana, Samyag darsana and Samyag charitra".[29]

Jain philosophy having vast literature on different subjects like Meta physics, epistemology, spirituality, karma theory and mathematics and many more subjects. The selected concepts are Jain religious principles. I choose the following concepts from Jain philosophy (1) Ahimsa (2) Karma theory (3) Anekantvada means non-absoluteness (4) Aparigraha means non possessiveness.

1.5 Methodology

The method means the technique adopted for welfare in economic and in Jain philosophy. The methodology is library research-reading books, articles and lectures given at various places, reports, statements and notes of Dr. Amartya Sen and writing of other eminent writers in welfare economics. Dr. Amartya Sen is renowned authorities on economics and especially on welfare economics.

Library research in Jain philosophy is of the literature on Agamas and interpretation on it by eminent writers and Jain scholars. Jain agamic texts were known as Anuyogas. It is the sermons of lord Mahavir kept in these text books written by learned monks.

1.6 Chapterization of Thesis

CHAPTER 1   Introduction of the thesis

CHAPTER 2   the concept of Humanism in Economics and Jain Philosophy

CHAPTER 3   Dr. Amartya Sen's idea on collective choice and social welfare

---

[29]   Umaswatiji, Tattvarthasutradhigam, Commentary by Pandit Sukhlalji, Ch.1,Stanza no.1, page no.4

CHAPTER 1   Introduction of the thesis: - The definition of philosophy and meaning there off is given. Use of philosophy in social sciences is necessary due to human factor. Ethics in economics is welfare of human. Various writers' opinion about concept of welfare and detail account of Dr. Amartya Sen about development and ultimate thought in welfare economics is explained in detail. The Vedic laws were the reason of unrest. Lord Mahavir was pioneer reformer. Ahimsa was the first principle of Jain religion. The four fold community and welfare of them are the issues. Welfare is the core aspect in humanism. Humanism is discussed in second chapter.

CHAPTER 2 the concept of Humanism in Economics and Jain Philosophy: Definition of humanism and views of Prof. J.K. Galbrailth about humanism are noted. The human needs, in all sense and importance of them in human life. The remaining part of definition is also discussed in detail. In Jain religion, man is at centre irrespective of having status of ascetic or house holder. Environment has a special reference in term of humanism for future generation. According to Jain religion humanism is through donation. It is for all six types of living being on the earth.

CHAPTER 3 First concepts of economics is discussed in this chapter. Dr. Amartya Sen's idea on collective choice and social welfare: - Person choice and society choice has to be determined. Individual preference is best in terms of Pareto optimal. Society choice can be ruled by Collective choice rule, Majority method of decision, social welfare decision and social welfare function. Inter personal comparison is another point. The equality and maximum criteria are also included in choice function. The pros and cons are discussed by various economists in light of different choice function. This has resulted in to Arrows Impasse. Finally Jhon Rawl fairness and justice has worked.

CHAPTER 4 First concept of Jain religion is discussed in this chapter. The doctrine of Ahimsa in Jain philosophy: - Definition of Ahimsa is important for understanding the subject. Himsa is opposite of Ahimsa. Acharang Sutra has described the feeling and effect of violence on all six types of living being. One has to learn the lesson from it. The pity, compassion is different than ahimsa. The cruelty gives the idea about the degree of violence. I have given an idea about Gandhi's thought for non-violence in this chapter. Non-violence should be the main aim for environment. Everyone should take vow of non violence in their life.

CHAPTER 5 Dr. Amartya Sen's ideas on Development as freedom: - Dr. Amartya Sen has given a new meaning to development as freedom via capability. We have to take in to account non-freedom also. Liberty is another aspect in freedom. Well-being of person comes in development. The poverty is deprivation of entitlement. Market Mechanism is not useful for welfare aspect. Incentive in various ways will not work. Democracy, political freedom and civil rights are the instruments for ultimate development in freedom. Globalization has its own effect on society. There are short comings in the society. Dr. Amartya Sen's capability approach is the right answer for freedom. Dr. Amartya Sen is in favour of capitalist system but with check and balance. Social commitments, responsibility and tolerance are important. Justice and freedom are in democracy.

CHAPTER 6 the doctrine of Karma in Jain philosophy: - Jain philosophy believes in rebirth theory. Rebirth is the result of Karma. Karma explains the difference in society in logical way. In Jain religion karmas are of two types. Dravya karma is as physical action and bhava karma is as psychological action. Bhava is the reason to have karma incoming and binding to soul. Soul is coved by veil of eight kind karmas; as a result it does activity with passions. This is the reason of incoming of karma known as Ashrav. The karma bandh with soul is the reason of transmigration. You can stop incoming influx of karma known as Samvar. You can annihilate all the karmas known as nirjara and get emancipation of soul.

CHAPTER 7 Dr. Amartya Sen's idea on Inequality re-examined:- Dr. Amartya Sen has basic question regarding equality of what and why? Inequality in terms of impartiality, liberty, income, freedom, and women neglects etc. Inequality and poverty as well as well-being are the point to be thought off. The answer is capability. In capability, functioning is important to achieve well-being and freedom. Justice is another important point which leads us to Basel equality which is the basic thought provided by Dr. Amartya Sen.

CHAPTER 8 the doctrine of Anekantvada in Jain philosophy: - This comes in the area of epistemology in Jain religion. The all round beauty of the anekantvada can bring peace and as a result prosperity in society. This provides a good structure in social atmosphere.

CHAPTER 9 Dr. Amartya Sen's idea on Poverty and Hunger, An essay on Entitlement and Deprivation:-Definition of poverty and different approach to poverty are discussed in detail. Prof. J. K. Galbraith ideas are also incorporated in the chapter. Various methods to measure poverty and remedial measures for the same are discussed. The remedy lies in entitlement approach. Deprivation is the cause of poverty in many senses. Starvation and famine are the causes of entitlement and deprivation and not of poverty. Poverty in social term is in family, particularly in women. Rich countries are also suffering from poverty in different way. Food availability and market mechanism are important issue in eradication of famine.

CHAPTER 10 the doctrine of Aparigraha, effective tool in Jain philosophy: - Jain philosophy allows you to earn maximum with certain rules of ethics and morals. The extra income should be used for fellow man and in good cause of society. Jain community follows the rule prescribed in religion.

CHAPTER 11 Conclusions: - Summary of all chapters and final view of the researcher is given.

1.7   Wish for final outcome of thesis

It was a fatal attraction for me to use my little knowledge of economics and my study of Jain religion in the form of research paper. The subject of welfare is beauty to adore the research work. The thesis is the right carrier to convey my thought to the people. It is an industrious effort to study the thing. It gave me good insight in economics as well as Jain philosophy. Historical, social, political and economical situation of Lord Mahavir time was very much different than present time. It is important to know Mahavir's philosophy as in the jigsaw puzzle of world philosophy and particularly in Indian philosophy.

Dr. Amartya Sen has work on most appropriate subject of philosophy of welfare in economics. The thought of philosophy incorporated in the welfare economics has changed the thinking of ruling governments all over the world. The value of man will be established by this. The conscious of man should work for fellow man is the best expected outcome. The burning problem of man's capability will start working for freedom through development. This will bring joy of tears in the eyes of poor. This will re-establish the kingdom of humanity and brotherhood amongst the population of the universe.

2 The Humanism in Economics and in Jain Philosophy

2.1 Concept of Humanism

Humanism is to bring the intrinsic value of man. Humanism is more a tendency than a system. Here the physical and mental capacity of man has to blossom next to the fullest capacity. Human capability is the key factor in welfare economics.

It is very vital to find out the right definitions of humanism from various dictionaries.

As per Cambridge Dictionary: - Humanism is a noun. The meaning is "A belief system based on human needs and values and not on a god or religion."

As per American Heritage dictionary: - Humanism means "The interest, needs and welfare of humans.

As per Oxford dictionary: - Humanism means (1) a system of thoughts that regards humans as capable of using their intelligence to live their lives, rather than relying on religious belief. (2) A renaissance cultural movement, which revived interest in ancient Greek and Roman, thought.

On examination of the above definitions we can say that man and his quality is the result. It is clear from the above that certain points are common in these definitions.

(1) Needs of human

(2) Value and interest

(3) Not to rely on god or religious belief

(4) Human capability

2.2 Needs of Human

One has to think in terms of other sciences and not only in terms of economics.

Now a day's all sciences are interrelated and interwoven in each other. We have to think in terms of (1) Economic needs (2) Social and political needs (3) Psychological needs (4) Philosophical needs (5) Environmental needs

(1) Economical Needs

Basic needs of human are three (A) Food (B) Clothes (C) Shelter.

J. K. Galbraith counted fourth most urgent requirements of men (D) an orderly environment in which the first three might provide.[30]

Economic theory has managed to transfer the sense of urgency in meeting consumer need that once felt in the world. At present the affluent society is behind increasing output. They want to satisfy themselves with more elegant automobiles, more exotic food, designer clothing, more exotic travel, and more elaborate housing and entertainment. This is the result of lethal desire to satisfy most modern things in life. The population lives below subsistence in many part of world. The minimum nutritional requirements are not satisfied of these people for their survival. Even in any modern sense, most of those are living above the subsistence level do not enjoy a standard of living that one can call well.

(A) Food

Man requires food to get energy. This energy is the work force for him. The work can be of physical or mental nature. This is a basic need for human to survive.

Malthusian Theory of population and reply to Malthus

---

[30]   Prof.J.K.Galbraith, the affluent Society, Ch.21, page no.234

Malthus in his book "Essay on population" says 'the number of people who can live in the world is obviously limited by the number that can be fed.' Any increase in supply of food would bring in, in Malthus view, an increase in the number of people to consume it. The Malthusian theory of population tried to prove that as population increases the food availability decreases. As a result, men will forever live on the verge of starvation.[31] This will result in malnutrition, diseases, and death. The nature has limited resources. Malthus established direct correlation between food and population.

It is felt that due to improved seeds, fertilizer, pesticides and increased use of irrigated land, rotating crop pattern has increased the food production. Over and above, fruits, vegetables, meat and seafood are available in sufficient quantity. Poultry and dairy products are also helping to reduce the food shortage. Surplus food production of a country can be exported to the needy country. Empirically it is proved that food shortage is not the cause for starvation of population.

Dr. Amartya Sen's basic question and role of welfare state

Dr. Amartya Sen raises the question philosophically. What exist is not important but who commands what is important question. Dr. Amartya Sen looks the question of food in all together different perspective. Dr. Amartya Sen has found out that at the time of famine people are not having "Entitlements"- buying capacity. They died due to absence of entitlement- no buying capacity for food. The starvation is the cause of death. Who is responsible for this? Government agency should create opportunity for the entitlement. This should be created by way of social services or unemployment allowance. Food became costly in rich countries. People spend more on to maintain the social standard; as a result they spend less on food.

It is a duty of welfare state to provide minimum entitlement to every able working human. Alternatively, state can distribute cash entitlements to the unemployed people, who are below poverty line. The welfare state can provide the food on subsidized rate and see that it goes to the real needy people. Welfare state has to make immediate arrangements to bring in the food grain from distance places by arranging rail and road transport in case of famine. Centre and State should take care that no one is without food. This will happen due to effective opposition and media.

---

[31]   Ibid, page no.23

(B) CLOTHES

21st century has arrived on the threshold of universe. Man requires clothes to cover his body. Decency comes from the clothes which human puts on. It is culture and moral obligation on the part of human to cover the body in the society due to opposite sex. Men should have surplus entitlements after buying food to buy clothes for his family. Many a times, the poor people in cold countries, suffer from cold in winter season and lost their lives.

(C) SHELTER

The availability of land on the earth is limited. Dwelling is another important agenda of welfare state. The population explosion and the urbanization have added fuel to the question of residential space. States can make compulsion to builders to construct some economic class tenements for poor.

The Welfare state should build minimum standard tenements and give to the economically needy people on ownership basis or give them on rent. It should not be a VOTE BANK policy in the democracy.

Social and political needs

It is universally known, in past, the great philosopher, Aristotle said, "Man is social animal". Man lives in society. The cast, creed and religious belief will create a chequered pattern in society. The natural good is an inborn tendency in every individual to assert him with limit. Democracy is the best cradle for humanity. The elected members should be honest people and are ready to serve the society. The honesty should be the prime virtue. They should be patriotic by heart and in their deeds.

Psychological needs

It is a basic ground from where the plant of good mental attitude will grow in such a way that it's' shed and fruits will be enjoyed by mankind. The psychological change will bring a long-term effect and chain reaction in society for benefit of man. The behaviour, attitude, motivation, emotion and feeling; thinking will play a great role in society.

Philosophical needs

Man came out of primitive stage to recent sophisticated stage. Man had acquired knowledge from experience. Man can have answer through science. Where science fails, shastra-religious texts give the answer. The metaphysical elements are important in men's life. Men have to search for reality. Testimony is elevated to a status as a source of knowledge.

Greek, Egyptians and Indus valley people tried to get knowledge of reality by way of intuition. Indian Philosophy has divided knowledge in two sections (A) Worldly knowledge – Para Vidya (B) Spiritual knowledge– Apara Vidya

Worldly knowledge means the materialistic approach, wellbeing of human to live happy life. The crude theory of materialism which denies future life is inconsistent with the emergent view of self. If the self is not produced by the body, it need not be ended when the body is destroyed. Spiritual knowledge means to understand the reality. Man should have ultimate freedom from all miseries and make his soul free from cycle of birth and death.

Worldly knowledge

This knowledge is necessary to live the life. There are number of thinkers, scientists and educationalist, who work day in and day out in every corner of planet to have more and more knowledge. This knowledge will bring all round prosperity and happiness in all sense for mankind on the planet.

Spiritual knowledge

Man started thinking deeply in the deeper and deeper structure of reality of thought. He thought that from where he has come. Where will he go? Is there any other world beyond this world? Is there anything other than birth and death? Which is the element that keeps body active, alert, makes thinking and acting for good and bad deeds? These philosophical questioning of man has tried to find out the answers. The search for right answer is still going on. The prophet, Messiah or the great Seers have given answers for the inner reality of man and suggested how to follow the ethical and moral rules.

Environmental need

Already almost 90% of world's rain forest annihilated. Every five years human causes 100000 plant and animal life forms to become extinct through deforestation. The havoc which have created environmentally through violent and exploitative behaviour in last 40 years, will take 10 million years to undo according to the scientists.[32] The materialism has ushered in unparalleled prosperity, While the weakness of human beings is, it is not been evenly distributed. Out of total world population, 25% of world population living in highly developed countries of North enjoys 83% of world income, 70% of worlds' resources, 85%of wood, 75% of metals and 60% of fuel. The rate of growth in the North is being 2.7 times greater than in the South. [33] Hence, the urgent need to make an earnest beginning by forging an emotional bond between nature and human.

Environment and U.N.O. report

The report of the world commission on environment and development titled "OUR COMMON FUTURE" has pointed out in 1987, lapses of environmental neglect and degradation of the perils of developmental failures. It pointed out that each year some 6 million hectares of productive dry land was turning into worthless desert and more than 11 million hectares of forest had destroyed.

Statistics
    Year 1960
        18.5 million Affected annually by draught.
        5.2 million By flood.

    Year 1970
        24.4 million Affected annually by draught.
        15.8 million By flood.

Number of victims of cyclone and earthquakes also increased. The tolerance limits of benign nature and the dangers are clear and present. As the U.N. commission had concluded, the environmental crises, the development crises and the energy crises are all one and the crises is global. [34]

2.3 Value and Interest

The human value is most important ingredient. Human is wealth of nation.

---

32   N.P.Jain, Ahimsha-ultimate Winner, page no.28
33   Ibid, page no.83
34   Shri L.M.Singhvi,A tale of three cities, page no.60

The philosophy of humanism is to protect, preserve and to make progress of human in any condition. Welfare state should see that human being should not be exploited and the women, children and old people should be protected. The welfare state should adopt such a policy that make human to think in "OUGHT TO BE" position. Our material progress is much ahead than our ethical progress. Human is tending to ignore and even forget human values.

Freedom in democracy

The person should be free to live his own life. This is only possible in democracy. In past, Gantantra-democratic system was existent in India. Confucius was the first philosopher, who advocated for democracy. Democratic form of government first established in the west in recent past. Many countries are choosing democracy as a form of government. Impartial judiciary is the only hope in democracy. Democracy is a method by which human attempt to raise the living standards of the people and to give opportunities to everyone to develop personality.

The socialist theory of Karl Marx, Engle, Lenin and Mao does not exist anymore. Socialist countries cannot withstand the pressure of market mechanism. More and more countries are now turning to democracy. Dr. S. Radhakrishnan says "democracy requires us to respect and develop the free spirit of man, who is responsible for all progress in human history."[35] Dr. Amartya Sen goes further to the root of welfare of human. He says capability of a person should be developed by welfare state.

2.4   Not to rely on god or religious belief, Human capability

The present age is an age of humanism. Philosophical interest has shifted, rightly or wrongly, from god, matter and science to men. Men are subject and not object. An Object will make man mindless, rigid and routine.

These are some most important conditions. (1) Not based on god or religion (2) Rather than relying on religious beliefs.

RUSSELL says, "Philosophy is meant to suggest and inspire a way of life. The value of life is lasting importance."[36]

---

[35]   S. Radhakrishnan, Indian Philosophy, Vol. 1
[36]   S. Radhakrishnan, The concept of man

SOCRATES says "KNOW THY SELF."

The Indian philosophy said "ATMANAM VIDDHI".

Humanist revivals occur when religion disintegrate and fail to attract men's attention. As against religion, humanism claims that this world is our chief interest and perfection of humanity is our goal. To humanist, the belief in god is blind thinking. If you rely on god and do not act, in that case, you will starve.

Man has the power to change his environment through action. Jain religion says that PURUSHARTHA can change the way of life and karma too. Aristotle agreed with Agathon that even god could not change the past; he did think that the future was ours to make-by bagging our choices on reasoning.[37]

Ancient age belief in god

In the Stone Age period, man was worshiping the light and clouds and other super natural elements subsequent to animals and there after he personified the god in form of divine things and started worshiping and adoring the symbols. People are constructing temples and shrines. They get mental satisfaction for doing these things even today.

Unfavourable practice in religion

Any religion is based on good ethical and moral principles. The oriental religions and other religions are incorporating the young age boys and girls in their cult to make the religion to survive and continue to flourish. The so called religious leaders miss interpret the religion which ultimately harms the society. Some time the religious beliefs are cruel and meaningless. Say for example- sunnat–religious ceremony for boy in Islam. The "female circumcision" practiced in parts of Africa and elsewhere actually a morally abominable genital mutilation.[38] Female genital mutilation also known as female circumcision is a practice that dates back to Pharaonic times in Egypt. It is common in a band that stretches from Senegal in West Africa to Somalia on the east coast and from Egypt in the north to Tanzania in the south.

---

[37]   Amartya Sen, Rationality and freedom, page.no.261

[38]   Editor- Christopher W. Gowans, Moral disagreement-classical and contemporary studies, pageno.1 and news report of Times of India Bombay edition dt.12-8-2007.

Religion should give education of good and bad things. Persons are losing their faith in religion due to fanatic approach, more of rituals and no change in present life from bad to good position. The doctrine of humanism thinks only of a human. If we bring religion in humanity than our good ideas, plan and its' implementation will be in danger.

Noble prize winner Gabriel Marquez has observed: "Accept nothing from the 21ˢᵗ century; it is the 21ˢᵗ century which expects everything from you". [39]

We must utilize economic and political power in service to humanity. Dr.Amartya Sen belongs to 20ᵗʰ century and the definition of all above things have changed drastically. Though, Dr.Amartya Sen thinks in terms of man's development with the inner value of soul. Dr.Amartya Sen emphasises improvement in present condition and value judgement in the behaviour of man.

2.5   Humanism in Jain religion

Importance of food in Jain religion

In Sraman traditions, Jain and Buddhist religion were in opposition to SACRIFICE OF ANIMAL as religious rituals. This gave a tremendous boost to vegetarianism. The food habit of Jain is quiet distinct. The limit of food consumption helps for health as well as to help save food for others. One of the Jain customs is not to leave the food in the plate. In case of surplus food, very rarely, the same should be distributed among the hungry people.

The Jain religion has prescribed number of vows and advice to monks and householder to restrict the use of certain types of roots, vegetables and fruits. They are advised to use hot water. They advised to eat some less quantity of food rather than their belly full. This practice is known as "UNODRI" vow. They advised not to have attachment for test; this is known as "RAS PARITYAG" vow. They advised not to have food after sunset; this is known as "RATRI BHOJAN TYAG". Jains are restricted to make use of leafy vegetables in monsoon due to small insects on leaves. They have been prohibited to consume any type of vegetable and especially roots vegetable during religious festival known as 'PAJJUSHAN' for eight

---

[39]   N.P.Jain, Ahimsha-ultimate winner, page no.56

days. The Honey, Liquor and Meat are prohibitive for monks for lifetime. Householders are also advised not to consume these items as far as possible throughout the life.

Psychological aspect in Jain Religion

Jainism has truly thought in terms of psychological aspect. The mind, speech and body are important factors and their activities are affecting to soul. Jain religion has separated the mental activities from speech and body activities. The mental activities are BHAV. This mental stage is of two types. First attachment and second is aversion. The mental activities are acutely relying on passions of a person. These two mental stage activities will bring good and bad thought. The thought will turn in to action by way of speech and body activities. The speech and body activities are DRAVYA.

The mental attitude is important to bind the soul with karma and make him to transmigrate in four gaties as per Jain religion. Jain religion prescribes the rules for control of body and mind activities. The purity of thought will make man more accommodative, soft and compassionate. The mental attitude is reason for fall and rise of soul in final emancipation.

Jain worldly knowledge

Jain religion is considering "SIN" for eight types of pride.[40] The pride of high position is one of them. Jain avidya is as a result of karmic veil. This karmic veil sends human into transmigration. Person is interested only in worldly things and activities. He has the feeling of possessiveness. He thinks in term of self only, as a result he became an utmost selfish man.

Jain knowledge about reality

Jainism uniquely stands here in responding many of the critical questions. It has always aimed certainly in the liberation of soul. The faith of this eternity of position can be acquired by all souls universally.

Jain religion environmental approach

The challenge is enormous for propagating Jainism as universal welfare in the new millennium. Jain religion had foresighted environmental

---

40   Edited by Dalsukh Malvania, Sthananag Sutra, page no.77

approach before 3000 years in the slogan of "Parasparopgraho Jeevanam".[41] The living organism is mutually interdependent on each other. The meaning is that irrespective of the degree of their sensory perceptions or size, all living organisms are bound together by mutual support and interdependence. This covers earth, water, fire, air, vegetation, animals, birds and human. Jain ecological perception views growth of life and evaluation on our planet. Jain religion recommends use of all natural elements as per man's need and not beyond that. Man should not hoard or store the things more than his basic necessity. Lord Mahavir found the truth. Lord Mahavir said to human to make FRIENDSHIP with every living being. Human being would have been happier, if friendship had seen in right prospective in term of environment. Jain religion has taken utmost care for environment in its preaching.

Human development in Jain Religion

Lord Mahavir was in favour of man's full development in material as well as in spiritual term. Jain religion talks about universal peace and prosperity with human welfare. Lord Mahavir had shown two ways. Vyavahar is the day to day conduct and Nischya is aloof from material objects and look for emancipation of soul. Lord Mahavir belongs to earlier time when the main lively hood was dependent on agriculture, dairy, small scale industries and trade and service in the society. The life was peaceful and man was equally concern for his material as well as spiritual matters. Spiritual development is dependent on material prosperity. Jain religion understands this concept very well.

Humanity in Jainism is through four-fold community. They are pillars on which edifice of Jain religion exists. They are 1) Male Ascetic-Sadhu 2) Female ascetic-Sadhvi 3) Male laity-male house holder 4) female laity-female house holder.

The rules for ascetic are MUNIDHARMA or ANAGAR DHARMA. The rules for laity are known as SHRAVAKACHAR or SAGARA DHARMA. The other name of laity is householder.

The rules for householder dharma are somewhat liberal compared to ascetic dharma. The reason is that householder is not free from worldly duty,

---

[41]   Pandit Sukhlalji, commentary on Tatvarthsutradhigfam of Umaswatiji, Ch.no.5, stanza no.21, page no. 15, Sanskrit text

family to look after, to take care of ascetics and other things. There for he is not in a position to fully adhere the rules of Moral and Ethics. The householder union known as 'Sangh' is doing various activities in welfare for Jain religion followers and ascetics. The detail is in chapter number one, Page No.18-19.

Humanism through Donation in Jain religion

Definition: - (1) Suddha-pure dharma is a transcendental stage of soul. This is above ascetic and householder religion. As you are unable to practice "SUDDHA DHARMA, you donate in The ANAGAR dharma–society of ascetic and AGAR Dharma-Society of householders, for their causes.

(2)The most important donation in JAIN RELIGION is to give "ABHAYA VACHAN"- to protect any living being. The person will protect the living being; who has come to take shelter under him. This is the most important principle in Jain religion. Jain religion believes and practicing AHIMSA-No killing thoroughly.

(3) Another important definition of donation is–you leave your own things irrespective of its value or usage to you, for benefit of yourself and for the benefit of others.

(4) Person acts with full sense and with a feeling to forgo his belonging, for fellow human, who are in need of it. The person is doing this even when he is capable and can enjoy worldly things, but offers voluntarily the part or full of his capacity for the benefits of others. This is a real donation as per Jain religion.

Mental situation for donation as per Jain Religion

In this process of donation, Jainism considers to whom you donate and what donor's mental attitude is. This will result as good or bad effects in a person who donates. This will be a meritorious act or non-meritorious act and accordingly you will enjoy or suffer fruit of karma. Desire for donation is the result of Dan antray karma. You wish to donate when the power of this karma reduced. Person fails to act as per his wish due to strong resistance of the Dan antray-obstacle karma. As a result, person is unable to give donation and does not get benefit of his good thought.

Donation in Spiritual sense as per Jain Religion

The poor person will be able to use his hard earned minimum entitlements for more urgent needs, looking to the type of donation he receives. Donation is silent and important factors in transferring the income smoothly from rich to poor, without help of any law, in lieu of redistributing agency and absence of government in between. Donation system is useful to some extant in a sense, person gets some relief from his guilty conscious. The person becomes lighter in terms of bad karma. This is good for society as the criminal activities will be at lower level. It prescribed in every religion to give certain portion of one's income as donation. Donor is earning meritorious act on his part, to have happiness in this or coming life. Donation will be a virtue in people. Donation will increase the purity of heart. The meritorious act of donation will uplift his soul. Donation will have effects in society in spiritual sense.

Donation to ascetics in Jain religion

The donation for ANAGAR-ascetic can be in four ways,
    (1) Food,
    (2) Cloths
    (3) Expenses for educational purpose and miscellaneous
    (4) Medical expenses.

Many a time, ascetics are proposing a projects such as subsidized housing, education subsidy, hostel and medical facilities for the benefit of masses, Seminar and lecture series arranged for spreading the general knowledge of religion in society, publishing the religious books, erecting the religious temple, renovation of old temple and pilgrimage centre at the Jain religious places. These activities are supported whole heartedly by householders.

Donation to householder and Classification of donation

Socially the donation can broadly classify in three ways
    (1) Financial Assistance
    (2) Physical Assistance
    (3) Establishment assistance.

(1) Financial Assistance: - Financial help extend to any good activities in society.

(2) Physical assistance: - The projects can run locally. One can include many services under one roof. Jain sang gives the assistance for food article, scholarship for study, medical assistance, legal assistance, to run employment exchange for their members.

(3) Establishment assistance: - Here we consider the projects in chain and at different geographical locations. The types of activities are for hospital projects, student lodging and boarding for higher education and repairs and maintenance of old religious places. These types of projects are run by either famous philanthropic Jain organizations or a big industry owned prominent Jain family. Mahavir Jain Vidyalaya is running educational and loading and boarding facility for the benefit of student at various places in India. Please refer chapter no. one as Chaturvidh Sangh. Page no.18-19

Ishavashya Upanishad of non Sharman tradition has beautifully framed the phrase that "TEN TETYAKTEN BHUNJITHA" means Person renounces and gives to others having pleasure of giving it. Here the feeling of sacrifice is supreme. Person does not think anything at that particular movement of donation and donate whatever he has for the pain of others. After doing this act, person does not repent or have no trace of selfishness. He feels himself honoured doing this act. He had utmost pleasure.

Other consideration for Donation

According to eastern religious philosophy, beggers are not beggers from economical point of view BUT from their past karma point of view. They suffer due to their bad deeds in past lives. Second thought, donor always like to pay back the financial assistance or other relief received in kind, which he had received in past lives. Donor does not what to carry the burden of donation in next birth. They think that if they do not pay back in this life than they have to pay back in future lives. People believe in rebirth theory. Donation is a kind of mental satisfaction and not a pride or ego but feeling to do something good for others.

Humanism through vows in Jain religion

Jain Religion is divided in to two part; Vyavahar religion and Nischya religion.

The economics comes in Vyavahar religion. The Vyavahar religion is working after taking in to account the ethics and moral rules established by Jain religion. The ethics for Jain society is 1) not to kill, 2) not to speak lie, 3) not to steal, 4) not to act in wrong way for celibacy and lastly 5) not to hoard. These basic vows are the pillars of Jain society. They are knew as Maha Vrats-Big vow for ascetics. The ascetics are not allowed to act in any way, in any circumstances to transgress the above five vows. The householder allowed some relaxation in light of their day-to-day economical and commercial activities. Five vows are known as ANU VRAT-small vows for male and female householders.

AHIMSA-NON-KILLING

This is a small vow compare to ascetic for householder. Householder is bound to make some himsa-killing in his/her day-to-day activities. There for minimum HIMSA is the vow for householder. This vow will give and save life to maximum number of plants, animals and human. This is the humanism of householder. To allow living more number of plants, will help to have more oxygen in air, to control pollution, to bring good rain and greenery on the planet. The rain will benefit to agriculture, in turn give fodder and grain. This will help to survive the birds, animals and human. The increased food production will give satisfaction to people. It will solve the problem of drinking water, Industrial water and irrigation projects. It will be a live and let live policy. There will be a maximum good for maximum number of human in society. Householder will control his activities and this will have minimum harm to nature. Householder is following this vow by two karan and three yogas. Two karan means (1) Not to give consent to do the act and (2) Not to encourage to do the act by others. Three yogas mean (1) Body (2) Mind and (3) Speech. Householder will control his activities as a result he will have less number of KARMAS. This will turn in to stoppage of new karma. This will help him to annihilation of past karmas and make rapid progress on spiritual path.

SATYA-TRUTH

It belongs to anuvrat (smaller vows) tradition compares to ascetic for householder. The householder has to speak truth only, but as he is in society and for survival, he may have to lie to some extent. He has to do this because he is in business, in political activities, in social relation or due to family affairs. As far as possible, he will speak in such a way that his speech is not far away from the truth as well as not harsh to others. He will develop a skill to be good to all persons as much as possible. This will develop courage in him to face the wrong situation. Truth is a virtue. Truth is strength. It gives inner courage to men to face layer.

NON STEALING-ASTEY

As against Mahavrat (big vows), this is a small vow compare to ascetic for householder. Householder will not do the act of stealing. This means in business, he will count, weight and measure in correct proportion. Nothing is more or nothing is less. In case, if there is any change than he will caution to public about it. The society will benefit by right weight and right measure. Society will pay right amount for just right thing. The householder will build his own prestige over a period of time. It will full fill his wish to observe vow. The state will have minimum control and face minimum problems. This will create an atmosphere of faith in society. A chain of faith will establish between people, people and state. Indirect effect of this will be a benefit to state in terms of; to have minimum conflict, minimum court cases, and minimum police force with minimum regulations will create peace in society.

CELIBACY

This is an anuvrat (small vow) for householders compare to ascetics. Here the male member and female member have to observe certain restriction willingly regarding their sexual life. First of all they have to take vow that they will satisfy their sexual urge by their partner only. As per Jain religion, a householder is not to have sexual relation with animal, infernal or celestial soul. The high family prestige will be the result of this vow.

Womanize or gay partnership will be the cause of economic or social or mental disturbance. The venereal diseases will on rise. The exploitation of women and woman trafficking will increase. This type of problem comes up in society due to unavoidable circumstances and beyond human control. This type of problem will be limited in a vow society. The benefit of a vow will reflect in control of child birth. There will not be a forced rape or seduction. Woman will have more freedom. Woman will have respect and say in family and society.

APARIGRAH- (NON-ATTACHMENT)

This is an anuvrat (small vow) for householders compare to ascetics. Householder requires number of things and in varieties. Householder can classify his need and accordingly he can control the number of items, control in weight, and size of thing, which he is going to consume daily and repetitively. He can have limit of his wealth, number of foreign trips and items of wealth. This will be his welfare in terms of satisfaction, mental peace and away from pomp and show business. There will not be a tug of war between RICH and POOR.

The environment will saved from excessive burden of unnecessary consumption. Human and society will saved from hypocrisy and demonstrative effect. The demand will be as per one's need. This will give equal distribution of goods and services at right price. The production of goods and services will be as per demand therefore it will save natural resources. The most important question of today is to save mineral oil, water, forest, wild life and other scare resources.

2.6 Conclusion:

Dr. Amartya Sen agrees to have economical activities for the benefit of people. Prof. J.K.Galbraith has discussed humanism. Definition throws much more light on the subjects with yes and no. Human development is humanism. State has to play an important role. Dr. Amartya Sen wants to increase the total benefit with a few changes in society through the democratic government.

Humanism in Jain religion is keeping man in centre. It is thoroughly on donation and practice of vows. Voluntary control of wealth is important point. In Jain religion, pity, protection and compassion are for all six types of living being.

We have seen the definition of humanism and related area, how they are important in present contacts. The welfare of human is the essence of religion and economics. Economics has to take care of the shortfall and religion has to wipe out the wrong thinking. It is not an easy and straightforward job, but certainly, I can say that it is not impossible at the same time. All religions have to think in this direction and economists have to bring the change in thought process to bring the human in centre. The profit, interest and exploitation have to be limited in the economic sense and people should be fearful to have excess of anything and everything. People have to have limit and control on desire and have to think in terms of other's unhappiness. Religion can bring this change by way of giving right ethics and moral to the followers. The number of councils, divisions and organizations of U.N.O. are working in the right direction under able guidance of world-renowned experts. Now it is the turn of all faith in world to unite and give proper guidance for ethics and morals.

Now onwards we will examine four concepts of Dr.Amartya Sen regarding philosophy of welfare economics and four main principles of Jain religion to understand the welfare of man.

3 The concept of collective choice and social welfare

3.1 Introduction

The title of chapter says that it is concerned for social policy and combines with preference and aspiration of members of society. When you consider society as an independent entity in that case preference of member cannot be the society preference. Karl Max objected idea of making society as individual and given no importance to the individual member of society.

The main thesis of the book is to find out the 1) Social choice plays great role for dependence of judgment and 2) public policy on preference of members.

The deciding factor is preference of members of society. Say to decide the percentage of tax on one commodity. Its optimal revenue is one thing and public opinion to build the flyovers in the city is a different thing. These things are in relation to society.

There is a big gap in the need and desire of people as stated above, in the collective choice to take a judgment. The collective choice is a diverse subject and number of things is incorporated in it. The field of collective choice is very vast. It can be subjective as well as objective. Here the social welfare is pertaining to policy and decision. Policy and decision implementation are very important. Therefore, it is objective.

Individual is the member of society and society as a whole is the aggregates of members. Here the individual will insist for his goal or a community may come in picture and force for their demands or the matter of equality

37

may crop up and many more things happen in collective choice. In this situation we may have many different theories in the collective choice. We have to decide the system, nature, operations and implication of the subject. After that, one can go ahead in these decisions.

Ingredients of collective choice

Social choice is based on individual preference than we have to find out the form in which it is relevant. Kenneth Arrow [42] took the orderings of the individuals over the set of alternative social states to be the main ingredient of collective choice. He made function of an individual preference ordering as a social preference ordering, a rule in collective choice. Now the ordering is a ranking in each other as well as with all alternates. The rank must satisfy the three things to begin with. Here the ranking termed as "At least as good as".

(1) It must be transitive. Here if X is at least as good as Y and Y is at least as good as Z than X should be at least as good as Z.

(2) The relation must be "Reflexive". I.e. every alternative X must be thought to be at least as good as itself. This is mild condition.

(3) "Complete". Complete means any pair of alternatives X and Y either X is at least as good as Y, or Y is at least as good as X.

It is understood that man knows full well about his choice. Sometimes man is in such a position that he cannot understand the difference between indifference and completeness. Indifference means not in a position to decide and completeness means a firm choice with full consciousness.

The example of indifference is 1) "X is at least as good as Y" and 2) Y is at least as good as X.

In case of completeness Y may be as good as X and X may be as good as Y.

Arrow saw a point that the Individual is seeing the ordering on alternative social state and society is supposed to have an ordering on the set of

---

42   Amartya Sen, Collective choice and social welfare, page no.2.

individual ordering. Arrow's view can be criticized in following ways. Dr. Amartya Sen says first of all the transitivity condition is violated in this situation. Example: - If X is preferred to Y, Y is preferred to Z, and Z is indifferent to X then there is a best alternative in every choice situation. Here Z is indifferent therefore transitivity condition infringed. In case of pair (X, Y) X can be preferred, (Y, Z) Y preferred and (Z, X) EITHER Can be chosen. Now X is selected in all the three (X, Y, and Z) because X is at least as good as rest of the pair. The rationality is violated. One can ignore the transitivity in social choice.

Second thing is regarding completeness. Example: - X is preferred to Y and Z. Now Y and Z are not comparable. This is incompleteness though we can choose X in x, y, z. The completeness is desirable. We can ignore this depends upon the nature of choice. When one is unable to satisfy the completeness than the transitivity and reflexivity is preferred. The preference relation known as "Quasi – ordering" in technical term.

Third thing is the social choice should take in to account the intensity along with individual ordering. The cardinal welfare function should be taken in individual case.

Example: - Person 1 strongly wants that society chooses X and person 2 chooses mildly wants that the society choose y and not X, in that case X is good case to choose for both the persons. Here we are doing interpersonal comparison which is misleading. Here personal preference intensity is not in measurement.

Forth point is Interpersonal comparison can be without cardinality and the concept can be applied in various modes. In interpersonal comparison we find new thing. Here the marginal gain and loss can be measure and or the welfare level. There is an argument that interpersonal comparison is meaningless as it is not based on choice.

Example: - The person A in social state of X or Person B in social state of Y. Person A in state X is an unemployed labourer and Person B is well paid engineer in state Y. Here the comparison is there. In collective choice you can introduce the preference and not comparison.

The nature of individual preference

The interesting point is one can say that the social choice is dependent on social preference than why to study the individual preference. This has less relevance. Individual preference configuration will decide the effectiveness of collective choice. The society in which man lives is as per his class, his economical and social position, his personal choice. These affect his value system and his notion for other members of society. Self interest of man was in traditional economics. Preference relation was in relation to consumption theory and demand theory which has not helped in collective choice theory.

3.1.* preference relation *(Technical Part)

*Binary Relations.

Dr. Amartya Sen has given lots of mathematical terms to explain the thing in better way. This forms as S x S. Earlier we show the transitivity, reflexivity and completeness. Now, out of so many mathematical terms we add three more for our purpose and they are Anti-symmetry, Asymmetry and symmetry. Let us examine these six things in relation to "at least as tall as" for measuring heights of all peaks of mountain.

1) When we say since a peak is as tall as itself, it is reflexivity. 2) Now if peak A is not at least as tall as peak B, than peak B will be at least as tall as peak A it is complete. 3) Peak A, being at least as tall as peak B which itself at least as tall as peak C. This is in relation to transitivity. 4) Peaks A and B could be of the same height without being the same peaks. This is anti-symmetric. 5) This is not asymmetric since A being at least as tall as B does not preclude the possibility that B will be as tall as A. 6) This is not symmetric as A being at least as tall as B does not at all impose any compulsion that B must be at least as tall as A. [43]

We can use the term "taller than" which will not satisfy three terms out of six terms. Different authors use different terms for the same thing.

* Maximal elements and choice sets

Here we define the relations of "strict preference" and "indifference". The definition of maximal elements is in binary relation; the elements of set which are not dominated by others in set. The "best" is defining

---

[43]   Ibid, page no.8.

as under. An element X can be called a "best" element of S if it is least as good as every other element in S with respect to the relevant preference relations.*

3.1.3.*, 3.1.4.*, 3.1.5.* A set of results of quasi-orderings, sub relation and compatibility, choke function and quasi-transitivity.

Here technically proved the naturally, to ordering and chains with partial ordering. Further it proved the rest of the two things.

* Preference and rational choice

The choice function is incorporating the rational function in it. This is in binary relation which is full of rationality property. We can think in other way and rationality condition in as a property of a choice function. The definition of rational choice is-if some lemon of subset S1 of S2 is best in S 2 then it is best in S 1. Finally it proved that preference and relation in binary term as well as rational choice.

Revealed preference is further development in preference theory. Revealed preference is the choice restricted to certain sub set alternative. The result may be useful in certain area only. Revealed preference has taken hold of choice theory in general and of demand theory in particulars. Revealed preference is used for market as well as non-market choice also. The weakness of revealed preference is choice is between two choices only.

Now onward we will leave the technical part as the discussion is not much of interest and beyond the general understanding.

3.2 Unanimity

The Pareto criterion

Dr. Amartya Sen says PARETO gave idea of criterion of comparison of social welfare. He proposed two rules. (1) If everyone in the society is indifferent between two alternative social situation X and Y then the society should be indifferent too; (2) If at least one individual strictly prefers X to Y and every individual regards X to be at least as good as Y, then the society should prefer X to Y.

In case of (1) an either choice is safe. In case of (2), no one is interested in y and someone is interested in X. The aggregate of individual is reflected in choosing X to Y as society, hence it is o.k.

We develop the concept of Pareto optimality. One has to choose X in alternative set. Now the alternative X is Pareto optimal and no other alternate is better than X as defined Pareto optimal. X is Pareto optimal as far as the society members considers at least as good as X and not a single member will say that one person will regard alternate better than X. [44]

Now one person prefers X to Y and another person prefers Y to Z in that case, it is not Pareto optimal. Pareto optimal is incomplete ordering, even though the reflexivity and transitivity is there. If two persons have opposite choice then also Pareto optimal will not work. Pareto optimal has limited use in precise circumstances.

Pareto optimal is very much useful in welfare economics in spite of its incompleteness. Some people are rich and some are extremely poor though the economy may be optimal. Here we have to tell rich to sacrifice for poor.

Pareto-inclusive choice rules

We are moving from individual ordering to social preference called "Collective choice rules". There are number of collective choice rules. The "method of majority decision" is one of them. Many people prefer X as good as Y as prefer Y to X. [45] The complete preference of ordering is here which was not in the Pareto optimal. In MMD the pair is in consideration. MMD is Pareto optimal including CCR. CCRs which generate preference relations are better than Pareto relation. You can find out this in aggregates of welfare or bargaining solution and of justice. Pareto optimal alternate is the best suitable for income distribution in the society. CCR inclusive of Pareto optimal is in a weak form because everyone prefers X to Y as X is better than Y. Pareto superior of X is not possible. Individual preference over the pair and the same pair is in choice between alternate pair then it is simple. One may think that the social choice over X and Y depends on individual preference over other pair. Pareto optimal is incomplete and it need more as conditions or limitation of application.

---

[44]   Ibid ,page no.21
[45]   Ibid, page no.23

Consensus as a Basis of collective action

The social action is heavily relying on unanimity. Dr. Amartya Sen says earlier Buchanan and Tullock [46] had made great efforts in this direction. One exception in unanimity is decision regarding unanimity is too expensive. Unanimity is the satisfactory base for choice. To arrive at unanimity one should apply the change. Change is not effective than you should remain in status quo position. This is very conservative because one man can oppose the change. The change blocked, no matter what everybody wants.

Buchanan and Tullock felt that politicians have forgotten about unanimity. The unanimity can come up during course of discussion and bargain. Unanimity may not exist in the beginning. People's compromise depends on own assessment and bargaining power. One social situation is accepted by society. Society is not binding for other social situation. Example: - In monopolistic labour market, labour accepts the term with an understanding that he may not get better term. This is a compromise position.

3.3   Collective rationality

The Bergson- Samuelson Welfare Function

All possible alternative state for the society has to take in to account for social welfare in scientific term. Bergson puts it in this way. "Social welfare can be thought to be a real valued welfare function, W, the value of which is understood to depend on all the variables that might be considered as affecting welfare".[47] We can examine the "social indifference curves" in Bergson approach using Pareto indifference rule and conclude that everyone in the society be indifferent. Scitovsky [48] approach is that it requires two alternative bundles of commodity and if everyone is indifferent in two bundles over the distribution of each over individuals. We can interpret this approach in Bergson way.[49]The result will be something like this. Person 1 may be better off in X than Y, and person 2 may be better off in

---

[46]   Ibid, page no.24

[47]   Ibid, page no.33

[48]   Ibid, page no.33

[49]   Ibid, page no.34

Y than in X, society might still be indifferent, if the overall social judgment is that the gain of one exactly compensates the loss of another.

Dr. Amartya Sen analyzed the Bergson approach and found the observation. The form of welfare function is not specified properly. The question of who provide the end-social welfare function-result is unanswered. Social order is not defined exactly. The choice in between alternate state, the function of W is not necessary to exist. Here the complete social ordering as R is necessary and this can be without welfare function of Bergson. Dr. Amartya Sen is not in favour of this idea.

Arrowian Social Welfare Function

Dr. Amartya Sen says Robbins attacked utilitarianism. Bergson and Samuelson [50] gave rational thought to social choice. This has cleared the confusion in welfare economics. Arrow asked how individual preference ordering can decide the social welfare function-W and what should be the collective choice rule. Dr. Amartya Sen says Arrow's social welfare function is different than Bergson and Samuelson. According to Arrow the collective choice rule that specifies "ordering" for the society is called social welfare function.(SWF) Arrow's SWF is different type of CCR. Second thing particular type of rule meant for SWF applied to CCR and the result is "Impossibility Theorem". SWF must satisfy certain condition of reasonableness. Again reasonableness is opinion therefore mild.

The general possibility Theorem

Dr. Amartya Sen discusses here Arrow's four conditions.

First, when we turn from individual preference to social preference than SWF should be wide enough to accommodate the individual ordering. In Pareto principal the unanimity is there but will not yield social ordering and hence it is not fitting in Arrow term. In case of MMD it falls in intransitivity area. The individual preference ordering should work in every configuration and in logical way. We will call it condition of unrestricted domain.

Second SWF must satisfy the weak Pareto condition.

Thirdly, Arrow requires social choice over the same alternate set on which individual ordering is only on those individual ordering alternatives sets.

---

50   Ibid, page no.35

Here the social choice should remain same i.e. between X and Y. Election involving between Mr. A and Mr. B. It should be A vis-à-vis B and not A vis-à-vis some other person. We will call this condition of independence of irrelevant alternatives.

Fourthly, SWF should not be dictatorial. Here individual prefers X to Y than society can prefer Y to Z. This is known as condition of non-dictatorial.

Opinion of Arrow is no theorem can satisfy all four conditions however weak it may be.

A comment on the Significance of Arrow's Results

Individual preference and social preference combination leads to inconsistency. This was reflected in the form of "Paradox of voting". [51] Consider three individuals 1, 2 and 3, and three alternatives X, Y, and Z. Let individual 1 prefer X to Y, and Y to Z, and individual 2 prefer Y to Z, and Z to X, and individual 3 prefer Z to X and X to Y. Here X can defeat Y by two votes to one. Y can defeat Z by same margin, so that transitivity requires that X should defeat Z in vote two. But, in fact, Z defeats X by two votes to one, here the MMD leads to inconsistencies. MMD applied to CCR. Here MMD satisfy the conditions of P, I and D but not condition U. MMD can be examined in "Rank ordering" system. This is not satisfying condition I. Here the position is of tie. In case of 'change' the value differs. This way we can examine number of possibility but in each case it requires specific conditions. We assume that there are at least two persons in the society and at least three alternative social states.

3.4   Choice versus orderings

Transitivity, quasi-transitivity, and Acyclicity

In SWF as collective choice rule, it requires reflexive, complete and transitivity. In case of 'choice' function transitivity can be skipped. The necessary of reflexive and completeness in choice function is defined as "Acyclicity". [52] If X1 is preferred to X2, X3, X4, and X5 and so on unto Xnth.

---

[51]   Ibid, page no.38
[52]   Ibid, page no.47

This is a weaker condition. In case of transitivity of indifference, it should X1 be strictly preferred to X nth. Transitivity is necessary for sets of three alternatives no matter how long the sequence is. In case of Acyclicity, all triple is acyclical and yet violate the rule.

Arrow's impossibility is applicable to SWF. Here the acyclicity in social preference can replace the transitivity. CCR generates the preference relation which is sufficient for choice functions and social decision functions-SDF. Arrow's impossibility is valid for SWF and not for SDF.CCR is sufficient for social choice and it satisfies all four conditions of Arrow. Arrow's impossibility theorem is the case of demanding social ordering and not the case of choice functions. CCR declares X to be socially better than Y if it is Pareto superior to Y and declares X to be socially at least as good as Y if Y is not Pareto-superior to X. Let us look at the 'paradox of voting'. The CCR specify will declare X, Y, and Z to be all indifferent to each other. We consider two persons in CCR. Acyclicity will be there. Every configuration of individual preference is true and satisfies condition U. SDF is satisfying Pareto condition and non dictatorship CCR failed on this count. "quasi-transitivity"[53] is for triple. This quasi-transitivity helps us to move from social ordering to social choice and away from Arrow's impossibility.

Collective choice and Arrow's Conditions

Arrow's conditions can be challenged and relaxation of a condition, the result will be demolition of theorem. According to Arrow, his conditions are inconsistent, but not sufficient for collective choice as satisfactory system. Arrow feels that they are necessary conditions for collective choice. Dr. Amartya Sen feels that he can prove that these conditions are sufficient and not inconsistent. Here you have to make Pareto optimal as indifferent; the distribution problem will be over. Quasi-transitivity will affect by way of dictatorial condition. We apply this result in all SDF than the conditions U, I, P, and D are satisfied. This will result in quasi transitivity and decision can be of "oligarchic" position. Here some people of society will prefer any X to any Y than society must regard X to be at least as good as Y and if all members of the group strictly prefer X to Y, then society must also prefer X to Y. In case of SDF, quasi-transitivity is not necessary as acyclicity is sufficient for choice function. In light of above Arrow's impossibility theorem is not at all important. SDF is able to pass the examination of Arrow theorem.

---

[53] Ibid, page no.49

Rationality and Collective Choice

Let us examine the Arrow theorem from one more point of view. Rational choice based on best alternative exists in each subset. There is indifferent condition in between X is preferred to Y, Y is preferred to Z and Z is preferred to X. Choice function exists and X is unique in all three choice function as X is no worse than other two. In case of two, each one is best as it is as good as other. You cannot say it is rational in case of one as X; it is to be chosen from the triple. The reason is it violates the property "b". If two alternatives and both are best in a subset, then one of them should not be best in the whole set, without the other also being best in that set. There is another condition in which if X is best in a whole set, than it must be best in all its subsets also. The both things are good in all respect for all CCRs.

If two alternatives are, both best in a subset, then one of them should not be best in the whole set, without the other also being best in that set. Choice function generated, in SDF, there for it is SWF. When we impose choice function on above proposition then it becomes impossibility theorem in SDF also. We have to forgo one of the conditions of Arrow for consistency in this regard. Here the property 'b' condition is better than all four conditions of Arrow in connection to SDF. We can go ahead without property" b" because it satisfy property "b" in choice function and get converted into SDF to SWF. There is many more dilemmas and many more conflicts other than Arrow impossibility which require thinking for collective choice function.

3.5   Values and choice

Welfare economics and value judgments

The term welfare is concern to the society. Society is a group of all people. Welfare can only be a policy recommendation. In case of choice between the social states is described as X and Y, in that case X to be chosen. The recommendations are in a sense value therefore welfare economics is value judgment. So many economists thought that welfare economics is value free. The debate is going on with notable economists on this subject. Earlier Hicks had define that "if A is made so much better off by the change that he could compensate B for his loss, and still have something left over, then the reorganization is an unequivocal improvement."[54]

The philosophical thought of "ought" is very much necessary in welfare economics rather than to eliminate from "is" proposition in economics. There are other propositions in ethics. Economists started doubting the compatibility of this in logical form as law. New welfare economics has nothing to do with this. When you say "value free" and "ethical Free" then it becomes the interpersonal conflict free. The hidden assumption is if everyone agrees on a value judgment then it is "objective".

Pareto optimal is for individual and comparison is between two. It is subjective. Robinson [55] thinks that the value judgment in economics is difficult in interpersonal comparison. Hicks were also of the opinion that when you talk about the compensation then the interpersonal conflict does not come in the picture. The compensation is paid to individual for better off. Samuelson concluded for welfare economics as "The only consistent and ethic-free definition of an increase in potential real income of a group is that based upon a uniform shift of the utility possibility function for the group." [56]

The value judgements in welfare economics cannot analyze but in common sense some are agreeing and some are not. The point is the value free in welfare economics is somewhat not suitable. Value judgment is acceptable to all.

Content of Welfare Economics: A Dilemma

We defined welfare economics concern with policy recommendations. This will be of three types (1) some factual premises (2) some value judgment and (3) Some on logic.

Now the factual premises concerns positive economics. The second proposition is of scientific type and it cannot argue out or discussed. The third one is related to logic. Someone will question that welfare economics exists or not. Mr.Graaff is not in favour of welfare economics.[57] Baumol put it "an ill concealed resemblance to obituary notices".[58] This is all due

---

54   Ibid, page no.56
55   Ibid, page no.57
56   Ibid, page no. 57
57   Ibid, page no.58
58   Ibid, page no.58

to the factor of reasoning. But the reasoning is grossly misleading due to it based on arbitrary definitions.

We discuss all three one by one. Dr. Amartya Sen proves that the logical exercise in policy recommendation in welfare economics cannot be ruled out. Logic is the heart of analysis or mathematical calculation or informal argument or formal as logic. One can accept as discipline or logic is his convenience. Logical reason is important for policy recommendations as a part of welfare economics. In traditional economics, existence, efficiency, stability and competitive general equilibrium were based on logic.

Secondly the value judgment set is based on individual ordering reflecting in social ordering. This is social welfare function in the definition of Arrow. The important point is, here we move from individual preference to social value based on public choice.

Lastly, economists think that the value judgment has very limited scope. The controversy is not useful for nature of value judgment, as it is not recognized fully.

Basic and non-basic judgments

Dr. Amartya Sen does a partition between basic and non-basic with specific reason. The definition of basic value judgment is it should apply under all conceivable circumstances. The opposite of this is non-basic. Let us examine this statement. "A rise in national income measured both at base and final year prices indicate a better economic situation". [59] This basic statement can be a non-basic in value system as soon as the person changes saying that "if circumstances were such and such." When some people say that killing is justifiable in that case it implies that person should not kill human being.

The relevance of factual consideration in ethical debates is the distinction in basic and non-basic partition. Someone makes a statement of value judgment more basic than it is non-challengeable, in a sense of factual or analytical. The value judgment is non-basic than it is disputable in factual and analytical sense. One should not misunderstand the value distinction. Factual circumstances cannot be taken as probable.

---

[59]   Ibid, page no.59

Example: - A says "Men and women should be allowed to dress as they like.

B says "Even if it turned out that mini-skirt caused cancer in the eyes of beholder?"

A says "Not in that case, of course. But I do not think that situation very likely." [60]

The analysis of this is not giving any result even though it is non-basic and factual one.

Value judgment can be made conditional in certain circumstances. In non-basic value judgment do not violate the conditions. Dr. Amartya Sen says "On rainy days, I should carry an umbrella". This is a basic value judgment. I want to make non-basic value judgment than I should suggest something else on rainy day.

All the basic value judgment sets are not consistent in terms of logic then they are non-basic. The example of perfect logic is as under. A man judges that "Consumption today should be maximized" and another statement "consumption a year hence should also be maximized".[61] These both the statements are in conflict only under factual circumstances. Here if you wish that every one's income should be higher than national average than there is analytical problem.

Facts and Value

One person puts a value judgment. Another person denies it. This happens because they differ on what should be chosen in some alternatives given for choice. Here they can discuss the reasons whether it is value judgment or not. There is no reason to accept or deny it. But it could be accepted or denied on factual or on logical grounds. Only the factual or logical propositions are not the reason to consider value judgment as non-basic. Hume said factual or logical could be one of the reasons amongst other reasons. One person's value judgment can be disputed on scientific grounds of validity by way of examination on factual premises or logical derivation. The reasons for rejection of value judgment could be only scientific. The

---

[60]   Ibid, page no.60
[61]   Ibid, page no. 61

basic judgment in value system cannot dispute by way of factual or analytical method. Non-basic judgment is dependent on particular factual assumption. You can move to another judgment independent of previous factual assumption.

Dr. Amartya Sen says Robbins said, "It does not seem logically possible to associate the two studies (Ethics and Economics) in any form but mere juxtapositions. Economics deal with ascertainable facts, Ethics with valuation and obligations." [62]This is true only in case of ethics deal with basic judgment. It is difficult to judge the end as a basic or non-basic. We disagree about means than it can be resolved by way of scientific analysis. The disagreement about morality of taking interest will be non argumentative. In this approach, it is very difficult to find out whether it is basic or non-basic.

We have to find certain judgment in this value system is basic or not. The answer to question may not be conclusive due to two reasons (1) person may not be able to ascertain all the convincible alternative factual circumstances (2) he would decide to change the judgment in any case or not. He will be inconclusive.

Person can have suitable revision in factual assumption and he can change his judgment in light of any factual assumption. By this process you cannot establish the basicness but it is basic in all sense. No value judgment is demonstrably basic but some are non-basic. We can assume that supposition is wrong then non-basic is basic. A constrain may convert the non-basic value judgment into basic judgment.

Look at this statement. "A rise in national income at every set of positive prices implies a better economic situation". This is non basic value judgment. Now we convert this into "basic" then we have two way results. (1) In case of fundamental value judgment to which a rise in national income corresponds, when the income distribution is no worse. (2) We can ask the person about the acceptance of the statement that "a rise of national income indicates a better economic situation, if the income distribution is unchanged". It is difficult in second method to ascertain that one value judgment belongs to this group only. You cannot decide the rational argument beyond point in value judgment.

---

[62]   Ibid, page no.62

Individual ordering and Choice rules

Let us start the discussion with individual position. Mr. A firmly prefers the social state of X to state Y. Mr. A is strongly anti dictatorial in his thought. Here Mr. A will face the conflict of opposite things. If Mr. A recommends choosing Y then he goes against his own choice. If he recommends X then it is dictatorial, against his principle. This thing happens in collective choice. Individual value affecting two ways (1) Individual preference (2) Concern with Collective choice rule. Here both sets of judgment are non-basic due to conflict. This conflict can be resolved with understanding that the CCR is incorporating the individual preference and convert it in to social ordering. One can see this thing in the process of selection of professor in university. In the first round they will vote to various candidates and in second round they vote chosen candidate. So selection becomes unanimous for the candidate.

In opposite case, individual will stick to their preference and preference R will be a way for public policy. Here R is social ordering. It is possible that the individual preference may not get included in CCR. Occasionally the individual preference can change the CCR mechanism. In the French revolution, the demand of equality, liberty and fraternity were extreme dissatisfaction against existing Collective choice mechanism.

It becomes tough when a person approves the CCR and wants his own ordering to be included in public policy. This is not possible. In special case, the CCR is the result of his choice social ordering included as recommendation in public policy. In general any one set is non-basic, possibly both.

Harsanyi has division the preference into "Subjective preference "and "Ethical preference". The personal actual preference is the subjective preference. Here the preference of individual will be called as ethical preference. The ethical preference is in which a person will get equal chance in any one position, if he had thought. Harsanyi is of the consideration that each person has maximum expected utility.[63] Person can choose moral value CCR in between possible CCRs. A chosen CCR will be called as an ethical CCR. This is a thing of aggregation and nature is of general approach.

---

[63]   Ibid, page no.66

Conditions on choice rules

Let us go deep and examine the value. Values can create conflict in the CCR. The best example is of Arrow's impossibility theorem. In this case, conditions like U, P, I, and D when imposed on CCR subject to condition O (i.e. on a SDF) will conflict. Here the logic of condition U is somewhat different. The rest of three conditions are suggesting what should be done given certain configuration of individual preference. Here it is a matter of specification or qualification. In case of condition U it is a positive aspect that CCR should work for all possible individual preference. It is quite possible that certain configuration of individual preference may not occur. If someone believes that some configurations will be ruled out in practice than condition U is not necessary in CCR as well as SWF. At subtle level conflict may prevail for not having plausible in a CCR but objectionable in some configuration of preference that might not be very plausible.

Let us look at the condition independence of irrelevant alternatives in CCR. MAY-economist has proposed a set of conditions.[64]The condition of anonymity, here you have my preference and I have your preference. This way it goes on. It means individual preference is permitted than social preference should remain invariant. Neutrality condition requires no discrimination in alternatives. Here the socially X is as good as Y then W should be as good as Z. The criteria of X are replaced by W. In the situation of positive responsiveness, individual and society preference have positive relationship. Previously X was as good as Y, now X moves higher status in some one preference than Y and not falling in any one preference than X is socially better. MAY says this type of CCR is only considered as MMD (Method of majority decision).

Dr. Amartya Sen has discussed the various things like, transitivity, acyclicity in the light of MMD and found that absence of any one condition will give result of impossibility position. The possible solution is, we should make responsiveness as "Negative responsiveness" then the problem of quasi transitivity and acyclicity will be solved. We can prove that Pareto incomparable pairs are socially indifferent by putting in CCR as X is socially better than Y and if someone prefers X to Y and every one regards X at least as good as Y in Pareto extension. Pareto

---

[64]   Ibid, page no.68

extension is not agreeable in the distributional judgment to some people. They may hesitate to reject other conditions. This proves that CCR is having Pareto extension. There is a difference between Pareto extension and MMD. The MMD is not satisfying quasi transitivity in social preference. Pareto extension does not satisfy positive responsiveness. Arrow's "Positive association" is still weak condition compare to "Non negative responsiveness". May's positive responsiveness and Arrow's positive association takes us away from MMD and Pareto extension rule. It is difficult to judge the conditions in isolation; The CCR nature will be non-basic and requires precise circumstances to examine.

3.6   Conflicts and dilemmas

Critique of Anonymity and neutrality

Many actual collective decision procedures violate the condition of Anonymity and neutrality though they are powerful. The anonymity condition is fulfilling in case of U.N.O. general assemble voting. It decides that procedure is simple majority and matter of substance requires two third majorities. In Security Council of U.N.O. special veto power granted to five countries. This violates the condition of neutrality.

The free market allocation procedures under capitalism or socialism are non neutral and non anonymous. I choose my consumption basket and you choose your consumption basket. After this our preference will result in different social outcome though social alternates are same. This violates the condition neutrality. Example of market mechanism: - I prefer my wall to be blue rather than white. You have opposite choice and society is indifferent. As per market mechanism I will get my wall painted in Blue. I want to substitute your colour but market mechanism will not allow the change. You will have your wall painted in white. This violates neutrality condition. The market mechanism failure will be defended as "externality". The values of individual freedom of choice are more important.

Liberal values and an Impossibility result

Some social choices are personal. Say. Mr. A lies on back when he sleeps (X) everything else being equal, Mr. A lies on his belly when he sleeps (Y). Now suppose Mr. A prefers opposite (Y to X) where as many other want to be opposite (X to Y). Here only Mr. A is involve---one person. Sometimes the one person choice may turn into CCR. This is a condition of liberalism. This is very weak. Here more than one pair and more than one alternative are available. The condition L is demanding more. We further develop this thing into two individuals and one pair of alternative. This will be known as L*--minimal liberalism. In SDF, if we impose the condition of L* than it is inconsistent with condition U and condition P. The result will be completely different than Arrow's impossibility theorem. Condition L* is stronger than condition D of Arrow but much weak in term of liberalism. Arrow's conditions are applicable only to SWF and not SDF. The SWF and SDF conditions can be explained by various examples. Let us consider the social choice with three alternatives. In case of three, the every alternate will be worst. There is no best alternative or no optimal choice possible.

Critique of Acyclicity

Any particular pair of alternative and unrestricted domain has no conflict between Pareto principle and minimum liberalism. One can reject pair-wise choice and not to generate choice function out of social preference relation. If condition P and condition L* is not relaxed and configuration of individual preference ordering in choice mechanism working than acyclicity has to go. There is no point in selecting A from A, B, and C and rejecting A in A and C pair. Property is most appealing condition. Rejection of acyclicity is a short of cheating. Acyclicity is social choice for non-pair wise. The discussion is highly technical and examining various things in alternative and opposite ways giving lots of new possibility in choice function at individual as well as interpersonal level and society level.

Critique of Liberal Values

Condition L* is minimal liberal. Here person's personal affairs are unsupportable.

Example Mr. A's wall colour may be disturbing to Mr. B. than it is Mr. B's business as well. If it makes Mr. A unhappy that Mr. B should read *"Lady Chatterley's lover"* while awake, than Mr. A is relevant party to the choice. Major thing like pornography, is a point of view for public policy. Here public policy is imposed on individuals, as others will, for which the particular individual is not concern. The condition L* is very weak as per the opinion of Dr. Amartya Sen. The condition L* is in relation to two person for one pair of alternative per person. This is a form of most limited expression of freedom of individual. This violates the privacy of individual as it is forced upon him.

Critique of the Pareto Principle

Everyone knows that Pareto principal is in weak form. We have to know who prefers what but also why he has that preference. Mr. A does not wish to read the book *"Lady Chatterley's lover"* himself if the choice is between his reading it but wants to deny Mr. B. the advantage of reading it. Here Mr. A's preference ordering diverts from value of Mr. A's preference. Here the preference for Mr. A's reading the book *"Lady Chatterley's lover"* vis-à-vis Mr. B's reading book. According to Dr. Amartya Sen one should not think too much about others preference. This should be ignored.

The above reasoning takes us to different stage than Pareto principle. First thing is does social choice depends on individual preference or something else. The reason can be other thing changes the status of concept of collective choice rule. The result will be the social choice cannot be an individual preference function. Second thing, one can argue that the collective choice mechanism cannot work on information of such a complicated nature. This can be a cause of individual ordering. It can take into account in to consideration by taking preference over other alternatives pairs. In such a situation, CCR is violating condition I. Now the condition satisfies Pareto principle even though it is objectionable. One can say that individual preference between X and Y is insufficient information for social choice in X and Y. To say that Pareto quasi ordering as "the unanimity quasi ordering" is not correct because unanimity is on a particular pair only.

The consequence of rejection of Pareto principle will be heavy in the field of collective choice in general and welfare economics in particular. The political choice mechanism is Pareto inclusive. The externalities are present in free market allocation therefore the Pareto optimality is absent.

The irrelevant alternative condition is in the Pareto principle. This condition is not useful against the concept of unusefulness of the thing. This is in indirect sense only. Mr. A's reason for preferring to read the book *"Lady Chatterley's lover"* himself rather than giving it to Mr. B may be based on A's expectation of B's social behaviour after he reads *"Lady Chatterley's lover"*. One can see that Mr. A's preference ordering has not given enough ground for not reading by Mr. B. In case of Pareto principle you can doubt the same.

Critique of Unrestricted Domain

Condition U is important in theorem of collective choice. Number of configurations of individual preference having the condition of P and condition of L* are in agreement. These terms are not in agreement in reality. The reason is individual freedom is not guaranteed in collective choice mechanism. The problem can be dismissed by way of respecting individual privacy and personal choice. When the individual preference falls under specific pattern than Pareto principle disturbs the minimal liberalism. This type of reasoning is to ridicule condition P in Pareto principle. In CCR, individual preference actually will decide the goodness or badness rather than the logical conceivable pattern. In CCR the certain restricted domain and secondly differently restricted domain may be in conflict then we might chose set of individual preference keeping an eye on it.

3.7   Interpersonal aggregation and comparability

Independence of irrelative Alternatives

Rank ordering covers in SWF where condition U, P and D is satisfied but not condition I. We saw the relation between condition I and liberal condition. Opening of condition I have number of possibility in which one of the possibilities is of rank ordering. Utilitarian approach is ruled out in condition I. The condition of independence of irrelevant has number of possibilities on relaxation and this should be explored. Individual utility aggregation is not dependent on condition I. The definition of CCR is negative for condition I. The CCR is completely unchanged when the utility measure is changed but individual ordering is not changed. This is applicable naturally to SWF and SDF type CCR. In case of change in definition of CCR and utility measure is admitted than in that case condition I will be a problem.

Social choice involving X and Y and individual ranking for third alternative is violating the condition I. This is "irrelevance" aspect. Social choice involving X and Y and individual ordering over X and Y called as preference of intensity. This we call ordering aspect. The irrelevance is mostly a part of "ordering" aspect of condition. Each individual has cardinal utility scale than irrelevant alternative has no place for construction of scale. Social choice is positive after adding all the difference in utility between X and Y for individual. It is declared that X is preferred than Y. Now the utility difference is negative in that case the preference will change to Y in place of X. This violates Arrow's condition of independence of irrelevant of alternatives. This is not true. It is the violation of "ordering" aspect without involving irrelevance. You have to fix two points on utility scale and this violates the other alternatives. Preference intensity is used for interpersonal correspondence in social aggregation. Here the preference intensity violates both the ordering aspect and irrelevant aspect.

Comparability, Cardinality and Discrimination

One can see the reflection of interpersonal comparability in individual utility units. Von Neumann-Morgenstern approach is to calculate individual utility scales than interpersonal comparison problem does not arise.[65] Interpersonal comparability will change as soon as you make unit double of one person, living others on same scale than it is individual arbitrariness. In utility, the measure is one to one. In behaviourist measure, it is degree Say Happy, happier, happiest. LITTLE [66] in 1950 put this concept. Here the interpersonal comparability is there. Here you can make marginal comparison.

Now we have to examine two things (1) cardinal measure of individual welfare and (2) rule for interpersonal comparison.

Cardinal measure of individual welfare is based on assumption that individual cannot have infinite level of discrimination because he cannot make fine comparisons. Individual can make out the minimum utility difference from one level to another level. We can get cardinal measure of utility between two discrimination levels. This can be put in positive linear transformation. Individual is indifferent between all alternative in same discrimination. Cardinal measure is originally belongs to Borda and further developed by Armstrong and other economists.[67]

---

[65]   Ibid, page no.92
[66]   Ibid, page no.92
[67]   Ibid, page no.93

Goodman and Markowitz made development in interpersonal comparison. [68] They assumed that the ethical level is the same from one discrimination level to another discrimination level for each individual and independent from the level effected the change. This is very easy thing. You want to compare the alternative X to alternative Y. Find the difference from original level to change level in one alternative in positive or negative sense. This approach is not practical in real life. From analytical point of view also difficult but it is important in the field of economics.

The criticism of this approach is observation of limited level of discrimination of individual in given fixed set of alternatives. A new commodity is available to person than independent effect is not there in X and Y alternatives. Ethical assumption is difficult for all people, as person's perception is different by emotion. The social welfare of individual will be different. One say "HORRIBLE" another say "GOOD". Here the ethical assumption is objectionable and not the condition I. The ethical assumption appears as arbitrary and objectionable.

Uses of von Neumann-Morgenstern Cardinalization

The behaviour of a rational person in no risk situation can be explained in ordinal utility. The situation may change in risk condition. Von Neumann-Morgenstern provides a set of utility number corresponding to set of alternatives for behavioural satisfaction to attempt the maximum utility numbers.

Marschak had given the simpler formula.[69] Marschak suggested a system with four things (1) Complete ordering (2) Continuity (3) non-different prospect being sufficient (4) equivalence of the mixture of equivalent prospects.

Number one, two and four are not sustaining on test from various type of alternative combinations. Say for complete ordering. A person climb mountain and survival in love of danger, percentage can be from 95% to 80 % to 1%, out of 100 %. In case of continuity, person is poor and has a thought of sin to play gamble. There is an equal chance for prosperity by playing the gamble and a chance of loss. As soon as he decides to gamble,

---

[68]   Ibid, page no.93
[69]   Ibid, page no.95

the purity destroyed. This violates the continuity. Neumann-Morgenstern correctly pointed out for fourth condition that it is opposite in nature. Person may play for "thrill" for once in his life. People are having simple attitude for gambling. Arrow commented that utility indicator is not useful for social choice.

Arbitrariness is objectionable in any cardinal scale and independence of action set. Arbitrariness is in cardinal as well as in other scaling also. In case of ethics, particular set is chosen even though it is having arbitrariness. One can justify the gambling for equal chances in individual preference in social choice. Cardinal measure is entirely personal. The method of normalization of Interpersonal invites criticism.

Partial comparability

Cardinal measurability is problem with first utilitarianism and after interpersonal aggregation. In case of aggregate welfare, one can debate the famous incident. When Rome was burning, the king Nero was playing fiddle. Here the welfare of Romans had gown down and Nero was delighted. The interpersonal comparison is between two Romans and not Roman and king. This cannot be done. The welfare has gone down in any case definitely. The sum total of welfare went down as a consequence. This is a case between non comparability and full comparability.

Dr. Amartya Sen says Robbins (1932) and others failed to distinguish between SOME and TOTAL comparability. Now let us go further and compare the welfare from one to one, to MANY to MANY in cardinal fashion. We take three people and three alternatives. We use the formula of worst for zero and good for one. This is cardinal fashion welfare.

Table: - Tentative welfare indicators.[70]

	Alternatives	Alternatives	Alternatives
Individuals	X	Y	Z
A	1	0.90	0
B	1	0.88	0
C	0	0.95	1

---

[70]   Ibid, page no. 100

In case of C the difference from Y to X is sharp (0.95) to (0) and in case of A the difference from X is mild from (1) to Y (O.90). If we multiply this by ten times than the difference for A from X to Y is only one point. Where as in case of C from Y to X is 9.5 (measure 0.95 x 10 = 9.5). Here aggregate result is incomplete but in choice function, Y is the best. The rest of writing is highly technical and covering many aspects of ordering in partial and full comparability.

Adding ordinal-type welfare

Utility measurement for individual is difficult. There can be more than one cardinal measure but ethically it is difficult to establish the superiority. All the systems are accepted than it will not transform in linear like cardinal. We say this as ordinal. We can obtain quasi-ordering aggregates for individual with ordinal and partial comparability. In special case of classical utilitarian approach, aggregate welfare maximization is for analysis in collective choice. Here complete comparability and cardinality is used as general frame work.

3.8   Cardinality with or without comparability

Bargaining advantages and collective choice

In collective choice, individual welfare has three problems (1) measurability of individual welfare, (2) interpersonal comparability of individual welfare and (3) Social preference relation in individual welfare function and comparison assumption. These three are interdependent. NASH gives solution for "bargaining problem".[71] He takes "products" as against sum in individual welfare. The failure to hit a bargain will create the status quo position. In case of bargain, the parties are in status quo position and problem will be trivial due to absence of bargaining contract, this will not hurt anyone. If both are choosing status quo position than in cooperative position, there will be a problem. In status quo cooperative position both are choosing same set than there is trivial and they can chose the outcome which will be best. In bargain and in cooperative position both will gain, where as in contract one will get more and other will get less. This is a case of individual behaviour in uncertainty. Here change of origins and individual utility function is in

---

[71]   Ibid, page no.118

invariant position. The original is out and units simply changed. In this process interpersonal comparability is absorbed.

One individual unit is in variance and systemically it relates with other unit then the social state ranking may not be sensitive. This relation is in correspondence to one to one, yield complete ordering or none; in case of Pareto preferences and indifferences which are reflected in social choice. Nash had wiped out this by making use of status quo. This different status quo point will generate different solutions.

The non cooperative outcome depends upon the objective of exercise. We have seen the status quo position in bargaining position and in contract position. Zeuthen had put forward the same idea like Nash and Harsanyi had noted that concession will bring the result like Nash formula. [72] Definitely Nash solution is not ethical. Example:-The best prediction is not fair or just out come in circumstances like unemployment workers agreed to work in subhuman wages and poor service term in absence of contract then to starve. There may be contract between labourer and employer, but labour has poor bargain power.

Harsanyi's ethical judgment model is useful in case if he thinks that he has equal chance in either party position. In absence of equal chance, what he will predict will be all together different. Apart from Harsanyi's ethical judgment model, there are other models also like aggregate welfare maximization with partial comparability or fairness and justice of Rawls and Economist Suppes model of "grinding principle' in collective choice mechanism as the method of majority decision.[73]

Dr. Amartya Sen says HARSANYI's (1955) model of "Ethical judgment" is useful here. Like that, MR. Braithwaite's (1955), [74] a tool for the moral philosopher is also interesting. The situation is somewhat like this. Mr. A likes to play piano and Mr. B is playing Jazz on trumpet. If both play simultaneously, there is disturbance due to imperfect soundproof walls. If Mr. B plays trumpet will be more harmful to Mr. A than Mr. A will play piano to Mr. B as less harmful. Author's final solution is to recommend the divide up timing. Here more timing given to Mr. B as Mr. B prefers

---

[72]   Ibid, page no.120
[73]   Ibid, page no.121
[74]   Ibid, page no.121

both of them to playing at once to neither of them playing; where as Mr. A prefers silence. Here Mr. B has a threat advantage in absence of contract. If Mr. B is unaware of this threat advantage, he might propose equal sharing of time. This will emerge as actual bargain. A solution based on the threat advantage of the two parties indeed manifestly unfair.

Some people are in favour of prediction of outcome. This is not correct. The ethical judgment is useful for three things. (1) This is an objective study and useful for improvement of collective choice mechanism. (2) The bargain power in society is a useful function for better social choice mechanism. The feeling of injustice will find out the agency to solve the problem. The Rousseau's analysis of "Injustice" and Marx's theory of "Exploitation" are the example of bigger impact on society. (3) There is often conflict between principle and action chosen by people. The principle is a part of collective choice and action is an analytical part for social decision. This will check in society the consistency of principle and action. The ethical judgments models are not useful in value judgment about principle of collective choice. Ethical judgement talks about 1) Status quo 2) Threat advantage and 3) Complete avoidance of interpersonal comparison are minus points.

Cardinality and impossibility

Social preference as individual welfare function redefined that the status quo position violates the condition of "independence of irrelevant alternatives". The social choice in two individual taken as cooperative then this will result in impossibility theorem. This is for cardinality in absence of interpersonal comparability. Social welfare function is one social ordering for one individual. The transformation of individual welfare function, in no comparability, leaves the social ordering unchanged. In cardinality it is a condition that transformation of any utility function in any individual is permitted. We can modify Arrow's conditions to suit social welfare function. We show that we have to make change in independence of irrelevant alternatives and remaining three will redefine easily. Here social preference invariant as individual utility measure remains invariant. These all four conditions will turn SWFL in to impossibility theorem. Earlier we show that variance is possible to some liner transformation in individual units for interpersonal comparability. With unit comparability of cardinality, aggregation of SWFL satisfies Pareto principle, condition of D and condition I. When cardinality is combined with non comparability will fail to generate from individual welfare function to social ordering.

3.9   Equity and justice

Universalization and Equity

Simple definition of interpersonal comparison is to put oneself in position of another person. Sidgwick explained it as whatever action any of us judges to be right for himself, he implicitly judges to be right for all similar persons in similar circumstances.[75] Hare explained it in detail. Hare converted it into meaning rather than mere principle. Suppose that I say to someone "You ought not to smoke in this compartment," and there are children in compartment. Here" Ought" refers to some general principle.[76]

Now let us see the difference between "immoral" and "ignorant". If a white South African claims that apartheid is good, but concedes that his judgment would have been different if he were himself black, then in Hare's system he would reveal an ignorance of "The way in which the word 'good' functions". In contrast, if the criterion was taken as a moral principle and not as a matter of meaning, then the white South African in question could be called, in some sense, immoral, but not, in any sense, ignorant. From the above, one can think of two things: 1) the question of universalizability of value judgment and 2) as if interpersonal permutations given other things should be taken as "exactly similar" circumstances. Arrow had argued the universalizability in another context. According to him, "Value judgments may equate empirically distinguishable phenomena, but they cannot differentiate empirically indistinguishable states".[77] The concept of universalizability had two problems. They are either to be considered as 'logical' or 'normative rule'. This takes us to scope of thing. You take it logical, than it violates, so called Hume's law. According to Dr. Amartya Sen, if this is taken as a logical necessity, two states being factually exactly the same(a fact) seems to imply that they are equally good (a value judgment) .

The scope of principle universalizability is important than logical or normative. As two things are not exactly alike, 'relevantly similar' comes

---

75   Ibid, page no.131
76   Ibid, page no.132
77   Ibid, page no.133

in picture. Relevant similarity is a value judgment. Example: if X and Y are exactly similar except in some respects, and if a person's judgments in question involving X and Y are independent of those respects then X and Y are relevantly similar. Person's judgement is similar for X and Y when the two alternatives are relevantly similar.

We have to examine interpersonal permutations in light of similarity. Here Sidgwick principle of equity is the direct consequence of universalizability as positive. The negative of this is the question of relevant similarity. Moral judgment criteria are difficult in Hare's use of interpersonal permutations. Individual cannot say honestly that he will hold exactly same judgment in interpersonal permutations. The mild form of moral judgment is in names of 'fairness,' 'justice' and 'ethical preference' has two things. These concepts apply to some limited categories of moral virtue and second thing individual is unaware of exact position.

Fairness and Maxim in Justice

Rawls principle of fairness is the result of fair agreement with no vested interest. He derives the principle of justice from this. Here the initial situation is fair and in original position. Interpersonal permutation is absence. Fairness and justice are applicable in cooperative bargaining situation in original position. Two principles of justice emerge from this fairness. (a) Each person has an equal right in liberty compatible in liberty for all (b) Inequalities are arbitrary unless they work for every one's gain and open for all. This means it works for welfare of worst-off-person of society. The first thing is for liberty and second thing is for interpersonal conflict. We can find out here the worst-off person with the help of interpersonal conflicts. Rawls' main theme is to apply for institutions to be chosen for maximum to order social state bases of individual ordering. This is useful in interpersonal welfare comparison.

Arrow suggested SWF. This procedure does not fit to Arrow's SWF as it is for one social ordering. The worst-off person welfare is going up in each alternative even though the individual ordering remains same. Here individual is I and X is state. The welfare of different people can be different. SWF does not permit this.

In case of CCR, the individual ordering takes place as ranking with interpersonal permutations. The statement would be Individual 'I' has a higher welfare level in state X and individual 'J' has in state Y can be translated. Now we consider M states and N ordering. In case of Rawls maximin ordering, one can obtained immediately as MN element, where as in case of CCR social ordering dependent on N ordering in M state. The ordering may be of individual or unanimous views of all. Unanimity will create the same problem like SWF and CCR. Maxim criteria in social decision will face some problem.

Example one: - Pareto stronger condition is violated. The welfare level of A and B in state X and Y is given in the table.[78]

	Welfare of A	Welfare of B
State X	10	1
State Y	20	1

The maximum rule will make X and Y indifferent. In case of Pareto Y is superior to X. The worst-off individual is no better off under Y than under X.

Example Two: - Here the inequality is not reflected in maximin rule, as it hides lot of issue related to equality in worst-off individual or worst-off individual group.[79]

	Welfare of A	Welfare of B	Welfare of C
State x	100	80	60
State Y	100	61	61

The maximin rule indicates that Y is preferred to X. Welfare of group B and welfare of group C is reduced compare to welfare of group A in state X and welfare of group A and welfare of group B is widen In state Y. Inequality is difficult to judge in worst-off position to best-off position. Rawls insistence is on institutional frame work than individual. The minor gain wiped out in big gain of others. Here no trade-off position emerges. Rawls maximin rule is justified in the relationship of fairness.[80]. Fairness

78 Ibid, page no.138
79 Ibid, page no.139
80 Ibid, page no.139

element is applying to all. Person does not know his attributes but joins in system which satisfies important value of moral system.

Person has pessimistic outlook than in fairness the uncertainty will not achieve definite conclusion. Here the utility is not distributed like utilitarian concept.

The institution comes in picture. The suffering of man by religion or otherwise will mutiny and the big gain cannot wipe out the small loss. Maximine approach is for institution. Rawl's insistences to accept the maximine principle in original is not convincing. Hurwitz developed the pessimism-optimism index in which maximine has last consideration.[81] You can apply it after generalisation. In Hurwitz concept the maximine original position assumption can be one out of many. Rawl should have taken the social ordering in centre. Institution approach against individual is different thing. Rawls approach to "principle of fairness" is more appealing than "principle of Justice". The application of fairness in collective choice mechanism is like uncertainty in the same approach.

Impersonality and expected utility Maximization

Harsanyi has two sets of consideration for each individual.[82] The first one is subjective preference as they actually are and second one is ethical preference which one can say impersonal. This impersonal concept is in line of Hare's universalizability and Rawls fairness. The impersonality concept requires assuming the equiprobability. The ignorance of Rawls is somewhat equal here in equiprobability. Harsanyi is of the assumption that impersonality is in individual term and will satisfy the Von Neumann-Morgenstern rational behaviour under risk concept. Ethical preference is for utility maximum and this will result in maximization of utility for all.

Harsanyi thought for social choice. He put a theorem that if social preference and individual preference satisfy Marschak postulate and if everyone being indifferent implies social indifference, then social welfare must be a weighted sum of individual utilities.

Let us examine the impersonality. Example: - In one society 99 are free man and one is slave. If someone wants to replace the slave then will society

---

81   Ibid, page no.140
82   Ibid, page no.141

morally supports his Idea? The answer is, in case of "fairness", this will not reflect as Rawls thinks for worst-off position. In case of Hare's test, it requires much more than this. Here the equiprobability is the solution with putting self in that social position.

Let us examine this from interpersonal point of view. [83]

	Welfare of 1	Welfare of 2
State X	1	0
State Y	1/2	1/2

The explanation is, both are indifferent in state X and Y but from equality point of view, they will prefer state Y than state X. Here we calculate the welfare of impersonal and the exactness of distribution of welfare in individuals. Diamond criticizes Harsanyi's "strong independence assumption" in social preference.

Let examine the table of Diamond.[84]

	0.5 probability		0.5 probability	
Lottery1	Ua=1	Ub=0	Ua=0	Ub=1
Lottery2	Ua=1	Ub=0	Ua=1	Ub=0

Comparison between two persons and two lotteries gives result of sure thing principle. Here Two persons are as A and B and two lotteries as lottery one and lottery two. Lottery 2 seems unfair to individual B, while lottery 1 gives B a fair shake due to probability. Here the sure thing principle is rejected. Let us apply little change. We will make B's value as two. We can say that lottery 1 is preferred now. No one has stated clearly about interpersonal comparability. We can conclude that Harsanyi needs unit comparability and Diamond needs full comparability in aggregation. Ultimately the lottery result will come as 1 to 0 and not egalitarian in independence assumption.

---

83   Ibid, page no.143

84   Ibid, page no.144

Utility maximization is doubt full proposal. We show earlier the argument of ½, ½ against 1-0. The first value is rather strong. Here the utilitarianism in general and Harsanyi criteria in particular will be indifferent, where as egalitarian distribution will favour this proposal. A Maximin criterion is for level of welfare. A utilitarian criterion is for social ordering with assumption of cardinality and unit comparability. Maximin do not require this. Ethical consideration is relevant for both. We compare the welfare unit of different people than it is utilitarianism with importance, where as if we consider welfare level than it is simple.

This type of evaluation for social judgement is worse than interpersonal comparison we make.

Grading principles of Justice

Suppes' model of "grading principles" yields the partial ordering. Suppe devise the ethical rules for two persons. Here the act and its consequences found out. This is Pareto-like judgment in individual's own preference. This can be explained technically with the assumption of two persons and action and likely consequences. Economist Suppe's theory proves the partial ordering over the pair of consequences for individual. Let us examine this for interpersonal relation. Asymmetric and transitivity are the consequences. Suppe admits the element of justice and each person decides his strategy for game. First rule is to choose each point and second rule is to choose one point. This will not work as the behaviour is arbitrary. Suppes grading principle of justice satisfy the requirement of universalizability. Suppes principle does not require interpersonal comparison of welfare. This does not require any Cardinalization. Suppes principle is incomplete in the rank ordering. The personal difference does not reflect in this principle.

In case of personal differences consider the "Test" of individual in case of choice of eating items. The Y is preferred in Pareto optimal where as in case of test; X is preferred by both of them. Here X is admissible in sense of justice. When you apply ethical than the result will be wrong. Here the person is having own test and for other's test also. Suppes model takes it as subjective. The same thing is absent in Rawls and Harsanyi. The problem can be solved by changing the view from objective to subjective in others test also. Suppes grading principle does not have justice in a sense that interpersonal comparison is absent which makes principle to reformulate.

Grading principle, Maximin, and utilitarianism

Grading principle can be extended from two persons to "nth" person societies. This will resolve conflict of maximin and utilitarian concept. In this case the larger welfare aggregates makes worst-off person to well-off person. The yield is strict partial ordering which is an incomplete criterion. The extended grading principle will give 3,628,800 different ways for "nth" persons.[85] This is much better in comparison to Pareto one to one position.

3.10 Majority choice and related systems

The Method of majority decision

Method of majority decision is studded more in collective choice rule.

Borda (1770) and Codorcet (1785) there after Laplace (1814) and Lewis Carroll (1876) [86] widen their interest in majority rule study. Majority rule has wide appeal and as a system in collective choice. MMD is satisfying most of the conditions of CCR and therefore decisive. CCR in which Pareto principle, condition U, condition D, condition I, Condition N, condition A, condition S are satisfied. MMD has minus point for intransitivity and acyclicity. The "paradox of voting" is the example of the same. MMD is not working for some configuration of individuals in SWF and SDF. MMD violates condition L and L*, which gives little scope for individual freedom. Problem of inconsistency will arise in MMD for some choices. You cannot change decision procedure. Still MMD is used in social choice. MMD does not take in to account the intensities of preference. Here not mere number but how much is also important. Aggregation procedure is special case in utilitarian with weak assumption and it was threat for take over on MMD. MMD ignores comparison between absolute levels of welfare of different people. The notion of fairness of Rawls and justice of Suppes works against MMD. At institutional level, MMD is used effectively. Interpersonal comparison, intensities of preference and measurement of wellbeing is difficult in MMD. We use these concepts for value judgment. In case of choice, it is difficult to find out the private and public choice. MMD is passing all these problems due to independence of irrelevant

---

85   Ibid, page no.151
86   Ibid, page no. 161

alternatives, neutrality and anonymity. The simplicity, symmetry and primitive logic attract many.

Probability of Cyclical Majorities

Inconsistency in MMD is a problem. We have to find out the probability in case of no majority winner. Many economists have work on this. We have to find out assumption about the probability distribution in different individual ordering for each person. First assumption is all ordering are equally likely for every individual. Guilbaud confirm 8.77% probability of cyclical majority in strong ordering.[87] He noted that there is less chance than 1 in 11 that no majority winner will emerge. Garman and Kamien also Niemi and Weisberge had obtained an exact pattern of equiprobability of there being no majority winner as number of voter differs.[88] Probability impasses increase on the number increases but never to 1%. Niemi and Weisberg calculated the probability failure. The probability of cyclical majorities travels towards 1(one) as the number goes up. The equiprobability assumption is in favour of society.

Individual preference is the result of pattern of social, economical, political and cultural forces. The patterns are different. The difference will produce consistent and transitive majority decision. The Class war between two groups results in to transitive. Individual preference will avoid inconsistency choice. The question of motivation and interpretation is there. This may be either subjective or frequencies of different ordering. Much depends upon a person, who is well verse with the subject. The MMD can be thought in connection of time say today and T time-in future. This cannot answer the probability. Further study can be done in light of more empirical data analysis.

Restricted Preferences

Black and Arrow defined the problem of cyclical majority as alternative approach as "Single-peaked preference". [89] According to them majority

---

87   Ibid, page no.163
88   Ibid, page no.163
89   Ibid, page no. 166

decision will be transitivity irrespective of the requirement for it. This approach makes use of qualitative pattern of preference provided total number of persons odd. The qualitative approach is different than probability approach. Here political rationality is major thrust. In single peaked preference individual alternative is in terms of some dimension and any pair-wise choice, vote for that alternative which is closer to one's position. There is extreme right and extreme left group both will decide their alternatives. In any case the number of voters is odd than majority decision will be transitivity. In absence of utility it will be single peaked because here ordering is taken in to account and not utility. Single peakedness does not require arbitrariness. Every triple alternative are arrange able in single peaked position. Single peakedness is a partial agreement. Alternative can be best, medium or simple. This is a case of value restriction. The violation of value restriction will not affect transitivity. You select one from odd and give him some position. This will make equal number. Here the selected person is willing or not is a question. You cannot omit the odd factor so easily. The oddness can be nullified in case of SDF and not SWF. In individual ordering strict value restriction is necessary than MMD is SDF. In individual ordering, other conditions are not strict, then value restriction will work as "limited agreement". In case of "External restriction" is in the pair of X and Y and Y and Z, if Z is best than X should be worst in that ordering. Everyone thinks that everyone agrees that some alternative is at least as good as some alternative in each triple. The external condition is also necessary. Limited agreement is easy to follow. The external restriction has three things known as "echoic preference", "antagonistic preference" and "dichotomous preference".

For majority condition of SDF rather VR, LA or ER which is necessary in each triple for majority decision of MMD in SDF. This is for rational choice under MMD. ER is a must in each triple for SWF in MMD.

Conditions of collective choice rules and restricted preference

Dr. Amartya Sen says, Inada (1969) [90] find out three approaches. VR works a wide class of collective choice rules I.E. 2/3 majority.

L.A. works for CCR. Condition I, N and R and P* may be applicable to many other CCRs. In case of VR, these conditions are not applicable.

---

[90]   Ibid, page no. 169

In case of E.R, it violets quasi transitivity even though CCR is N, A, R, and P* is there. If we convert R, negative response in to S positive response then it becomes MMD. When one takes MMD then E.R. is sufficient for full transitivity.

These are all technical terms. Further discussion is of high level and proves that it requires thinking in various ways for restricted preference.

3.11 Theory and practice

Systems of Collective Choice

There are different ways for base of social preference. There are number of preference of members of society. These two things are different. Arrow defined social welfare function in which social ordering specified for each set of individual ordering. Social decision function is based on choice. Social preference relation based on individual ordering. We can say that SWF is a part of SDF. Consistence factor is strong in SWF than SDF. This has resulted in to "impossibility theorem" and other results. SDF is having problem due to choice factor. SDF is having quasi-transitivity and acyclicity even though have problem for collective choice. The conditions are not reasonable then various types of SDF come in to existence. When you demand less from SDF, is not necessary, social preference must generate choice function. A quasi-ordering is giving guidance in many cases though weak but useful in many CCRs.

Individual preferences are also of various types. The collective choice systems are based on more information regarding individual attitude to social alternatives, than conveyed by ordering. We can take help of utility function in cardinal, or ordinal or intermediate type and measure utility or welfare in interpersonal comparability. This comparability can be partial comparability for welfare and non-comparability to complete comparability.

We can switch from comparability unit welfare to level of welfare. Individual ordering for state can be converted into any individual and any state. We can use the criteria of fairness and justice at this place. This way we can analyse CCR in different types and have different results.

Institutions and Frame work

Wide varieties and different angles give different CCR problem. Out of this we discuss now the institutional part for decision taking.

Here three possibilities are there (1) Majority rule (2) Rank order method (3) Social choice based on individual preference. Recommendation had from individual ordering set to every individual ordering sets. Second thing, in place of cardinal welfare, you can replace it with aggregate gains or losses on national level. Here you can have partial comparability. This will help planner to give policy recommendations.

Let us list out few important collective choice theories than many of them, some may be illusory.

Institutional mechanisms: - In institution majority rule is applied. This satisfies the anonymity, neutrality, positive responsiveness. Complete free market is justified on the ground of Pareto optimality with Pareto extension as principle. Social institution can choose the condition L for individual freedom.

Planning Decision: - Here some body or committee responsible to government takes decision on the bases of individual preference for aggregate welfare and to improve the condition of worst-off people. The maximin rule works implicitly or explicitly.

Social criticism: - This is used as protest against dissatisfaction from existing system. The CCR has to satisfy many conditions as problems are many and in different forms. The problem regarding the advice to government till overthrow of government. Many practical things have come from eminent person in the interest of public.

Problem of committee decisions: - Every institution has committee, may be large or small, may be formal or informal. The procedure may not be open for general public. They take into account the intensities of preference and formal decision will come forward and like vote trading, it is informal. In all cases transitivity is important.

Problem public cooperation: - Here the evaluation of collective choice by public is important. Many problems require justice and implementation of that justice in interest of public. Some economic decision will effects to public, in that case fairness, justice and gains and losses have to take into account. Population sacrifice and accept the future debt burden. This is in interest of population at large. The success and failure depends upon the cooperation of population.

Expression of individual Preference:

Individual preference can be decisive in collective choice. There are difficulties. The game consideration may change individual preference. The honesty is important factor.

In some theory, voting is not in favour of personal interest. This point is examined from various method of collective choice system even than it is not sure that it will work in proper way as desired. In social ordering, cardinal measure and communication are serious problems. Murakami[91] is of the opinion that non negativity response to individual preference will limit the scope of distorting their preference. This is true for MMD. There are three people and three preferences. In process it can say that X is most preferred. Y is next and Z is thereafter. Now some one wants to bring Y in the position of X, he cannot do it, but can knock out X in the decisive vote in MMD. The example of four people and three preference, result can be distorted, in spite of positive responsiveness and rank ordering in MMD. Game consideration and voting may bring in measure of intensities of preference and can compromise conflicting interest. This is social choice and ethics is effective element. The probability is important factor in individual preferences. This is like lottery in which result is probable. One can say that individual vote does for maximizing his utility. The answer is negative. The probability is to record the presence more than true purpose of voting. Person may indifferent even than vote or prefer to absent in light of cost. This may be one problem out of many but it affects to choice theory.

Efficiency and Pareto Optimality

In collective choice, ordering is less problematic than ordinal measure. In economics, Pareto Optimal is most widely used approach. It is seen that most of the conditions are satisfied by Pareto Optimal. The condition of indifferent is disturbing. This condition of indifferent restricts the general conditions of collective choice rule. Pareto optimality is necessary but not sufficient condition for optimality. In case of two individuals and

---

[91]   Ibid, page no.193

freedom given to them, even then, it violates acyclicity which is weaker than transitivity. Pareto optimality cannot be taken as a goal.

Concluding observation

Pareto principle is mildest. Pareto optimal cannot use as universal principle and as absolute in collective choice rule. Simple principle is non basic and use of it with suitable facts can play havoc with general principle in universal application. The unversilazition and generalization requires ethical theories to make application in economics. General Principle can work on the above basis but general principals are not that type. In general principle conditions are based on very limited view such as anonymity, neutrality, relevant similarity, and information between individuals and alternatives along with preference intensity. Independence of irrelevant alternatives, preference incentive and personal motivation are the factors in Pareto principle. Here the criteria are more important than approach. Simple principle is useful in some cases and not in all cases. Simple principle is useful and provides shortcuts than it is welcome. Arrow's general principles and impossibility theorem should be considered as a positive contribution to collective choice system.

As soon as we know the nature of principle as non-basic, we should over rule it. In traditional welfare economics the Paretian judgment is compelling as well as non Paretian judgment as arbitrary. Paretian consideration is on one hand put traditional welfare economics in narrow box and on the other hand ethical invulnerability will not survive. The evaluation of non basic principles could depend upon nature of society. "Pure" system of collective choice in social decision is good for theories and studies. This pure is well known but limited with impurities. The "impure" elements may be more practical and useful to institution. This is the system of collective choice for society.

3.12 Philosophy of Welfare in collective choice

I have selected four chapters in my thesis in continuation to find out the philosophy of welfare in Dr. Amartya Sen's writing. Dr. Amartya Sen was chosen for Noble prize for his outstanding contribution in economics for collective choice theory. This leads us to welfare rather than mere development or economics activities. The human value is established by way of introducing philosophy in economics.

Welfare economics is not value free. "Ought" has to come in picture. Ethics and unanimous judgement are the bases of welfare economics. Welfare economics concern with policy recommendations. Welfare economics require help of Logic, factual premises and value judgement. Value can create conflicts in CCR (Collective Choice Rule), MMD (Method of Majority Decision) and Pareto optimal by applying different conditions. Ethical are basic judgement. The interpersonal comparison is not possible in welfare economic as it is for society. Harsanyi divided the preference in 1) Ethical and 2) Subjective. The condition of anonymity and neutrality is requires to be examined in CCR. The condition of anonymity and neutrality does not work in market mechanism. Market mechanism gives maxim to individual by way of sale, exchange or buy.

Preference and aspiration of society members is the social policy. Need and desire are different for member as well as society. Kenneth Arrow took individual ordering in collective choice. The comparison standard is "at least as good as". The preference is used as alternative in collective choice. The interpersonal comparison is meaningless in choice. Preference relation was in demand and consumption theory which is not that helpful in collective choice theory.

Pareto gave criteria in social welfare. These criteria are known as Pareto optimal and used everywhere. Pareto optimal does not work in opposite choice, weak in case of inclusive in CCR. MMD is another type of CCF (Collective choice function). CCR and Pareto optimal are included in this. Unanimity is a social choice and expensive in decision. Politicians have forgotten this. Unanimity suggests compromise. This way unanimity is useful in choice function. Social welfare has to take into account rationality and all possible alternatives. Bergson gave idea of real value function should examined as W (Welfare). It is incomplete as who will provide the social welfare. Scitovsky though that when individual is indifferent than society should indifferent. This social ordering R is necessary in CCR.

Arrow gave another CCR imposing four conditions. One condition of them is not fulfilled than it is not considered as CCR. The reasonableness is mild condition in CCR but puts hurdle in SWF (Social Welfare Function). An individual preference and social preference creates inconsistency. MMD failed in four conditions for SWF and rank ordering failed in four conditions. SDF (Social decision function) has choice function in Arrow impossibility theorem. Quasi transitivity is in CCR which goes away from impossibility. Rational choice requires three conditions.

When the change affected in individual preference, it violates condition of I in Arrow theorem. The Preference intensity is in interpersonal correspondence violet both the aspects. In cardinal measure individual is indifferent. This is a practical problem and difficulty is in analysis. The behaviour of a rational person can explain in utility. Arbitrariness is objectionable in cardinal.

The bargain problem solve by taking product in place of sum. Sidgwick proposed the principle of "Equity" or "Fairness". The principle of "Exactly similar" has come up in line of equity or value. Rawls principle for fairness and justice is in favour of worst off people in institutional approach. Hurwitz contributed by way of pessimism-optimism index. Suppe grading principle resolves the conflict of maximin and utilitarianism criteria. Interpersonal comparison is not possible in MMD. MMD is having defects but favoured by institutions. Harsanyi has two sets of preference-1) Subjective 2) Ethical. Ethical is "impersonal" type. They are in line of universalizability and fairness. The impersonality is like equiprobability.

This collective choice function has to examine in connection of utilitarian and libertarian as well as in cardinal and ordinal fashion. We have to examine the possibility of interpersonal comparison. Pareto optimal is the better than best position.

Dr. Amartya Sen made it clear that the choice and preference are different. The reveal preference is amongst two sets only. In welfare, individual and his/her wellbeing is the prime thing.

Rationality is a part of preference. Pareto optimal is useful in welfare function. Dr. Amartya Sen has very correctly observed the effects of ethical judgment. The principal is a part of collective choice and action is of analytical part which is two different things.

The bargain, co-operation and contract are the worth examining substances. The co-operative formula will work well and in benefit of all. The contract requires full knowledge otherwise the threat and ignorant person has to pay heavily. The equity is important for welfare thought. The Universalization is the result of equality. Here we have to talk about moral law, fairness and justice. We have to apply the value to interpersonal comparison and find out the likely effects on CCR, MMD, SWF and SDF. Here requires the transparency in government act. This will curtail people freedom in economic sphere, freedom of speech; freedom to express opinion etc. Here it costs to individual in welfare term and government purpose is not served in collective choice function.

The technicality of the subject is complex and it is beyond common man's understanding. The base of collective choice requires the discussion from all the angles. The above things come under broad theory of collective choice. Dr. Amartya Sen has discussed collective choice elaborately to give precise idea of the effect of the each and every function. Dr. Amartya Sen has solved the Arrow impossible theorem which was up till now a problem to take a decision at government level to implement the welfare program. This has given a new horizon in public economics and new direction to welfare economics.

The collective choice decides the human way of working to maximin the fulfilment of desire. The next topic is development as freedom. In this the freedom is best variable option for person in political and economical term. We will study the same in detail.

4 The doctrine of Ahimsa in Jain philosophy

4.1 Definition- Ahimsa

Ahimsa means non-injury to living being, by all persons to the maximum extent possible. It is further extended like not to deprive a living being of its' life and or give pain knowingly or unknowingly. This act should be free from mental feeling with negligence.

Violence is opposite of non-violence. Violence in Jain philosophy is interpreted in the following ways.

(1) Definitions of Violence

    (a) Person creates violence by body and speech. This is a physical violence. Person does an act of violence by way of words. This means the quarrel and verbal fights say abusing, use of threatening words and back biting. Actual act of violence is DRAVYA himsa-violence.

    (b) Person creates violence by way of thoughts- mind. Person hates, thinks to do harm to others. This is mental violence. This is BHAV himsa-violence.

    (c) Violence defines as doing injury to living beings through pramatta yoga or subjective disturbance due to passions. The subjective disturbance is your mind; speech and body come into agitating condition. This disturbance creates vibration in soul. The vibration creates an unstable condition in human and than human hurts the living being. Here the degree of passion-"mental position"- is important. The karma comes into existence due to vibration of soul

80

and attracting the karma pudgal to soul. The intensity of passion will decide the Pradesh, Stithi, anubhag and bandh of karma. These four things are the determinant for karma formation. These four things are discussed in detail in the chapter on karma.

(2) Another classification of violence
Violence is distinguishable in the four ways.

(A) The Sankalpani or intentional violence

(B) The Virodhini or a return violence in self-defence

(C) The Aarambhani or the act of violence

(D) The Udyogini or industrial violence.

(A) The Sankalapini or intentional violence: - Here the act of violence did intentionally to harm the living beings. Here the person involves body and mind together. The reasons of violence are beyond ones' imagination. This type of violence is not encouraged in any circumstance. Violence is done in an intake of intoxication of passion. This form of violence is beyond hate limit. The civilized society will never encourage and/or support this type of violence.

The Art of War: - War is a kind of intentional violence. Computations made on an electronic computer by a former president of the Norwegian Academy of Sciences, aided by historians from England, Egypt, Germany, and India, have produced some astounding figures on the frequency and severity of wars. Included in these findings is the fact that since 3600 B.C. the world has known only 292 years of peace. During this period there have been 14,531 wars, large and small, in which 3,640,000,000 people were killed. The value of the destruction inflicted would pay for a golden belt around the earth 156 kilometres in width and ten meters thick. Since 650 B.C. there have been 1,656 arms races, only sixteen of which have not ended in war. The remainders have ended in economic collapse". (RAND Internal Publ., 1961)[92]

(B) The Virodhini or return violence: - The virodhini or return violence is in self-defence. This is for self protection against any kind of violence. All living beings are protecting themselves by their nature. Society is making law for human. The two senses to five senses living beings other than

---

[92]   RAND internal Publ., 1961

human, animals and vegetation are not protected. Human and animals protect themselves against their enemy. Jain philosophy believes in six kinds of living beings and giving protection to all of them. Human has to establish suitable laws to protect rest five types of living being in the name of environment. Jain says Virodhini is a milder form of violence. It could transform itself into sankalpani with providing justification and not in strict requirement of self-defence.

(C) The Aarambhani violence: - Here the daily acts of minor violence are accommodated. Householders are doing various types of acts-cooking, sweeping, washing, to light the fire for various purposes. These acts injure innumerable living organisms daily. This is a kind of violence but unavoidable due to human requirements.

(D) The Udyogini or industrial violence: - This is the requirement of twenty-first century. The violence is undertaken purposefully for human society. The industries are—the agriculture, milling, chemical, textile, petrochemicals, steel, mining, and many more. One can take lots of precautionary measures to minimize violence. People put huge industrial complex surroundings with all type of trees, flower beds and decorative plants in the vicinity to defend themselves saying that they take good care of environment but in fact they NEED PURE AIR, MORE OXYGEN AND COOL ATMOSPHERE. They are the most selfish one. Second thing; it is not as sankalpani or virodhini in which the act of violence is done with intention or self-defence. The economic supremacy has given rise to killing. Technology has taken a Himalayan leap. Unfortunately, the rapid technological development has not recognised "COMPASSION" factor.

The third and forth type of violence is as good as second type with strict minimum demand for survival. The third and forth type violence is milder than first one. The first one-sankalpani violence is to be prevented at any cost and as early as possible.

(3) The very appropriate and perfect definition of non–violence in Jain philosophy is as follows. I with equanimity firm in soul and take a vow of samyaktva and with consciousness and by way of body; mind and speech to stop any activities of violence and have repentance for full life. I do this with three KARAN – (1) I will not do the act of violence (2) I will not endorse the act of violence by others and (3) I will not consent any act of violence by others and three YOGAS – (1) Body (2)mind (3) Speech.

Acarya CHANDANAJI of Virayatana says "Ahimsa is a true and unconditional surrender of our own identity for the welfare of others. Ahimsa is not mere a principle of a particular religion, and it is in consonance with true nature of all living beings." [93]

Tattvarthasutradhigam of Shri Umaswatiji described, "The killing which is done through the careless action of mind, speech and body is violence." [94]

(A) Nine ways of violence

Jain philosophy divided the human activities in three parts (1) Mind (2) Speech (3) Body. The technical word is "yoga" in Jain philosophy. When the action takes place,(a) it may be, done by you, (b) Act done by others and supported by you, (c) Act done by others and consented by you. These three types of acts are known as KARAN. When you do violence, it can be in nine ways. There is a multiplication of Yoga 3 X karan 3 =9. You are responsible in nine ways for violence.

(B) Violence done in 108 ways

The real cause of violence is FOUR types of passions–kasayas (1) Anger-krodh (2) Conceit-ego of man (3) Deceitfulness-maya (4) Greed-lobh. These four types of passions are indulging in violence. Violence is done with the help of instrument in three ways (1) To prepare for violence is called "SAMRAMBH" (2) To collect the instrument for the act of violence is called "SAMARAMBH" and (3) To perform the act of violence is called "ARAMBH".

Four passions x three instrumental ways 4x3=12 type of violence.

The act of violence by yoga is three ways. Earlier 12 types x 3 yoga = 36 types of violence.

There are three karan as explained above. This way, earlier 36types x 3 karan = 108 types of violence.

---

[93]   N.P.Jain, Ahimsha-ultimate winner, page no.23

[94]   Umaswatiji, Book- Tattvarthasutradhigam, commentary by Pandit Sukhlalji, ch.no.7, stanza no. 8, page no.260

4.2 Violence in Jain Agamas

(A) AACHARANG SUTRA

The first chapter is known as "SASTRA PARIGNA". Lord Mahavir had given the details of various types of instruments used to kill the six types of living beings.

Stanza No. 11 -"People knows this act of karma (Violence), they should know it and avoid it" [95]

Lord Mahavir had described in detail in Acharang sutra about one sense jiva known as Earth, water, fire, air, vegetation. Lord Mahavir said the specific things about them. Lord Mahavir had described the types of instruments use for violence to them.

Earth is physically unconscious but in subtle state, it is conscious. Earth supports other living beings. The greedy person does the act of violence to earth. Here along with earth, other small insects and other living beings also get killed. The greedy person does the act of violence to sustain himself, for praise, honour or worship, to get rid of the cycle of birth and death and to get out of the difficult situation. One, who does an act of violence, gets it done by others or gives consent for the act of violence, is doing harm to one self. Some people realized that this is an illusion, death and hell. Earth feels pain like unconscious person on doing various types of injury, unhappy like old person on doing violence to it. The "SUMMUMBONUM" person will not act as well as not endorse other's act and not give consent to the act of violence to earth. The person is ascetic.

In case of Water, life of water should be made free from all danger. One, who accepts the existence of water life, is accepting the existence of self. One, who does not, accepts self existence is denying the existence of water life. Some ascetics are claiming that they have left house and livening controlled life. They can use water in many unwanted manner. They are doing violence to water life. One who does violence by three karan is ignorant person and doing harm to one self. The water life feels pain like unconscious person on doing various types of injury, unhappy like old

---

[95]   Book-AYARO, narrated by Acarya Tulsi, Edited by Muni Nathmal, Ch.1,Udashyak-1, stanza no.11, page no.7

person on doing violence to it. The "SUMMUMBONUM" person will not act as well as not endorse other's act and not give consent to the act of violence. This person is ascetic. Water is life-sustaining element for all. One should avoid violence to water.

In case of Fire, one, who accepts the existence of fire, is accepting the existence of self. One, who does not accept self-existence, is denying the existence of fire. Fire body living being feels pain like unconscious person on doing various types of injury, unhappy like old person on doing violence to it. The fly and static living being are getting shrink due to hit and they become unconscious, fall in fire and died. The "SUMMUMBONUM" person will not act as well as not endorse other's act and not give consent to the act of violence. This person is ascetics.

In case of Vegetation, one, who accepts the existence of it, is accepting the existence of self. One, who does not accept self-existence, is denying the existence of vegetation. Vegetation is like blind, deaf and dumb and without legs. Vegetation is static. The vegetation feels violence exactly like person who is blind, dumb and deaf and without legs. One who does violence to vegetation is doing the violence to the other small and big living being too. One must avoid the violence to vegetation. You should not cut and make harm with sharp instrument to the vegetation. You should not make the vegetation in the state of unconscious to kill them. You should not put fire in forest. Vegetation has the same symptoms as living being has. The "SUMMUMBONUM" person will not act as well as not endorse other's act and not give consent to the act of violence. This person is ascetic.

The Movable living beings are from two senses to five senses. They are of various types as per birth. They live in different type of bodies. They are peace loving. They are frightened from all directions. They should not torment as they have the same feeling of violence as a blind, dumb and deaf person has. They are not too lamented as they feel tremendous pain and not to be killed. The person kills them to get skin, meat, blood, heart, stomach, fat, wings, tail, hair, horn, tusk, teeth, nail, bones, etc. Some people kill intentionally. Some people kill unintentionally. Person kills with a thought that moving living being had killed his kin in past and person feel that moving living beings will kill my kin in future. Person feels that he will get attacked by moving living beings. The "SUMMUMBONUM" person will not act as well as not endorse other's act and not give consent to the act of violence. This person is ascetic.

The person, who sees the terror of hell will be away from violence to air borne living being in self-interest. One who knows spirituality knows the world and one who knows the world knows the spirituality is ascetic. (Aacharang sutra, first adhyanana, seventh udesak, stanza no.147).The ascetics knowing the violence towards the air borne living beings, does not make use of fan. The greedy person does the act of violence to air borne living beings. Here other small insects and other living beings killed along with air borne living beings. The greedy person does the act of violence to sustain one self, for praise, honour or for worship, to get rid of the cycle of birth and death, and to get out of the difficult situation. One, who does an act of violence, gets it done by others, or gives consent for the act of violence is doing harm to one self. Some people realized that this is an illusion, death and hell. Air borne living being feels pain like unconscious person on doing various types of injury, unhappy like old person on doing violence to them. The "SUMMUMBONUM" person will not act as well as not endorse other's act and not give consent to the act of violence. This person is ascetic.

A wise person and ascetic will take these things into account in their mind before doing any acts of violence. Lord Mahavir preached like this to protect six types of living being. Lord Mahavir said, first you should obtain the knowledge about violence and thereafter do not act for violence. [96] This is a symbol of "SUMMUMBONUM" person.

"LOK VIJAY" is the second chapter of Aacharang sutra. The meaning of Lok Vijay is one who wants to win a prize to get out of transmigration - the cycle of birth and death. Lok means to be born and reborn in this world. Here the cause of transmigration is the passions- (Kasayas). If you know how to overcome passions you are winner. The person should not make use of violence to fulfil his smallest desire. The person has to give up intense desire for anything. Person should control himself and should not be lazy for a single moment. He should abandon the idea that no one can do what he has done in connection of violence.

Stanza no. 63 and 64 gives very important message to the mankind. "All living being like to live. All living being are interested to have pleasure.

---

[96]   Ibid, stanza no.91, page no.29

They do not like pain. They do not want to get killed. They want to live. They want the life. All living being wants to live the life". [97]

Lord Mahavir had clear vision for medical treatment for ascetic. A doctor will say that I will give you a medicine for your health, which is not given to you by any one. A doctor will do killing, tormenting, making disable and doing all sorts of wrong things to tree, animal, and other living being to prepare medicine. The ascetic, who uses this medicine or getting treatment, is child. The true ascetic does not indulge in this type of medical treatment. Lord Mahavir said, you should know all types of violence and you should leave it permanently. Modern giant pharmaceuticals companies of world are carrying out all types of experiment in the laboratory on rabbit, mice, monkey and other birds and animals to find out sure cure for various kinds of pains and diseases likely to occur to humans. This is a very crude method. It is a CRUELTY on these animals and birds. This increases the feeling of vengeance in the animals, who are suffering the laboratory pain. They are not able to speak in our language but the danger on their faces and hatred in their hearts and mercy in their eyes and trembling of their bodies are the hidden message to mankind to stop such activities. This should be stopped in the name of medical science. The research medicines are not giving full proof results.

The third chapter is "SITOSNYA" – hot and cold. Lord Mahavir said all souls are equal. By knowing this, one should avoid violence. Violence is the root cause of pain. Violence is the cause of karma. Karma gives you transmigration. One should avoid the acts of violence. They should avoid it by three karats and three yogas. Ascetic should not act for any violence.

The forth chapter is "SAMYAKTVA". The forth chapter is for Ahimsa sutra. Lord Mahavir and all Tirthankar said that any animal, living being, soul and matter are not to be killed. You should not rule upon them, do not make them slave, do not trouble them, and do not kill them. This is pure, eternal religion. The religion of non-violence is science, faculty, perception and opinion. [98] The person who is keen for violence will go in the transmigration. The Vedantin Brahmin had encouraged the violence in the name of yagna was not correct. They were ANARYA. One, who practices the non-violence, reduces his karma.

---

[97]   Ibid, stanza no.63 & 64, page no.83 & 85.
[98]   Ibid, stanza no.4, page no.153

The fifth chapter of Aacharang sutra is "LOK SARA". The person does an act of violence knowingly or unknowingly due to unlimited desires. He kills all six types of living beings with much cruelty for this purpose. He always remains in the circle of birth and death. The person does the violence because he loves violence in his life. The pain is the cause of unlimited desires. The unlimited desires are the causes of violence. So, one must keep himself away from the violence. Regarding violence, it is said that, if you kill, torment, make disable, make slave to six types of living being is going to affect you in the next birth, as you are transmigrating in this world. You look at the person, who controls all his senses. One should not show the desire of violence for a second; to whom you are thinking fit to kill that is you. To whom you want to keep in obedience, to make slave or to give trouble and to kill, that is you. [99] You are the sufferer of your karmas. The ascetic will not do this.

The sixth chapter in Aacharang sutra is on "DHUYAM". Dhuyam means dissect and vibrate the one sense living being. The mining, digging and any other activities done on earth is violence to one sense and none moving living being. The dissect thing is in connection to animals and birds too. This is in connection for medicine, pleasure games, cruelty and other things. There is nothing much about direct killing.

The seventh chapter of Aacharang sutra is lost and no reference is available in any agamic literature.

The Eighth chapter in Aacharang sutra is on "VOMOKSH" – regarding non-violence. It said that people do the act of violence in all directions. The directions are east, west, north, and south, four directions in between four main directions of east, west, north and south, upper, lower and slant. Lord Mahavir was against any type of large scale industries which emit hot air, hazardous chemicals and poisonous gases and corrupt water sources; which harms the environment I.e. water, air and vegetation, earth, animal and human. Subtle living organism and human are killed due to this. This should not be done by three karan said Lord Mahavir. The wise person avoids all directional killing. [100] The ascetic is supposed to bear cold and heat. In case of cold, due to any reason, he should not encourage to ignite fire. He should save the life of fire borne living being.

---

[99] Ibid, stanza no.101, page no. 201
[100] Ibid, stanza no.18, page no. 269

The ninth chapter in Aacharang sutra is on "UPDHAN SUTRA". Here Sudharma swami described the glimpses of lord Mahavir's ascetic life. How he had preserved the Non- violence- ahimsa and religious thinking in his life. Sudharma swami said that lord Mahavir never encouraged the violence toward the six types of living beings and never hurt any animals in spite of trouble created by them. [101] This way lord Mahavir practiced non – violence in his life time and set an example to follow it. Lord Mahavir preached lots of things for ahimsa by way of giving useful slogan regarding each and every type of living being. Lord Mahavir preached the principle of tolerance and receptiveness of other living being in the life. The compassion was another main principle, from lord Mahavir, for human being; in a sense that in any way human should not enter into any type of himsa-killing in small or big way. Lord Mahavir's preaching is applicable to human race irrespective of time. The things, which were relevant, in those days are relevant even today.

(B) Non-Violence in Jain literature

Learned, intelligent ascetics had interpreted agamas and related literature from 5th century to 18th century. The famous work of them are as follows (1) Sutrakrutang sutra (2) Upasakdasang sutra (3) Prasna vyakran (4) Niriyavali (5) Uttradhyayn sutra (6) Aavasyak sutra (7) Dasvaikalik sutra (8) Pravachansara (9) Samyasara (10) Niyamsara(11)Purusharthsiddhiupay (12)Mulachar (13) Ratnakarandupaskadhyayan.

I do not go into details of all of them. The salient features about non-violence are as under.

(1) One who kills or supports to kill animal is increasing the enemy feeling in them.

(2) One who kills or gives trouble to animal certainly goes into hell.

(3) If you trouble to another living being, it is violence. This is an immoral act. In moral sense, killing is a one kind of vice and accepted by all.

(4) Person remembers the pain of hell than person stops violence, with a fear of pain in future which he shall suffer in hell.

---

[101]   Ibid, stanza no. 17, page no. 325.

(5) The householder, who observes non–violence, certainly goes into heaven.

(6) The suffering is considered as a himsa–violence.

(7) It is understood that, if person gives trouble, torment, keep hungry, kill the other living beings than as per rebirth theory, those living beings will act in the same way as person acted with them in past. Therefore, ascetics are living the life of non–violence. This is an advice to human that better he should refrain himself from such acts.

(8) Violence can be defined still in another way. Violence means cruelty. The act of cruelty is sin. One should save himself from sin. One should have meditative attitude for all acts of violence.

(9) Ahimsa–non–violence defined, as not to give any trouble to any living beings. This is a principle of Ahimsa. This is a supreme knowledge. The philosopher will not give any kind of trouble even to smallest insects. Ascetic is supposed to put into practice the principle of non-violence by body, mind and speech.

(10) It said that the truth, if it is going to hurt or giving suffering to other living beings, it should not be said directly. It should made mild, not to hurt his feelings and told in pleasant way to a person and other living beings. This is non-violence.

4.3   Six Duties of House Holder

Six duties are prescribed in Jain Religion daily for house holder. Pratikraman is one of them.

Pratikraman: - Pratikraman is the daily duty to carry out by male and female householder. It is described in 'Aavasyak Sutra', 4th adhyanana. Pratikraman means to come back from sinful activities. This is a daily act in which person remembers his sins, including the act of killing, which he/she did during the day and repents for it and resolves not to do it again. Lastly, a prayer sung. The meaning of prayer is to give and accept pardon. Lord Mahavir said- "I forgive all souls, let all souls forgive me, I harbour friendly feelings for all. I have animosity towards none."

The very important point is, as soon as you think of any violence, that very moment you are committing sin. The sin converted into karma and sticks to person's soul. It is unimportant that whether you had acted or not acted, at that very moment.

Jain householder prohibited making use of Madhya-wine, Makhan-butter and Madhu-honey. This is known as three Makars. These three words are starting with "M" in Sanskrit language. The consumption of these three things is instigating passion in you. Passion is the cause of violence. Householder prohibited using eight types of fruits, which contains many seeds. Each seed can grow into a tree and therefore it is containing many lives. When you consume such fruits, you commit violence. Simultaneously, householder supposes to observe the vow of "RATRI BHOJAN TYAG", not to eat, drink after sunset. Technically, physical position of the parts of body, the heart which is in downward position and stomach which is in upward position get closed after sunset. As a result the food did not get digested. Another reason behind this is you cannot see the minutes living organism with naked eyes during night. Jain religion has thought very deeply in term of non-violence.

Ascetics put into practice samities and gupties. Ascetic is supposed to sweep floor or place before seat or sleep and even before walk to avoid the killing of tiny insects and other living things. Ascetics use RAJOHANA – made out of woollen threads tied on piece of wooden stick. Ascetics are advised to use the broom of peacock feathers to avoid killing of small insects before seating, sleeping. This is in a particular Jain sect only. Ascetics do the act of repentance for any violence unknowingly done by them.

4.4   Non-violence in relation to Living beings

In case of six types of living beings, all are interlinked and dependent on each other. There is a famous sentence of wisdom in agamas "PARASPAROPAGRAHO JIVANAM". When person kills one sense living being earth, water, air, vegetations then the other two to five senses living being also gets killed as they are dependent on them. There is a special reference in Jain literature about fire. It said that when you lit the fire than you are killing living being, who had taken the shelter in it. When you extinguish fire, then also you are killing fire living beings.

Mental stage for violence

Your mental status is the reason of violence. The non tolerant person is engaging himself in the act of violence. The person, who performs an act of killing on six types of living beings, is violent. He argued that from one sense living being to five-sense living being, consciousness develops gradually. Degree of violence increases from one sense living beings to five sense living beings. One can kill lower sense living being. Here the answer is, one sense or five senses living being killing, is not important. Ultimately, from one sense to five senses living being killed is the most important factor in case of violence.

There are four types of meditation. Out of four types, two are good and two are bad. Arta meditation is first and of worst type. This represents the worst mental condition. The person is in cycle of doing bad things. Person does the act of violence due to this. The passions instigate person to perform the act of violence. The intensity of passion will decide the degree of violence. When you do an act of violence for one sense living being than your degree of intensity will be lowest. When you do the act of violence for five sense living being than the degree of intensity will be the highest. This fact has following reasons.

(1) Person requires more CRUELTY in his mind to perform an act of violence on five sense living beings. The pitiable condition of the five sense living beings may bring compassion in the action.

(2) Person may fear the retaliation of five sense living beings for his act of violence. Person takes more precautions and protection.

(3) Person has to collect and make use of precise instrument and make use of precise method to perform the act of violence.

(4) The five sense living beings may try to escape and will have tremendous movement for safety, will cry, the body will be trembling and have feeling of compassion in its eyes.

(5) No one should take life of other at the same time no one can give life to other.

One can argue that the possibly more than one person can do the act of violence. Say two. Here, one who has intense passions will suffer more for the act of violence out of two. There are various interpretations on the ground of various possibilities. The very interesting point is, in case of war, the solders are not responsible for violence but who give them command to fight war is responsible for total violence. People who indulge heavily in the act of violence; people definitely will have rebirth either in hell or in Tiriyanch living beings. Tiriyanch means birds, animals.

Mercy or compassion

Mercy or compassion is no substitute for non-violence. These words can be a one of the aspects of non–violence. Mercy is of four types (1) Substance mercy (2) Feeling mercy (3) Own- self mercy (4) Mercy to others. Mercy is having degree. Mercy can be discriminative. Mercy does not mean a total killing. Compassion is used in a limited and unlimited sense. Compassion in limited sense means up to human being only. It is important that in case of one sense living being, the compassion cannot be limited. It is unlimited in a sense for all six types of living beings. If selfishness increases, compassion will decrease. If compassion increases than selfishness will decrease. It should be in balance.

Donation and non-violence

Charity is another aspect of non–violence. Some eminent thinkers in Jain philosophy have given all to gather different categories to donation. Donation can help non–violence in four ways (1) Knowledge donation (2) Not to kill and/or protect a living being, one who comes under your shelter–ABHAYA DAN (3) Donations of things for religious purposes (4) Compassion.

The donation number TWO, Abhaya Dan considered the BEST. This is synonymous of non–violence with slightly less in degree.

Nurturing non-violence

The question is WHY non-violence? What are the substances nourishing non–violence.

I repeat, Lord Mahavir Said "NO one likes to get killed nor wants to kill someone. Every living being wants to live full life with peace and freedom". When a person adopting a vow of non–violence, it is a good cause & will lead him/her on the path of emancipation. It will be an obligation on other living beings. Non–violence in terms of philosophy is a pure and best step for self-purification and self-uplift. It is a character-building. Non–violence in terms of non-absolutism is a very strong principle of Jain religion. The meaning and scope of non –violence became wider and wider. Its scope well interpreted. Its fine analysis reaches to the depth of non-touchable in end. Non-violence has different form at different time and at different place.

4.5   Five transgressions of non-violence Vow

First five vows, greater for ascetics and lesser for householder and other seven vows have a certain prohibitive orders. You should not transgress twelve vows.

The infringements of non –violence in first vow are as under.

(1) Bandh: - Person should not tie the animals, birds with hard knots. This is equally applicable to slave or bonded labourers. In present time, slave factor is redundant. The persons serving under your control should not be the victim of any of inhuman treatment. The people in position are taking undue advantage of their position. This is violence.

(2) VADH: - lame the animals. VADH as per Sanskrit language, it is to kill. The Prakrit word vadh means to give trouble to birds, animals and slaves by beating with stone, to beat with wooden stick, or lame and tormenting. Person does this act of violence for negative pleasure.

(3) Chavichiya: - A person in anger cripples the bird, animal under his control. Person will give body injury to the people working under him. He will pay less to labourer; give less grain then agreed as per term against cash remuneration, not to give proper facility to work and leisure. These are act of violence.

(4) Aibhare: - Heavy load. A person will put more loads on animals and man than their carrying capacity. He will ask labourers to carry more loads on their head. He will load more load on animal than its carrying capacity. He will ask his subordinate to work more than prescribed time limit. This is violence.

(5) Bhattpanvochhoya: - Person will not give enough fodder to animals, food to human. He will not allow eating and drinking in time. This person will suffer from the ANTRAI karma in next birth. This is violence.

These five transgressions are to be interpreted in modern terms and to be put in to practice.

4.6 Comparison of non–violence between Jain religion and Thoughts of Gandhi

(A) Gandhi inspired by Count Leo Tolstoy, Ruskin and Shrimad Rajchandra. Gandhi changed his mind from violence to non-violence before going to U.K. for round table conference.

Gandhi firmly believed that the act of non–violence is SUPREME.

Gandhi believed that non–violence is conscious and it is a virtue of soul.

Gandhi believed that act of violence can be by body, mind and speech.

Gandhi believed that ego and ego related activities are violence.

Gandhi described non–violence as a mental stage from which the man comes out of selfishness, ego and passion for worldly things and sacrifice for the benefits of world. Person sees his own development in the development of world.

Gandhi thought that a person should develop such strength of non-violence that he can love to dreaded animal like lion and tiger and make friendship with them.

Gandhi was of the opinion that every soul having body is doing violence in one or another way. Non–violence is a mental stage.

Non–violence is supreme human religion. The benefit of non–violence is equal, to men as well as nation.

Non–violence is limited up to human in western thought. They make use of violence for things to be used by people. Against this, in east, a non–violent person will die himself rather than to kill human, animal or other living being. The believer of non–violence principle wishes the benefit for all in this world.

The feeling of non–violence is an act of soul. Soul is not active. Mercy and compassion are active virtues of men. Mercy is seed and non–violence is a tree. Pity for living being is a virtue of soul but it works in limited sense.

A non-vegetarian person makes a limit of consumption of non-vegetarian items due to pity, compassion. This is an act of limited violence and from that very point it starts spreading non–violence. This is admirable thing for such people. More and more people should think and act in this way to make world peaceful, coherent and worth living.

The social barrier for lower class people should remove; Gandhi wanted class of untouchable should abolish. This is a great work of non–violence in society.

Gandhi told that truth is biggest religion and non–violence is biggest act of mankind. The truth is ultimate aim and non–violence is instrument for it. The balance sheet of non–violence is ZERO in terms of profit as well as loss.

(B) Jain religion and non-violence

In Jain religion violence is prohibited by nine ways. Such a thought is not there in Gandhi's non–violence philosophy. Gandhi agreed only for three ways, body, mind and speech, but not three karan.

Jain religion talks about six kinds of living beings, Gandhi agreed for man, fire and vegetation.

Jain religion gave sixty names for non–violence and more than 30 names for violence where as Gandhi compared with selflessness, welfare of mankind.

Gandhi and Jain religion, both believed that (1) Truth (2) Non–stealing (3) celibacy and (4) non–hoarding which are essential for non–violence.

In Jain religion, the non-violence vow is total for ascetic and partial for house holder. There is a clear and distinct demarcation. Gandhi thoughts were not that deep, precise and clear.

Jain religion did not believe in god and made men solely responsible for the act of violence as well as an act of non-violence. Gandhi believed in god and believed that by prayer and belief in god, non-violence will work.

Jain religion very broadly discussed the donation aspect in detail and forms various angles; Whereas Gandhi is in favour of donation to disable human.

Jain religion is in favour of TOTAL prohibition of violence from one sense to six sense living beings. Gandhi advocated violence, if animal is suffering from acute pain than that animal should given freedom from pain by way of violence.

Gandhi pleaded the case of hand spun cloth–KHADI in favour of non–violence. This non- violence is in comparison to mill made cloth and exploitation of labourers.

Gandhi pleaded non-violence for society in the form of welfare, in politics by way of non-cooperation and SATYAGRAH means science to oppose thing with the act of non-violence.

In India, Jain, Buddhist, Sikhs, Vedantin and other religions believe fully in non– violence. These religions are pedestal on strong foundation of non–violence.

4.7   Non-Violence And Environment

Cyanide sprayed in coral waters to scoop up tropical fish. Fun farms breed confine, strangle or asphyxiate foxes, minks and rabbits, cosmetic industries squeeze or scrape openings near the reproductive organs for perfumes, which harpoon whales for lipsticks, rouge and other products, which kill musk deer for scent. This involves enormous cruelty, violence and environmental devastation and to what end? We talk of human rights day in and day out but choose to ignore the rights of the mute animals!

In order to quench our selfish desires and ambitions, we are sincerely and painstakingly moving towards self–destruction. George Bernard Shaw: - "When a man wants to murder a tiger, he calls it sport; when the tiger wants to murder man, he call it ferocity."[102] The evolutionary journey from being an animal to becoming a human being has been long but that from human to animal is very short.

4.8 Philosophy of Welfare of Ahimsa in Jain Religion

"Ahimsa parmo dharma"- Non-violence is the supreme religion. Jain religion considers violence as a sin. It is very difficult to practice non-violence by mass having heterodox of race, religion, climatic conditions, sociability and countries, having certain principles and values. In Jain religion, ascetics are prohibited from all types of violence. Jain ascetics are very particular about religious preaching and they follow lord Mahavir preaching thoroughly. They advise the Jain religion followers not to commit violence. The non-violence will save the person for himself and opponent too. Non-violence will help to resolve quarrel amicably. The positive side of non-violence is as important as the negative side but it is something not fully appreciated. The positive aspect implies forgiveness, kindness, charity and service. The greatest welfare of men lies in their happiness.

Jain philosophy prohibits the violence in nine ways. Ascetic is bound to practise non violence by nine ways. House holder is bound to non violence by six ways (Two karan and three yogas).The effect of karma in violence is tremendous. This is at personal level but have far reaching effects in the society. There are four things comes in kasaya-passion. They are (1) Krodh- Anger (2) Man-Pride (3) Maya-Deceit (4) Lobh-greed. Each person try to control and gradually progress in controlling passion than there will be an atmosphere of peace in society. This will give boost to have full development of their spiritual capability. The subsidence and or reduction of passion in them are a great help to person to become mild, soft, straightforward and fearful of bad activities. It suggests for not having intense desire for anything. Passion will be a cause of doing wrongful act like violence & suffering. Intense desire is a part of passion, which is negative and never positive. Passion covers following four vices.

KRODH-Anger: - Anger is the main cause for violence. Men should learn to control it. The partial control of anger will play an important role at

---

[102]   N.P.Jain, Ahimsha-ultimate winner, page no.145

personal level and to control it at full level is an important achievement. Anger makes men blind as far as his sense of understanding is concern. Anger will make men to go to any extent. The last limit of anger will result in death of opposite person. The man in anger is not allowed to take the life of other man. It is heinous crime. When man comes into senses, he will realize that what great offence he had committed. On his part, it is impossible task to make a dead person alive.

MAN-PRIDE: - Ego is a part of Charitra Mohaniya karma-character deluding karma- as per Jain philosophy. Pride is a negative virtue in one's character.

MAYA-DECEIT: - Deceit means an ownership of anything. Here deceit is not in term of fraud or cheating. Deceit is a mental stage, in which person wish to have control on each and every thing.

LOBH-GREED: - Greed is another enemy of men. Greed has polluted the habit of men all over the globe. Greed breeds corruption. Greed means a limitless desire of possession. This is a very serious incurable mental feeling. Human greed had made havoc in the field of mining of earth, in the field of environment, in the field of making deforestation and polluting water, air.

All religions preach to their followers to have control on passion. Jain religion preached that passion is the strongest enemy of men. Person should control passion in his own interest. Jain religion showed the ways and means how to reduce the passions. This is over all in interest of mankind. The person will be contented due to happiness.

There is a detail account of violence in Aacharang Sutra, in all eight chapters. Lord Mahavir had given detail of violence and its' effect on six types of living beings. You give importance to other's existence is the welfare. Such good thoughts will bring peace in society and will create harmony in like minded people.

The earth considered as a single body living being. The wealth of nature is grabbed by greedy, unscrupulous people for their selfish motive and depriving fellow people for their share. Another important point of welfare; earth supports other living being from two senses to five senses. Here the men do the agriculture with the help of soil and gets food grain, fruits and vegetables for mankind. This is a greatest welfare in terms of survival of mankind. Earth supports vegetations. Erath supports the storage of water. Men have enough oxygen to live because of this. Earth supports flora and fauna for birds and small insects to live. This is welfare in a beautiful way.

Water is considered as one sense living being. The unlimited use of water will create a famine in coming days. Water is important life supporting ingredient. One can understand the value of one glass of water in desert, where scorching sun is on head, no near or far place to get water, man is thirsty for more than four hours. At this point of time a glass of water is most precious thing in his life. The importance of water is to give life to men, vegetation, birds, animals and all other living beings. Salty water is equally important to get salt. Salt is essential raw material for food preparation, for soda and alkaline base industries. Men processed the salt water and get sweet water for drinking purposes. The sweet water of rain improves the desalination process and converts salty land into productive land. The NO WAR situation for water is in best interest of mankind.

Fire is of two types (1) Outer fire- on earth (2) Inner fire- in body.

An Inner fire is helpful for metabolism for human. An inner fire is necessary for good health and to sustain diseases-free life. The fire on earth is of various types. Fire will help to have heat in cold seasons, for cooking, for industries and other essential services. Fire is essential elements existing on the planet. Fire is having devastating effect therefore it should be controlled. Fire is an angel as well as devil.

Air is a basic thing for mankind. Air contains various types of gases in which oxygen is most important one. An atmosphere is necessary to live the life for all living beings. An atmosphere is a cause of rain, heat and cold, wind which are important elements for cycle of life.

The vegetation on the earth is a great help in many ways. (1) It produces the oxygen which is essential for all living beings. (2) Vegetation helps to prevent soil erosion. (3) Vegetation gives different fruits and other jungle products for mankind. (4) Vegetation gives shelter to birds, small animals and various insects. (5) The deforestation had made many species vanished. (6) Vegetation gives green cover to fight against natural heat radiation and excessive rain or chilling cold wind. (7) Vegetation treats the toxic gases and gives pure air. (8) The flora fauna gives sweet fragrance in the atmosphere. (9) Vegetation near residential complex is a good natural beauty as well as help in many ways. Vegetation has symptoms like living beings. Therefore to cut, hurt, make unconscious, burnt and deprive from water and food to vegetation is a crime. Vegetation is static. Men should not take advantage of its non moving position.

There are more than one sense living beings on this earth. They need protection and need assurance for all help; in turn they are friendly and cooperative for work or assistance to mankind. There are number of stories in world literature about men and two to five sense living beings for their help in critical time, their faithfulness, fight against danger and peaceful living with mankind.

The religion of non-violence is science. Science serves mankind with useful discoveries in all fields. These discoveries will help to mankind to have material benefits. The material satisfaction may bring the spiritual betterment by contented position of human. Science is a slave of mankind to serve in all possible way.

Samyaktva is a faculty of people who understand meaning of violence and adhere to not to commit sin of violence. The non violence is perceptions. One should adopt a rule OR vow in ones' life. The perception is true to fact and it should nurture fully. The opinion for non-violence will strengthen the moral courage and person will work with ethics in life. This will be a good welfare proposal.

It is important to remember that if any living being is going to create problem to you than you should be calm and quite. You should not get hurt mentally or encourage violence physically. The welfare is to save the other living being's life due to non-violence. You create a faith and sympathy in living being for you. This is the welfare teaching of Jain religion.

The five sense living being will retaliate. Jain religion considered the killing of five sense living being a most sinful act. As per eastern philosophy, all religions give importance to non-violence. Jain religion gives importance to ABHAYA DANA - life protection - of living being in non-violence. The very idea of non-violence to living being is a reflection of pity, compassion and tender heart of human and his/her feelings. This is a great welfare in terms of friendship of living beings to men. There are number of examples in history, where person had repented after war is over or an act of massive violence was done.

The hate is another form of violence. In the long run, hate will create feeling of violence in you. It requires a great strength and courage to bear the person who hates you. Here the hate factor will be measured in terms of degree due to your calmness.

Jain religion recognizes the fundamental natural phenomenon of mutual inter- dependence known as "PARASPAROPAGRAHO JIVANAM"– interdependence. Lord Mahavir said that One, who understand the meaning and merits of reverence for nature, has understood the grave merits and determent caused by destruction of plants and trees. It means that all aspects of nature belong together and are bound in a physical as well as in a metaphysical relationship. Life is viewed as a gift of togetherness, accommodation. In present circumstances, Jain religion thinks that waste and pollution is an act of violence. This should be prevented in interest of future generation of mankind.

Lord Mahavir said, today's economics is not of peace or of non-violence at all. Economics talk about the greed and competition. Gandhi talked about the decentralization of industries and trusteeship of wealth. Lord Mahavir was thinking for control, peace and non-violence. Economics is thinking in terms of maximum utility for all. Lord Mahavir was in favour of earning for house holder. Lord Mahavir said in between labour and economics put an element of control. This will dampen the tempo of economics but it is in interest of human welfare.

Lord Mahavir suggested non-violence in three things. 1) Do not produce the war machinery. 2) Do not collect the war machine. 3) Do not give training to manufacturing, storing or using the war machinery. The industries which give rise to killing should be made limited. They should allow manufacturing of war machinery up to the own defence requirement. This will help to have non-violence. The war making machine manufactures are trying to ignite the war in any part of world to sell their product. They have hypocrisy. On one side they talk for peace and at backdoor they supply the war machines with latest technology[103] Non violence is the strongest message for welfare of mankind from Jain religion. We have seen the first and most valuable principle of Jain religion named Ahimsa and its' importance in life and welfare of man.

We will move on the second doctrine name karma. Karma is the force behind each and every activity and karma is the sole thing for your progress and downfall. You can get out of the illusion of life and death.

---

[103]   Acarya Mahapragnya, Mahavir ka Arthsastra, page no.38 to 49.

5 Dr. Amartya Sen's idea on Development as freedom

5 Introduction

Development in terms of G.N.P. or rise in personal income or industrialization or Technological advances is the incorrect term. Development as real freedom is the correct term.

Dr. Amartya Sen puts emphasis on subjective value of (Human) man. Freedom defined in much bigger term. Freedom depends on social and economic arrangement with development. This includes political and civil rights with liberty to participate, modernization, and technological progress as greater freedom. Development should remove lots of non-freedom from man's life and it is the blockade of human capability and hindrance into development.

Everybody loves freedom. People are ready to die due to starvation for freedom. Asha Mukherjee has different opinion. "Instead of liberty one may, for example, value food much more. In a state of object poverty one may think it better to sell oneself to feed his spouse. Individual's preference must be respected if we are to arrive at meaningful criterion on the basis of which we can act to reduce inequality." [104]

---

[104] Asha Mukherjee, Applied Ethics, Edited By Dr.A.P.Dubey, page no.43.

5.1   The perspective of freedom.

Dr.Amartya Sen has given the example of Maitreyee and Yajnavulka and tried to say that there is something more important than income, wealth. The point is for eternality of soul.

The living of life has concern with income and achievement, commodities and capability and economic wealth and our ability to live the life. Development lies in between economic wealth and life which we can lead. Quotation of Aristotle is important here. "Wealth is evidently not the goods we are seeking for, it is merely useful and for the sake of something else".[105]

Forms of unfreedom

There are many types of unfreedom. Unfreedom for survival is due to famine, in terms of medical facilities, morbidity, sanitation, clean water and pre mature mortality. Richer countries are no exception for unfreedom like gainful employment or education or social security and longevity along with restrictions on woman. The LEE Theses-[106] Prime minister of Singapore feels that no grant of political freedom gives higher economic growth. Freedom should allow to have action and decision on one hand and to have opportunities in personal and social circumstances on another hand.

Two roles of freedom

The Evaluative reasons: - We will measure enhancement of freedom of the people.

The Effective reasons: - The free public agency is how far a cause in development is to be examined.

The combination of both should result into the best as development and freedom.

Freedom achieved by people through the economic opportunities, political liberties, social power and good health, education, encouraging and cultivating institutions. Constitution has given some rights to human. The

---

[105]   Acarya Mahapragnya, Mahavir ka Arthsastra, page no. 195.
[106]   Amartya Sen, Development as freedom, page no.15.

democratic countries adopt constitution in best interest for their people; gives fundamental and subsidiary right to live in the country. The human will make organization and agency to work for their development and freedom will follow. Public freedom is in bigger sense.

Evaluative system: income and capabilities

Let us examine the evaluative system. This can examine in three ways. (1) Utilitarian (2) Liberation (3) Economic

Utilitarian is mental process. Liberation is concern with liberty. Economic is to increase income and wealth. Here income is defined as creative discontent and constructive dissatisfaction. Low income is connected to deprivation in two ways 1 ill health, illiteracy, hunger and under nourishment 2) High income can give good health, nutritional food and good education. The study will give us an idea about Income deprivation and capability deprivation. It has policy importance.

Poverty and inequality

Dr.Amartya Sen narrated an example. Person had gone in search of employments. All of a sudden communal violence erupted in the market. The person became the victim of mob and got the death instead of employment. This is economic freedom in terms of extreme poverty, which made a person helpless prey in the form of other kind of freedom.[107] Poverty should define as deprivations of basic capability rather than low income. In affluent countries, poverty is in the form of unemployment, deprivation of social security and social dishonour. Poverty is in physical and psychological term.

Income and mortality

Income is the ability. Sometimes discrimination is done for income on the bases of race, colour and gender. In U.S.A. Black citizen earns less compare to white citizen but earns more compare to black citizen of Africa, Brazil or Namibia. At the same time, the citizen of Brazil, Namibia is enjoying higher life years compare to black citizen of U.S.A. Income is not equal to freedom.

---

[107]   Amartya Sen, Argumentative Indian, page no.109, Book- Development as freedom, page no.8.

Freedom, Capability and market

Freedom is quality of life. The ability to survive is more important than mortality. The quality of life and substantive freedom is more important than income. Importance of income is only instrumental. Commodity consumption and its effect on human working are worth exploring. Joseph-Louis gave a formula to convert the nourishment value from wheat and other grains. Freedom for market mechanism is another force of development. Government policy should encourage and people should have freedom of market mechanism. This increased the capability of men. One should be free to exchange his entitlements, which may be the result of own labour production, inheritance by law, shared entitlements or ownership of something. Denial to access of the market mechanism is deprivation and non-freedom. it is a denial of his improvement on capability and freedom. Bonded labour is a denial of freedom. Market mechanism and freedom has a positive relation to expand his income, wealth and opportunity. Deprivation is the denial of economic opportunities by law. This is a case of social loss.

Generally market mechanism thinks in term of utility, income and wealth, competition but not freedom. The centralized function can do it. For example, a dictator takes a decision on behalf of people. He takes it for granted that it is in benefit of people. Here the freedom comes in picture. The freedom is preferred than slavery. In U.S.A., after slavery laws were made effective, the labourer employed with higher wages to work like slaves, did not succeed. The free labour has produce more than bonded labour. Bonded labour system abolished and wage labour can go anywhere and earn the wage as per his capacity. Dr. Amartya Sen said Aristotle had use the "Flourishing" and "Capacity" clearly to relate the quality of life. Adam Smith had analyzed the life in term of "Necessitate" and condition of living. William Petty has made pioneering work for this.

Values, tradition and culture

Freedoms are diverse as we discussed earlier. Individual freedom is more in a sense that he is freely participating in debate and value priority of choice. Individual freedom should work for (1) Social arrangements to expand and (2) Social arrangements should be more appropriate and effective. Tradition and culture has to change with economic development. Here the "CHOICE" of people comes in picture. This is the freedom of liberty.

5.2 Types of freedoms

There are two general attitude of process of development - 1) Economic analysis and 2) Public debate. The development is expanding in real freedom as primary end-constitutive roll and principal means-instrumental role. Primary end define as freedom for human life and principal end define as freedom for elementary capabilities and freedom of speech, right to know and active participation in public life. Each one of these will help to advance the general capabilities of a person and will help to achieve freedom.

Instrumental freedoms

There is much diversity in instrumental freedom. Instrumental freedoms are for human development. They are (1) Political freedom (2) Economic facilities (3) Social opportunities (4) Transparency guarantees (5) Protective securities.

Political freedom means a right to person to choose the government, watch the policy and freedom of speech and many political opportunities.

In economic freedom, person can utilize the resources for consumption or production or exchange. Economic freedom increases the national income and wealth, which should be distributed amongst individuals for their economic entitlements.

Social opportunities are in terms of education and health care and others. This will help economy by quality control and education; health care by way of political activity participation.

Transparency guarantees based on trust. The Transparency requires in government and private dealing regarding corruption and financial irregularities.

Protective securities in terms of social security like unemployment benefit, subsidies income, famine relief and flood or crop failure for farmers.

The above instrumental freedoms are interconnected and complementary in each other as an engine of economic growth. This will increase income in private sector. Public education and health care programme can reduce mortality rate, child birth rate and morbidly. Japan was ahead than Europe in education in nineteenth century in Meiji regime.

China adopted economic reform in year 1979 and India adopted economic reform in year 1991. China had literate population and India had half of the population literate. The time frame is earlier in case of China than India. In socialist regime of China, the social commitment had given good response to health care programme where as India was much backward in health care.

Income and longevity and other matters

GNP of country and public health care expenditure are worth exploring. The study shows that very low level of income of people of Kerala state in India, or China or Sri Lanka are enjoying higher life expectancy than much richer countries like, Brazil, South Africa and Namibia. Richer countries have put forward an argument that the fund for public health should be curtailed or postponed because of high cost. Poor countries need less money due to labour oriented medical services and wage rates are low and need advance facilities in health care.

In last century, Britain had lower life expectancy compare to low income countries. Britain adopted support oriented policies for nutritional food, health care and under nourishment and mortality had declined to good level.

5.3   Freedom and foundation of Justice

There are number of reasons for one decision. The information part is very important. You can say that there is (1) Classical utilitarian approach (2) Libertarianism (3) Rawlsian justice in individual freedom.

Information- included and excluded

Information is necessary for evaluation in making judgment. In case of utilitarian approach, which is the development of Jeremy Bentham, speaks in term of mental achievements. He has no interest in individual for actual distribution of utility as total utility is taken together. Here the individual freedom and right along with quality of life is not included. Libertarian talks about liberty and right of individual. In case of Rawlsian justice, the sensitivity of information is incorporated which is absent in two theories.

Utilitarianism based on principle of utility. R.M.Hare said "everybody to count for one, nobody for more than one".[108] In classical utilitarian approach; they use utility as pleasure and pain. Jeremy Bentham had used this. This is a mental stage. Here interpersonal comparison is difficult. The mental condition of two people will not be the same and difficult to transform in statistics. The actual distribution of utility to individual will be difficult. If we consider the utilitarian approach as welfare than it restricts the judgment. Now if we take utilitarian as sum ranking than it is not taking into account the inequality and other matter in purview. The new definition of utility is fulfilment of desire or personal choice behaviour. This is fitting into numerical representation. Here the scaling of utility will give the answer for superiority of X over Y.

Utility, merits and demerits

Here the utility is in terms of total utility as well as pleasure and pain in terms of merits. It is mental, difficult for interpersonal comparison and consequential. Utilitarian evaluation is in welfare. This judged only the particular state of affairs and no more than this. Utilitarian evaluation on SUM ranking is another way of looking at utility. The sum is total of utility by all. The utility reflects in statistics is a new method to see the utility in person's observable choices. The formula is "If a person would choose an alternative X over another, Y, than and then only that person has more utility from X than from Y." [109]

There are Merits & Demerits of utilitarian approach in a sense that useful in judging the results of social arrangements as the well being of the people. Property right is constitutional but Political opposition will be there. One has to find the solution. The tax on property will help in terms of environmental protection, unlawful acquisition from poor and others, in light of information. Demerits have limitation. This is a mental approach. "Sum ranking" has limitation here. An inequality, neglects the right of freedom and it takes care of individual only.

---

[108]   R.M.Hare, essays in ethical theory, page no.232.

[109]   Amartya Sen, Development as freedom, page no.59-60.

We adjust our pleasure and pain capacity to make our life bearable, in case of over worked and less paid worker, hopeless housewives in severely sexiest culture. In such a situation, information can help them a lot regarding the education and employment opportunity and health care programme to improve their capability.

JOHN RAWLS and the priority of liberty

JOHN RAWLS and his thought for the priority of liberty are very important. John Rawls theory of justice had many components. Dr.Amartya Sen took one part – known as "priority of liberty". This theory turns into libertarian theory for personal liberty to property right. Robert Nozick had developed it fully. Priority of liberty discusses the essential rights including political and civil rights. Herbert Hart argued for priority of economic need for survival than rights. John Rawls had acknowledged this. Dr. Amartya Sen is in favour of priority of liberty, in case of poor countries and raises a question that personal liberty should have the same importance such as income.

Robert Nozick and his theory of libertarianism

As per Robert Nozick: - [110] your entitlements of rights must be exercised; let the nasty result comes out of it. You cannot ignore freedom of a person on the ground of liberty. The freedom of person is in good mortality, good health, education etc. Dr. Amartya Sen gives an example of famine. It is there. You do not have enough food even though you have entitlements. Here no one's libertarian right is violated. Theory of political priority not bothered about people having freedom or not. The liberty given cannot be considered as a merit to libertarianism theory. It needs broader information to justify.

Utility – real income and interpersonal comparisons

Now utility considered as a numerical representation of person's choice. This change has come due to methodology. Interpersonal mental comparison is not possible as per Lionel Robin.[111] This happens due to no common denominator of feelings. Now the question is, if interpersonal comparison is made for same choice and under the same circumstances in welfare

---

[110]   Ibid, page no.65.
[111]   Ibid, page no.67.

economics, but to justify it in numerical term is a matter of question. The answer is negative. Utility comparison on choice behaviour can be in terms of "Real income" or commodity based utility. This is also not advisable due to different people and diverse demand.

Well being: Diversities and heterogeneities

The income or commodity bundle is our welfare depends on our personal as well as social circumstances. It varies in our real income and well being and freedom.

(1) Personal heterogeneities: - Sick person, pregnant woman and disable person needs more income. Older person needs support and help. This will not be comparable even if you transfer the income.

(2) Environmental diversity: - Seasons, rainfall, heat will change the equation in terms of income. The presence of infectious diseases can change the balance of real income.

(3) Variations in social climate: - The public educational system and state law for prevention of crime can bring change in real income. The state law for prevention of crime does help in real income change. The community relationship is important. This is known as "Social capital."

(4) Difference in relational perspective: - The commodity requirements differ from community to community and may change according to customs and conventions. You may require higher standard of clothing and visible consumption in rich society than poor society. This was noted by Adam Smith before 200 years ago.

(5) Distribution in family: -The Income is shared by earning member and non-earning member in a family. It is difficult to judge one's achievements and opportunity in overall level of family income.

Incomes, resources and freedoms

We have to go in detail for inadequacy of income in welfare economics. John Rawls's analysis of "PRIMARY GOODS" is important in broader sense, which includes real income. The primary goods meant for getting ends including the right, liberty and opportunity, wealth and society based self respect. Person takes his own responsibility for his preference. The relationship is between income and resources and well being and freedom. The actual living concept also thought by some economists. They study the relative desire of person in this regard. As per Adam Smith necessity means food and things as per custom to the lowest order should get. The poor society has no criteria.

Well Being – freedom and capability

As per Dr.Amartya Sen not the "space" but "CAPABILITY" is to choose for welfare. We concentrate on individual's opportunities to peruse his goal. This is Rawls's recommendation. This will not be true in case of disabled person in comparison of able man. The functioning concept of Aristotle is working from simple to complex activities of a person. The "Capability" is an alternative combination of function and feasible to achieve freedom. The capability set is a combination of such various functioning sets. Function sets are the achievements and capability is freedom to achieve. You make best use of available sets.

Weights, valuations and social choice

The benefits of interpersonal comparison lie in to assess the end by using capability. You have to make aggregation for overall interpersonal comparison and not heterogeneous components. This is Pluralist due to (a) different function (B) weight attached to capability and vis-à-vis achievement and (C) for evaluation applying weight to capability.

The evaluation reasoning will be reduced in one metric which will not serve the purpose. The partial ordering will narrow the function and weight will not be unique. You have to give weight as per reasoning. Interpersonal diversity can say little about the life they live. The public debate is necessary to arrive at agreed weight in social-choice. Public opinion may not in fully agreed position.

People have to decide whether they want the park in their area or they want a primary school. Here School is better option than park. Again, if sufficient number of students and fund is not available, than the first option is useful in larger interest of society.

Capability information: alternative uses

The capability perspective is necessary for evaluation and policy analysis. There are three alternatives available. (A) Direct approach (B) Supplementary approach (C) The indirect approach.

(1) Direct approach: - You are directly examining and comparing function or capability vector in three ways (1) Total comparison (2) Partial comparison (3) distinguishing capability comparison. Total comparison is much ambitious. Here you have to take in to account many things. The partial comparison is in connection to distinguishing capability comparison but not that useful.

(2) Supplementary approach: - Income space is supplemented by capability in interpersonal comparison. Here some more information is available for poverty removal program and to solve the problem of inequality.

(3) The indirect approach: - Here you work on information to determine capability. Say for example, the family income level will be adjusted on lower level for illiterate family and higher level on literate family. This has many advantages.

The indirect approach is not different than direct approach due to trade off and influence of income on capability. A little change in income gap on higher side shift can increase the chance of survival capability.

5.4 Poverty as capability deprivation

Poverty as capability deprivation

Dr. Amartya Sen defines poverty as deprivation of basic capabilities rather than low income of an individual. The lack of income is reason for person's capability deprivation.

(a) This approach is concentrating on capability deprivation. (b) Capability deprivation influenced by other factor along with low income. (c) The instrumental relation between low income and low capability is variable between different community, different family and different individuals. The third criterion is important for public action, evaluation of policy making for poverty reducing or inequality reducing.

(A) The capability and income is affected by age of the person, gender, family obligation as social role, by location due to flood or dry area, by insecurities etc, the relationship is affected between income and capability.

(B) Real poverty will be more intensive. The person is unable to convert his functioning and deprivation due to old age or ill health. More income makes him unable to enhance his capability.

(C) The unevenly distribution of income in family will create deprivation of capability of a member. This type of family discrimination is clearly seen in the countries of Asia and North Africa. In Europe and North America, poverty and inequality is existing along with gender inequality I.E. Italy has highest ratio of "Unrecognized" woman labour force. If you accord for reduction in freedom, it is true for Europe and North America. The interfamily division is all over the world.

(D) Relative deprivation in terms of income can yield absolute deprivation in term of capability. The low-income person in rich country can have capability handicap. This low income will exclude him socially.

The poverty analysis and informational demand of social justice helps us to understand the deprivation of capability.

Income poverty and capability poverty

Poverty as inadequacy of capability is important fact. The better basic education, better healthcare can improve the capability of a person to earn more. The economic reform has improved the capability of people to earn higher income in India. East Asia and South East Asia have made up improvement in capability much earlier than India. India has learned opening of economy and importance of trade from them. In India, in Kerala high education and good health care suffered due to anti market policy. Northern state (U.P., Bihar, M.P.) have suffered for not making social development as required. Kerala made moderate economic growth but remove poverty faster. Punjab made high economic growth and reduced poverty. The capability improvement will help directly and indirectly to make human deprivation less acute and more ease.

Inequality of what

The inequality is difficult to evaluate in social, economical and fairness terms. Adam Smith and John Rawls had tried for this. Adam Smith was very much concerned about poor and imagines that "Impartial spectator" will take care of the inequality. A.B. Atkinson gave formula known as "Equally distributed equivalent income".[112] You have to reduce the accounted value in proportion to aggregate income to the extent of inequality in income distribution.

Inequalities are of many types. Inequality of income differs from inequality of "Spaces" in many respects. "The income and capability can differ in terms of freedom. Say for example – A person with high income but enable to participate in political opportunity. Here the person is poor in a sense of freedom. A person is rich but cannot afford to buy alignment, which is expensive. The person is not poor in the sense of income distribution. A person, who denied employment, but given "employment benefit". This person is a deprived person in opportunity sense.

Unemployment and capability deprivation

The judgment of inequality is different from capability of income. In Western Europe, unemployment is higher. The person is given financial support but it reduced the capability in many terms. In financial term, Western Europe has done well compared to U.S.A. Nevertheless, in terms of reduction of inequality in capability is a big question. The inequality is higher in U.S.A. than Europe and unemployment is higher in Western Europe than U.S.A. Inequality in racial group in the U.S.A. is distinct in the sense of income – spaces. The American white is earning more than African American Black. American black is earning more compared to African black.

Health care and mortality

In case of mortality, U.S.A black has lower life compared to Kerala person and Chinese person. The white female of U.S.A. has higher life compared to Kerala-India, china and U.S.A. black. U.S.A. black woman is lowest in the list. Now the mortality ratios of U.S.A. white and black women are as under. All index is 1.6 after adjustment of

---

[112]   Ibid, page no. 93.

income compared with white and black, where as men index is 1.2 and woman index is 2.2 which is higher than white of U.S.A., in both the cases.[113] In America, health insurance is in private hand as a result those who cannot pay the health insurance premium are depriving of the benefit. In case of Europe the situation is different. Here it is considered as a fundamental right and state government has to fulfil the responsibility in spite of political unhappiness.

Poverty and deprivation in India and Sub-Saharan Africa

Extreme poverty is in South Asia and Sub Saharan Africa. In 1991, life expectance below 60 years was in 52 countries and total population of 1.69 billion people. 46 countries, out of these 52 countries, are of South Asia and Sub Saharan Africa. Indian population is half of these 42 countries but life expectancy is of 60 years. Infant mortality and adult illiteracy rate is the same in both region. Infant mortality was worst in Ganjam district of Orissa and illiteracy in women was worst in Barmer district of Rajasthan state. Mali, Mozambique and Guinea-Bisau are African state, where the worst situation prevails as per 1991 estimate. In India, median age death takes place at the age of thirty seven where as in sub Sahara African states it is five years and in five countries of sub Sahara African states, it is below three years.

Under nourishment in terms of %
India   40% to 60%
Sub Saharan Africa   20%to 40 %

Sub Sahara African states are in much better position.[114]

In case of life expectancy, India is in a superior condition due to no famine, no warfare and health care program started by government. African countries were surrounded by the warfare, uncertainty to economy and political turmoil. The literacy rate was very low in India and Sub-Saharan countries. The capability deprivation of woman is eye catching. This is due to high mortality rate and artificially lower survival rate of women in many parts of the world.

---

113   Ibid, page no. 96-97.
114   Ibid, page no. 102.

5.5   Markets, state and social opportunity

Markets, state and social opportunity

The Market mechanism has new meaning. The result of market mechanism reflects in income OR utility yield. We buy sale or exchange to make transaction to flourish our life. Therefore, freedom in this area is important. The business ethics has to follow. The absence of behavioural rule and absence of freedom is also major issue itself. African Americans in south U.S.A. were in slavery, even though their income was more and better living condition, but deprivation of legal freedom was there.

Markets, liberty and labour

The development of free market and free seeking of employment is very necessary. Karl Marx has endorsed the idea of free seeking employment in interest of labour. The bondage labour is in many parts of the world. They did not have freedom of employment as well as ownership of land.

There was a failure of bureaucratic socialism in Russia and Eastern Europe. This fails in terms of economic development. Earlier life expectancy was very high compared to present 58 years after desolation of communist rule. The socialist community was taking care of all health related problems and about mortality and under nourishment. People do not want to return to old communist system. The market function came into existence. The people denied using market function. The market function wiped out their freedom and economic development.

There were child labour in India, Pakistan and Bangladesh. The root of this was economic deprivation to the family. The children were force to do unwanted work and denied primary education. The parents were forcing them to work. This can be prevented by law with alternate arrangement of income to the.

The freedom of employment outside the family was an issue. The denied is a violation of woman's liberty and gender inequality with women economic empowerment. In Afghanistan, woman working out of family is brutally executed. Women have started open discussion and established an organization to bring substantial social change. Such women's social organization has good combination of complementary assistance and the market function, right of employment and earning which gives them freedom.

Markets and efficiency

The basic freedom of transaction is important issue in market mechanism, irrespective of positive or negative result. In market mechanism, we have to take note of types of market such as competitive or monopolistic, using general equilibrium model to achieve economic efficiency.

The Pareto optimality is another method. In this situation the utility of no one can be raised without reducing the utility of someone else. Arrow – Debrue model is thinking in terms of enhance the utility sum without reducing the utility of anyone else. Dr. Amartya Sen is in favour of individual freedom than utility. Dr. Amartya Sen sees that the Arrow – Debrue model can transform "space" of utilities in individual freedom to choose commodity basket and in terms of capability function.

The final analysis is in competitive market equilibrium guarantee that no one's freedom can be increased any further while maintaining the freedom of everyone else. In case of individual freedom achieved and enjoyed is the matter of motivation.

Coupling of disadvantages and inequality of freedom

There are inequalities in distribution of utility and freedom in Pareto Optimal. We may not be able to increase the utility or substantive freedom of a person, without reducing someone.

The inequalities in the distribution of utilities and or freedom will be there. As a result, income cannot get converted into capability and into well being. Example: - A disabled or sick person is unable to earn more and facing difficulties converting income into capabilities for well being.

Problem of Inequality in freedom and inefficiency in freedom requires attention. The government support for freedom efficiency is necessary in market mechanism. The market mechanism will be weak in achievement and equity is promoted due to this. Europe, by offering good health care and unemployment allowance keeps employment level high. U.S.A. is offering high social security and keeps employment level high. The efficiency and equity is equally maintained here.

Markets and interest groups

It is important that in market mechanism what things they can do and what things are allowed to do. Market is working in its own way. Some people's vested interest may hurt. They will disturb market mechanism. In monopoly, high price and below standard things will be sold. The producer will maintain his profit due to protection. The consumer suffers in economic term as well as in terms of freedom.

Adam Smith advocated for competition in better interest of consumer and for market mechanism. He was in favour of public education. It is happening in developing country today and it had happened in socialist country earlier. The general restriction in competition is favoured on politically influential people to have substantial material benefit from restricting trade and exchange. Many eminent economists have supported the competition.

Wilfred Pareto said that "Certain measure A is the case of the loss of one franc to each of a thousand persons, and of a thousand franc gain to one individual, the latter will expand a great deal of energy, whereas the former will resist weakly; and it is likely, that in the end, the person who is attempting to secure the thousand francs via A will be successful".[115] Pareto agreed that one-person benefits at the cost of thousands, but when it is made known in democracy, than all will oppose. The more freedom will come by way of public discussion. This will help to have freedom of one kind helping to realize another kind of freedom.

We live in this world, where political influence is in search of economic gain, is very real phenomenon. Adam Smith said that the vested interest tend to win because of their "Better knowledge" of their own interest.

Need for critical scrutiny of the role of the markets

Critical public discussion is necessary for good public policy as you cannot rely on market. Adam Smith was in favour of market but in favour of restrictions too. Adam Smith was advocating the maximum limit of rate of interest on loan by law rather than exorbitant rate of interest. It is quite possible that private profit motive can act against social interests. Best example is environmental loses.

---

[115]   Ibid, page no. 122.

Need for a many sided approach

A many sided approach to development is important due to success and difficulties faced by developing countries. The need to balance the market functions with government role and of politicians and social institutions. It must be an integrated process in which progress on different front, with different institutions to work as reinforcement to each other. India was lacking in elementary education and social opportunities. In India, Manmohansingh was successful to open liberalization in the year 1991. This was not combined with social opportunities as required. Year 1991 reform with education and social opportunities would have changed the face of India.

Extensive use of market with liberalization and social opportunities might give more freedom to people. The different instruments of freedom are (a) economics entitlements (b) Democratic freedom (c) social opportunities (d) transparency guarantee (e) Protective securities. These freedoms recognized of their role as well as their complementarities.

Interdependence and public goods

We have to find out the limits of market mechanism. Market mechanism is effective with supplementary activities of institution. "Public goods" will make market mechanism weak in case of efficiency. Market efficiency is argued that there is no "Non- marketable" thing. This is true in case of individual. The definition of public goods is people consume together than an individual. Public goods are hard to sell in the interest of human capabilities, welfare. Market mechanism is faster for private goods. There can be a limited reach of public goods in case of market mechanism. Example – Defence, policing and environmental policy.

There is a case for mixed property. The basic education is for benefit of community and capability enhance of individual. Literacy will help to develop economic growth and to bring social change. Western Countries, Japan and East Asia made rapid progress due to low cost basic education. Some people argue for free market for education in developing countries. This will withheld the expansion of progress in free education and rapid literacy in developing countries. Adam Smith said that with very little expanse on education, benefit can reach to larger group. Public goods are the need of basic capability apart from market mechanism with social provision and efficiency consideration.

Public provisioning and incentives

An argument can be against public spending for economic development and social change. (1)Fiscal burden:- Public expenditure depends on big or small planning and budget deficit. This will increase inflation in economy and increase public debt.(2)Incentive: - Public spending is an Incentive may discourage man for initiative and individual efforts.

Dr. Amartya Sen said that redistribution of income and free provision for public goods does affect the incentive system in economy. Europe had experienced that unemployment insurance as costly affairs. The unemployment allowance was to give part of an income and not whole. The incentive will work as catalytic. The social scheme provides only part of income. It requires finding out the adverse effect on incentive and having balance in equity and efficiency.

In case of incentive, for free education and health scheme, it is important to examine from two points of view (a) The extent of need by recipient and (b) how much he can afford to pay for that services.

Financial resources has limit in developing countries. The choice of the society should be a share system for cost and incentive, in such a social provision, which is the best solution.

Incentives, capabilities and functioning

Incentive helps to identify deprivation. In poverty analysis, the use of information shifted from low income to deprivation of capability. This is better term compare to low income concept. Person actual functioning and information will help capability concept. If a person dies prematurely due to any reason then, in most cases, conclude that it was a capability problem. In some cases, it may not be true, Example: - person commits suicide or decision to fast. The supplementary information will tell us the intention of person but again this is a matter of going beyond functioning and to check the capability deprivation expands upon circumstances. Supplementary information is also necessary to examine in the light of practical feasibility. It is possible to hide the income. This is happening in developing countries. The focus on capabilities and functioning will help to arrive at judgment. Incentive only on poverty can be manipulated, where as the capability and functioning information will restrict them to do so. Functional deprivation can be much more difficult to handle than income deprivation Example-old age, and handicapped person. Capability handicap will use public provision as it is meant for a person who need this and not transferable to anyone else. There is in built matching in such provision. This will not distort the provision of incentive to capability deprive people.

Targeting and means-testing

After finding out the capability deprivation and not low income, we have to think "HOW" to distribute the public provision to them. We have to find out two things (1) person's Capability handicap (2) person's economic condition. This will help to specific class of needy person and information requirement will be minimal. The misuse will be minimal in case of capability. In case of economic condition, it is difficult because of information limit as people can hide income.

The whole approach of finding capability deprivation and provisional public service can divide in following ways. (a) On the bases of information. (b) People can give wrong information to have the incentive. (c) Personal stigma of poor condition will prevent people to take benefits. John Rawls argued that self-respect "perhaps the most important primary goods"[116] This is the heart of a theory of justice as fairness. (d) Substantial administrative cost for resource expenditure and bureaucratic power employed. This may cost privacy and autonomy of person and breed corruption to get benefits. (E) The beneficiaries are poor and need political support to get quality benefits which is against democratic norms.

Even after right targeting, the programmed result is doubtful. This is equally true for rich as well as poor nations.

Agency and informational basis

There are for and against for mean testing programmed. The circumstances have to check for nature of public service and characteristics of society at universal. You have to look in to behaviour of individual, which effects to his choice and incentive. The importance of agency is to find out capability deprivation. When you target the beneficiary than the identification will reveal the capability deprivation. The result will help for public provisioning.

Financial prudence and need for integration

---

[116]   Ibid, page no. 136.

Financial conservation is necessary. The equation is of "What" and "why". The total income is equal to total expenditure is not in demand. At present, all states are spending more than their income and gap is filled by borrowing. State should see that inflationary pressure is not there and prices are more or less stabilized.

Dr. Amartya Sen says that Michael Bruno noted that 20% to 40% inflation has negative effect on economic growth. The stabilization will bring growth in medium and short run. Nation should go for less than 15% to 20% inflation rate which is costing less. Dr. Amartya Sen says the moderate inflation can hamper the economic growth. It is a strong case to reduce budgetary deficit in moderate form and not to eliminate it. There is a case for larger budget deficit which gives debt and interest burden on nation. Normally budget deficit should not be more than 3% of gross domestic product. Financial conservation should be seen in light of objective of policy. Public expenditure will help to generate and guarantee the capability development. In most of the countries the public debt is the result of higher inflation.

5.6   Importance of democracy

Economic needs and political freedoms

It is a general thinking that poor country cannot afford democracy and political liberty. Poor person's priority is economic need. Vienna conference held in spring 1993 discussed about human rights. It was majority view to give political and civil rights to all countries particularly in third world. This was forcefully opposed by China, Singapore and other East Asian countries. Dr. Amartya Sen says political freedom and economic need is interconnected. Political freedom will help to provide incentive and information to solve the economic need. Public should debate the economic need with civil right and political liberty as (1) Human being associated with basic capabilities – direct action. (b) Instrumental action – People expresses and supports their claims for political freedom. (c) Constructive actions: - People should spell out their economic needs.

Arguments against political freedoms and civil rights

(1) Lee – effect: - Lee Kuan Yew, prime minister of Singapore thought that freedom and civil rights hamper economic growth and development. China thinks that individuals must put the state's right first there after their own.

(2) If people are given choice to choose the political rights on one side and fulfilment of economic need on another side than definitely the people will choose the another one.

(3) The political freedom, human right and democracy are western thoughts, where as East Asian people believe in discipline and order.

(4) In Vienna conference the danger was shown that if you put human right as universal, it masks the reality of diversity.

Democracy and economic growth and Do poor people care about democracy and political rights?

'Authority is the key to economic growth' is not correct. The Lee thesis has limited information and not tested on wide range statistical data. Against this India, Costa Rica and Jamaica have made progress in democracy. Fastest growing Botswana is democratic state. These are the real policies guiding factor to make development with democracy. The GNP is correct barometer to measure economic growth. Political freedom has impact on the lives and capability of person. This is an instrumental role of democracy.

Put the democracy for free election and freedom of expression and opposition. The political leader in third world does not give enough political right and people have less opportunity to express views against government claims. In India, Indira Gandhi declared emergency in 1970. Poor people of India were interested in basic political liberty and rights. The people of Pakistan, South Korea, Thailand, Myanmar and Bangladesh are struggling for democratic freedom. In military regimes of certain African countries, people have shown their opposition. Political freedom is a part of basic capability approach for human.

Instrumental importance of political freedom, Constrictive role of political freedom

We have reason to value our liberty and freedom of expression in our life. Our demand attended and freedom of speech allowed. Political incentive should work as an effective instrument. Famine has not accrued that heavily in any democratic country than dictatorship or intolerant single party rule or in ancient time authoritarian types of government. The freedom of press, election fear and freedom of speech has made democratic government to work at the time of famine. There is a connection between political freedom and economic need. The exercise of political right helps to conceptualization of economic needs. This will result in information of value and deciding priorities. The effectiveness of open dialogue will help to solve social and political problems. The discussion has helped to reduce fertility in educated state and it is ineffective in illiterate state. Kerala fertility rate 1.7 is as good as Britain, France where as China is 1.9.

Working of democracy and the practice of democracy and the role of opposition

In democracy, the relevance, constructive importance and protective role are important. The political right can be tested in case of the problem of Famine but not problem of under nourishment, illiteracy or gender bias. These problems require greater political attention and more effective use of discussion. People go for less number in voting than they cannot expect good governance. Freedom is there, but it is important how it is exercised.

The achievement of democracy depends upon rules, procedure and its' adoption as well as safeguard along with to use the opportunity. Democracy has to work for ordinary people by way of instrument and with constructive role. Opposition should work effectively. The opposition in dictatorial countries is also effective. There is an example of South Korea and Pinochert's Chile. The gender inequality and elementary education are important issues in India. This requires public debate and support of opposition. In India, democracy has survived due to stability and security in spite of heterogeneity of culture, language, religion.

5.7   Famines and other crises

Introduction

It is our fear that due to population increase, wide spread hunger, frequent famine and under nourishment will be a big problem. We can change the situation of hunger and deprivation in the world by effective policy and action. Poverty and endemic hunger is different from famine. It was preliminary thought that the population increase is the cause of hunger. Individual and family has freedom over adequate amount of food by way of growing or buying from market. The results of famines show that it was for Individual and family, those who were not having enough economic power to buy the food and not the food supply. Economical and political crisis in East Asia and South Asia are the causes of hunger due to sudden loss of economic entitlements.

Entitlement and interdependence

Increased food production, agriculture expansion with functioning of economy and political and social arrangement affect to the person ability to acquire food and nourishment. In government policy, N.G.O. and other political parties with social organization, Media should be incorporated. Under nourishment, starvation and famine are the result of working of economy and society and not just food production. We have to think of entitlement by which individual and family can establish their ownership on food and abolish hunger.

Family has entitlement by way of endowment as ownership and assets which has price in market.. Entitlement can be generated by way of agriculture, wage income in absence of land. In industry, person's services will give endowment to buy food. The defect will affect their endowment and as a result hunger, not food production.

The exchange condition of labour and craftsman generate the endowment. The change in exchange condition makes person to the threat of famine due to shift in price. The fall in prices is due to many immediate changes. During 1943 Bengal famine, fisher men had to suffer most in exchange of food.[117] The high quality food-fish-were sold to get low calorie food-staple food.

---

[117]   Ibid, page no. 163.

In case of many other occupations like carpenter, mason or barber the price may drop or person alters his decision about taking services. Bengal 1943 famine had a tremendous effect on price of service and food price. The difference was up to 70 to 80% and poor became poorer. On one side he has to sale services at either low rate or forgets about endowment. In both the cases he has low or NO entitlement. The speculative hording had increased the price of food grain in high proportion. The food production did not decline sharply.

Famine causation

Famine is due to various reasons, as a result, failure of entitlement. People like Industrial worker, service provider and agriculture labourer has to acquire the food from market. There are three things to get food 1) his earning 2) prevailing price of food item 3) non food expenditure. These people can get food from market as per their wages, production of other things and other factors.

Famine will occur not due to decline in food production. Farmer sales his expensive products at cheaper rate and buys low calorie food at market rate. The pastoral people sold their high value animal product and got cheap food at high price. In famine labour will lose income. The loss of income should be substantiated by social security system in economy.

Famines can occur in spite of high food production in the economy. In Bangladesh, the food availability per head was high in 1974 even though famine occurred. Flood situation created regional unemployment and starvation. Famine can occur in case of food production decline for other reasons. The production loss in one part of country results into no income situation. Actually the food had moved out of famine district due to higher price available at other districts. Famine can happen in case a sudden increase in income results into high purchasing power of urban people and the rural people income shrank. This had happened during war boom in Bengal 1943.

The occupation changed and shift in gainful activity results into famine, in absence of income or entitlement. This has happened in sub Saharan Africa due to dry land converted in to irrigation land and shepherd has to face the famine due to no grassland for their animals. The landless labourers have to face famine situation in 1974 after the flood in Bangladesh, as they lost the gainful employment for rice transportation. To understand famine, average food availability per head will not help. Famine hardly affects 5% to 10% of population.

Famine prevention

The loss of entitlement can be re-arranged, as small portion of population effected at particular region due to famine. Poor country with little cost and systematic efforts can avert starvation of small group of large population in difficult time. Suppose the 10 % of population is in danger of potential famine and their food consumption is of 3 to 5% of national food consumption. The total income going to this people is say 3% of GNP. The preventive measure will take care for supply of food to needy with efficient organization. Famine is associated with mortality due to disease and sanitary breakdown and population movement; infectious diseases endemic in the region. This can be controlled with the help of community health arrangement and public action. Famine prevention depends upon political arrangement. In rich countries antipoverty programme and unemployment insurance are there. The developing countries may not have this type of arrangement but they provide emergency public employment caused by natural or non-natural calamities.

Famine and alienation

The political economy works for prevention of famine with the help of institutions and organizations. The distance between public and government may be a cause for non prevention of famine. Famine occurred in Ireland in 1840. People migrated in terrible voyage condition. At present the original Irish people are small in number in total population of Ireland. The food was exported to England. People were dying due to hunger. It is the effectiveness of public policy for prevention of famine. Famine in Ireland was due to reduction in food output due to potato blight. The fund was sufficient with United Kingdom but was not available to Irish people. The small group of potato grower of Ireland were affected and food prices were high. The result was the economic power was meagre in such situation.

The famine of Ireland was cultural alienation with political will. British poor were given enough help. British were interested to teach Irish people the lesions of civilization and live like human being. Winston Churchill remarked for Bengal famine of 1943 that it was the result of population explosion.-"Tendency to breed like rabbits".

The overall slump in economy had encouraged the food counter movement. This was happened in Wollo famine-Ethiopia in the year 1973. Here in both the cases the market force has encouraged the movement of food from one place to another place where they get higher price. Income should have generated which might have stopped the food counter movement and famine can be restricted.

Production, diversification and growth

Growing economics will provide better entitlement and more resource to prevent famine. This fact is applicable to Sub-Saharan Africa. The incentive provided by government to guarantee the growth of output in production and income by way of technical change, skill and improvement of productivity in agriculture and other fields which will help them to come out of traditional life style. If we compare food production per head figure of year 1992-93 with the year 1979-1981 than food production had declined by 1.7% in South Korea, 12.4% in Japan, 33.5% in Botswana and 58.0% in Singapore but these countries were not starved.[118] The richness of the people of these countries was able and affords to import of food.

In contrast to this, Sudan was having 7.7 % increases and Burkina Faso had 19.4% increases in food production even though they were having famine situation. This was due to general poverty and lack of entitlements. Sub Saharan Africa had experienced decline in food production and famine in absence of high economic growth and dependence on food output. Other countries did not experience famine because they were not dependent on above things.

The employment route and agency issue

The country with no presence in international trade and the economic situation is not good though famine can be averted. In this condition, equal share of food grain and employment opportunity to all will help to save from quick starvation. This will regenerate the income of people. These types of arrangement have helped India, Botswana and Zimbabwe. The employment route makes people active. The different social institutions are employed to eradicate famine. The public policy measure will help in three ways 1) State support to create income and employment 2) Operation of private market for food and labour 3) Reliance on normal commerce and

---

[118]   Ibid, page no.176.

business. It is in interest of famine prevention and important for economic development.

Democracy and famine prevention

Famine can be prevented in democracy due to political interest for election, multiparty politics and free press and electronic media. Rich or Poor democratic county can prevent the famine. India, Botswana and Zimbabwe are poor countries but prevented famine successfully. Botswana and Zimbabwe were democratic country and food output was less by 17% and 38% respectively between 1979-1981 and 1983-1984. Dictatorial country had 10% to 12% decline in food production in Sudan and Ethiopia. The decline in food production was moderate compared to Botswana and Zimbabwe. They face the music of famine.

Incentive, information and the prevention of famines

Democracy gives the incentive to ruling party to take preventive measure for famine. The fear of next election, opposition, the press and electronic media will bring the story of famine; will force the ruling government to work for famine. In China, before taking preventive measure, 30 million people died in 1958-1961 famine.[119] The opposition, the freedom of press and electronic media were absent in China during this period.

Protective role of democracy

China suffered for famine due to wrong policy. The economic incentive was there. The Sub Sahara African countries, authoritarian regime has made good loss to the fellow citizens in economic and political freedom. The leaders of various African countries were not in a position to decide to join with west or with communist countries. This hampered the progress of democracy. When newspapers suppressed and political parties were banned and there were no international protests. The absence of news, electronic media and opposition in Sudan, Somalia, Ethiopia and Shale countries have suffered a lot for famine. One party African state like Cape Verde and Tanzania had successfully avoided famine. The democratic countries like India, Botswana and Zimbabwe had made good progress in preventing famine.

---

[119]   Ibid, page no.181.

Transparency, security and Asian economic crises

Multiparty election and media gives a protective security in instrumental freedom. The positive role of political and civil right prevents social and economical disasters. This type of institutional right comes in to picture and becomes significant when laps come in light. The change in economy and mistakes in policy will bring insecurity in system. The undemocratic governance of East Asia and South Asia brought out problems.

There is no transparency guarantee in business. The IMF has stress the importance of this to avoid unscrupulous businessmen and to save fund. This will create confidence in international community. The public participation could be effective instrument to avoid government apathy. Trust is important factor in business and banking. This is lacking in many countries. The money was not invested in proper development projects in Indonesia or South Korea. These countries are not democratic therefore the non-accountability and no transparency. The financial crises lead to economic recession in non-democratic country will not make the ruler responsible. In democracy, it will be opposite.

5.8   Women's agency and social change

Women right movement started in 1792 by Marry Wollstonecraft. She wrote a book "A vindication of the rights of woman". She spoke about right, women well-being and women agency. Agency aspect is now in lime light. The well-being of women is concentrated. It is a combination of welfare and agency. Now women are considered as an active agent of change. The men and women are working together for women's cause. This is a social transformation.

Agency and well-being

The women cannot allow inequalities. They are thinking about the well being. These things are overlapping with each other. Inequality has to be solved by way of agency. Women's well being comes through agency. Both the aspects are intersection. Woman is, as a head of the institution, as well as member. She is having dual role. The matter of deprivation in well being of women is a matter of social injustice including injustice for women. Justice requires in respect of biological aspect, mortality and missing women in term of gender bias, for health care and other necessities. One argument is the agency aspect will affect the well being aspect of women. It proved contrary. The agency has helped women to get independent income, to find employment outside home, to have ownership right and improved literacy and made them to discuss the matter in and outside family. The result is, respect in family due to extra income, improved social status and property right. This has created far reaching impact in society for women entitlements.

Co-operative conflict

In family, the interest is of two types (a) Congruent (b) Conflict. How this will turn into cooperative interest of man and woman in family is important. Men and women have to get equal benefit out of this. The partial unresolved conflicts are solved in terms of behaviour. The cooperative arrangement distributes joint benefits to both of them. Woman may not be able to assess the right thing in deprived condition. In such cases, it is difficult to judge the production and contribution of her to the family. This may be relative deprivation of women.

Perceptions of entitlement

The perception of individual contribution and entitlement in family plays a major role in dividing joint benefit between man and woman. The women agency can help here to get proper benefit to women. The impact of woman entitlement will correct the situation and agency will be strengthened. This will help to reduce child mortality rate. The agency voice will help in case of education, employment and in turn the nature of public discussion such as women fertility ratio and environment. Woman empowerment will have definite impact in value systems of community. In case of poverty, mostly in many communities, women will make sufferer due to gender bias. At the time of famine, loss of entitlement will affect the intra family food distribution program and under nourishment for women.

Earlier male was the earning member of family. The wage earned by woman is now visible in family. This helps her to have better division of food and enhance position in family. She becomes independent and little powerful. We can say that freedom in one area helps to have freedom in another area. The woman empowerment has great bearing on fertility. The fertility is in check because of woman education and earning.

Child survival and the agency of women

Women education helped to reduce child mortality. In family, mother's decision helped the survival of children without gender bias. Mother attached to children's welfare. India, Pakistan, Bangladesh, China, Iran, North Africa and West Asia are having the problem of gender bias. The female child mortality rate is more compared to Europe, U.S.A. and sub Saharan Africa. Women agency has played important role in education and literacy. Woman had say in family decision about children care. Women agency was successful in economic effect as the women had started earning. In intra country comparison, it is found that the female literacy had given good result in child mortality rate under the age of five. In India, women agency is playing successful role in reducing gender bias because of education and literacy amongst women. Therefore WOMAN AGENCIES are important.

Agency, Emancipation and fertility reduction and Women's political, social and economic roles

Women well being and women agency are essential for the reduction in fertility ratio. Asian and African women are denied the freedom for reduced birth-rates. Educated woman is not ready to bear the child and care the children. Education has brought knowledge of family planning in women. The all India fertility ratio was 3.0 where as women agency in Kerala has brought down fertility ratio upto1.7 compared to 1.9 in China. Women agency in Kerala has given property right to women.

Women, given opportunity, are highly successful in the field of politics. The women were president of Sri Lanka, India, and Prime minister of India and Pakistan, Bangladesh, Philippines. The social initiative of women is also important. Women have done good job in the field of education and reduction in fertility rate. On economic front, women have less excess to resources. The ownership of land and capital is in the hand of men. Women have very less resource to start enterprise. Given opportunity, women have proved their ability in economics and provided social benefits to them as well as society.

The Gramin bank in Bangladesh is running successfully for women against discrimination of credit to them in society. The repayment of loans is 98% to the bank.[120] Agricultural activities, land ownership of women have played

---

[120]   Ibid, page no. 201.

greater role. Naila Kabeer's study of Bangladesh for economic involvement of women has shown that in local environment, it has a great effect.

5.9   Population, food and freedom

Introduction and is there a world food crisis?

In prosperous world, hunger is the worst enemy. Famine with hunger comes in some part of the world regularly. Millions of people dead and this is a tragedy of modern world. There are three factors affecting the hunger, under nourishment and famine. 1) Food output of world 2) The price factor at which people buy the food and 3) decline trend in food production. World cannot import food from nowhere.

The question is - is world food production falling behind world population? The answer is no. Malthus published "Essay on population" in the year 1798. He predicted a situation that the "The proportion between the natural increase of population and food" will be imbalance. After two centuries population had increased SIX times and the food consumption per head is higher due to general increase in standard of living than Malthus time. United Nations, FAO quarterly bulletin of Statistics, 1995 and 1998 and FAO monthly bulletin of Static August 1984 proved that there is no food production decline; on the contrary the densely populated countries are having largest per capita increase in food production. The production figure may vary from year to year but the trend was upward.

Economic incentives and food production

It is a fact that world food production per head had increased and it resulted into price reduction.

Table – year 1950-52 and 1995-97 price comparison.

Food	1950-52	1995-97	% change
Wheat	$427.6	$159.3	- 62.7
Rice	$789.7	$282.3	- 64.2
Sorghum	$328.7	$110.9	- 66.2
Maize	$372.0	$119.1	- 68.0

Note: - The unit is constant 1990 U.S.Dollar per metric ton adjusted by the G.5. Manufacturing unit value index (muv)

Source: - World Bank, Commodity market and developing countries. November 1998. Table A (Washington D.C.) World Bank price prospects for major primary commodities vol.2 Table a 5, A 10 a 15 (Washington D.C.) 1993.

(A) In mid 1990, panicky statements do raise the price for short run. Since 1970, prices are falling in long term. In 1998, world prices for wheat and coarse grain declined by 20% and 14% respectively. The downward price trend has affected the production.

(B) Generally the food production has increased well ahead of population growth. This will help the hungry people.

The food production governs by market mechanism. The rise in food production brought down the price. India and China had biggest increase in food production but domestic market was insulted against world effect. The yield rises per hectare by 42.6 Kg. during 1981- 93 in world as a whole. The cereal production rises 94%, due to increase in production to per unit of land from 1970-90 and 6% increase in area of world as a whole.

Beyond the trend of food output per head

World population has to slow down the growth. The environment and overcrowding are issues. The increase in population will not be the reason for food production decline. Dr.Amartya Sen says the entitlement approach is important.

Population growth and the advocacy of coercion

We have to look into the rate of growth of world population. Growth of World Population

One billion to Two billion In 123 Years.

Two billion to Three billion In 33 Years

Three billion to Four billion In 14 Years

Four billion to Five billion In 13 Years

Five billion to Six billion In 10 Years.

If this is so, the world will be over crowded in 21st century. It is necessary to slow down the birth rate. China applied the coercion method and kept the birth rate low. The point is, was this method right?

Coercion and reproductive rights

The slowdown of the birth rate has two arguments. (1) Family must have priority to decide how many children they should have. (2) The potential mother should have 'SAY' in this. If a mother is not willing for abortion, then that should be her right.

The normative right is important. The political philosopher has denied the right. Jeremy Bentham is not in favour of right. He says it is "NONSENSE".[121] If you give priority to right then you have to accept it unconditionally. Libertarian system is in favour and says that let any consequence came because of it.

Dr.Amartya Sen gives a "GOAL RIGHT SYSTEM" which is fulfilling the necessity of both thoughts (Utilitarian and libertarian). John Stuart Mill accepts that there is "No priority" between utility generated from different activities. The reproductive right must be protected irrespective of disaster to happen.

Malthusian Analysis

CONDORECT – a French mathematician had predicted that "Increase in number of then surpassing their means of subsistence resulting in either a continual diminution of happiness and population, a movement truly retrograde or at least a kind of oscillation between god and evil".[122] He further thought of voluntary reduction in fertility.

Malthus was thinking that individual reasoned decision would not work. He was of the opinion that population will reduce food supply. He was sceptical of voluntary family planning. He was in favour of "Moral restrain". He identified "Forced" route. The population growth will bring down standard of living; increased mortality would force to have smaller family due to economics.

---

121   Ibid, page no. 211.
122   Ibid, page no. 213.

The fertility rates have come down due to social and economic development. It has come down in Europe and North America and coming down in Asia. Fertility rate remain highest and constant in Sub–Saharan Africa, where economic and social progress is not much and backward in terms of education health care and life expectancy.

The "Development is best Contraceptive" is half true due to various reasons. In the West, there are many reasons. (A) Rise in income (B) Expansion of education (C) Greater economic independence of woman (D) Reduction of mortality rate (E) Family planning opportunity.

Economic or social development and Empowerment of young women

Gary Becker's analysed that prosperity is the reason or reduction in birth-rate. The economic development will help to have better education to children. Social theory is in favour of education in general and female education in particular to control birth-rate. Dr. Amartya Sen says that Becker believed-change of costs and benefits make a change in desired number of children. Whereas CONDORECET thought that social changes brings the decision to limit number of children. The sharp decline of birth rate in Bangladesh was due to knowledge of family planning. Fertility rate has come down from 6% to 3.4 % in ten years. [123]

It is difficult to separate out economic development from social change. People chose small family due to economic reason. High fertility nations should follow the route of economic and social change to reduce fertility. Women education has lowered the fertility due to economic empowerment by way of employment, property right and women status in social culture in the world. The rich states in India, like Punjab and Haryana has higher per capita income and higher fertility rate. Southern states with low per capita income and high education and job opportunity has lower fertility rate.

Externality, values and communication

Woman education and particularly school education help for standing in family and her social standing, her ability to be independent, her power to articulate, her knowledge of outside world, her skill to influencing group decision etc. Inter family study shows that fertility rate has not decrease and also independence of woman.

---

[123]   Ibid, page no. 216.

How effective is coercion? And Side effects and speed of fertility reduction

China adopted one child policy in 1979 and gave economic punishment to child and adult. The fertility rate came down to 1.9 compare to India's 3.1. This route of lowering fertility rate has a cost and violation of fundamental right of reproductive freedom. The human right commission is worried about this. The woman organization is particularly thinking the loss of freedom. When one child policy is applicable, the heath of child will be neglected and mortality rate will increase. China, India and North Africa population prefer the male child than the fate of girl child is in question. The social and economical change has made concrete effect on fertility rate in China. The concept of low birth rate is not fitting psychologically in the mind of people. The social ingredients of education, employment and health care has helped to bring down the fertility rate. Compared to China, Kerala in India is having all the same ingredients along with property right to woman which is an important point. Kerala birth rate is 1.8 compared to 1.9 of China. Kerala achievement is without compulsion, which China had.

In China, woman had performed abortion due to compulsion by government. In Kerala, infant mortality (16 for girls and 17 for boys) is much lower than China (33 girls and 28 boys).Kerala accepted voluntary control for child's birth. Kerala is as much as same of China in fertility rate.

Fertility Rate	Year 1979	Yaer1991
China	2.8	2.0
Kerala	3.0	1.8
Tamilnadu	3.5	2.2

Low education in the state of Bihar, Utter Pradesh, Madhya Pradesh and Rajasthan, had resulted into the high fertility rate which is from 4.4 to 5.1.

Temptations of duress

In mid 1970, Indira Gandhi declared emergency. The government policy was to meet the family planning targets by officers. The two child policy made effective for local self government, state and central government staff. The discrimination in service for two child norms was there. Indian government tried to pass a law to this effect in parliament but unsuccessful.

The poor people voted in election against Indira Gandhi and her party defeated. People were suspicious about family planning program. As a result, up to 1985, long stagnation of birth rate was there.

5.10 Culture and human rights

The importance of human rights is accepted now a day. A committee examined the position every year. It is prominent but the priorities have changed then what it was before few decades. The human rights become an important part of literature on development.

Three critiques

There are three critiques. The first one is "Legitimacy critique" of human right, they said it is natural. This is not natural. It has to acquire by way of legal system. The governing state has to pass the law. It is not natural but established through constitutional right. This gives people well defined right.

The second one is Coherence right. Here the matter is related to ethics and politics. You give the right to Mr. A but there should be a fulfilling agency named B too. The duty is recognized. In absence of agency, the right is a vocal and not effective in life.

The third one is cultural critique. This is not a legal or instrumental. This comes in social ethics. Ethics are not universal. The culture differs from country to country. Person has to become tolerant to the other culture than and then only universal human right can work.

The legitimacy critique

The ethical issues are based on reasoning of rights. The best thing is right must be seen as an instrument rather than ethical entitlement. The point is all human being should have certain rights. This is supported by ethics and has to be fulfilled. The wife has every right to take part in family discussion, every one accept this. In practice it cannot be forced by police. Here the 'right to respect' comes into picture. This is an ethical reasoning based on political demand. The other side of the picture is freedom.

The Coherence critique

When we talk about rights, we have to see that somebody has to give guarantee to fulfil it. The point is how you know that your right is realized. Immanuel Kant called it "Perfect obligation". Agency has specific duty to realize the right. The claim must have legal merits but rights considered as an entitlement. Human right has to come to every citizen without discrimination. The claims are addressed to anyone, who can help and to see that they realized through no particular person or agency. The rights formulated, sometimes end unfulfilled. Here we bifurcate the right in following categories of a) right have and not fulfilled and b) does not have right. Ethical value affirmation is to get help for right within limit of freedom. Here the right can help freedom.

The cultural critique and Asian values

Are the human rights universal? Do they have ethical value? Confucian culture does emphasis a discipline than rights and loyalty rather than entitlements. Political liberty and civil rights are a part of human rights. The authoritarian political arrangement of Asia had tried to suppress the Asian values. You cannot generalize that Asian value is opposing human rights. About 60% of world population is in Asia. You cannot separate them due to vast heterogeneous population from the rest of the world. The Asian values mostly considered for East Asian region. It is compared with west, than it is only Korea, Japan, China, Vietnam and NOT INDIA. Korea, Japan and China have vast difference in their culture. Singapore is a glaring example of intercommunity amity and friendly coexistence.

The contemporary west and claims to uniqueness

Asia is having authoritarian line of thinking. West indirectly backs this idea. West is giving preference to political freedom and democracy. Aristotle supported the idea of political liberty. In Asian tradition, these thoughts are from beginning. The idea of personal freedom is in (a) the value of personal freedom (b) quality of freedom. Here the freedom guaranteed for one and for all. Equality to women is a recent development. Freedom was valued in higher class in Asian society as well as in Greek society.

We can define tolerance in 1) the value of tolerance. Here you have to tolerate the diverse beliefs, commitment and action of people. 2) Equality of tolerance means offered to someone must be reasonably offered to all. In western literature, democratic and liberal idea is a part of personal freedom. In Asia, Buddhism is thinking very much in personal freedom. There is a room for violation and free choice in Buddhism. Nobility of conduct has to achieve in freedom. Confucius in China also believed in above virtues.

Interpretations of Confucius

The present Asian thinkers are not giving enough justice to varieties of teaching of Confucius. Zilu asked Confucius how to serve prince? Confucius replied "tell him the truth even if it offends him". Singapore or Beijing might have different view. Another good example "When the (good) way prevails in the state, speak boldly and act boldly. When the state has lost the way, act boldly and speak softly". Confucius gave two great things of Asian value (1) Loyalty to family (2) Obedience to the state. The role of state should be an extension of the role of family. There can be conflict as per Confucius. Confucius did not emphasise the authority of state but gave varied preaching about ethics and moral.

Ashoka and Kautilya

We see variety of views on freedom, tolerance and equality in Indian history. Emperor Ashoka of third century B.C. had vast kingdom. Ashoka started thinking of public ethics and politics after victory in great Kalinga war. Ashoka carved stone with the list of things of good life and good government in his country. Ashoka gave special importance to tolerance in diversity. Ashoka covered the forest people-native in tolerance.

Kautilya was a contemporary of Aristotle in the 4th century B.C. and worked as a senior minister of Emperor Chandragupta Maurya, Emperor Ashoka's grandfather. Kautilya wrote ARTHASHASTRA-the economic science. The treatise is on political economy governance. He was rational and believing to promote happiness in kingdom. The impressive work was in the area of famine prevention and administrative effectiveness. At the same time, he advised king, if necessary violate the freedom, to win over opponent and adversaries. Kautilya specially identify as the duty of the king to "provide orphanage, the aged, the infirm, the afflicted and the helpless with a maintenance" and "subsistence to helpless women when they are carrying and also to the (new born) children, they give the birth to".[124] He denied the personal liberty to upper class and prescribed penalty for crime along with acceptance of slavery. This is perfectly in line with freedom valuing ethical system as per Dr.Amartya Sen.

Islamic tolerance

Mughal Emperor Akbar was ruling India during the year 1556 to 1605 A.D. Emperor Akbar accepted social and religious behaviour and human rights of various kind including worship and religious practice though it was not a democratic kingdom. In Europe this would not have tolerated in those days. Emperor Akbar gave the specific instruction that (1) The person is free to follow the religion of his will (2)If Hindu child is converted to Islam against his wish than the child can go back to his father's religion at will. This was in the year 1591-92.The Muslim lover was living with his Hindu wife. The above resolution goes in favour of Hindu father in spite of opposition by Muslim. This is an example of tolerance and equality.

Middle East history of Islamic region is the proof of intolerance due to wars. Emperor Akbar proved contrary opposite of this. Turkish emperor was more tolerant than European ruler. A Muslim Scholar had to run away from his birth place to Cairo to save himself from brutality of Jews. Alburani was advocating mutual understanding and tolerance in 11th century.

Globalization: Economics, culture and rights

You have to value others culture in democracy. The western style and culture cannot dominate others. Globalization gives the free movement of labour due to trade and economics. The technological evaluations give competitive edge in economics. You cannot stop the import of other culture. According to Adam smith, Globalization will bring economic prosperity. It is true, if the gain is on positive side. Globalization has effect in employment, traditional living and transformation to new atmosphere. Globalization carries equity in culture and opportunities in economics.

In case of economy some looses will be there, due to method of production and new technology. However, in case of culture it is total LOSS. It is up to society to preserve old tradition with economic cost. You can compromise in your own way.

---

[124] Ibid, page no.237.

Cultural interchange and pervasive interdependence

Cross-cultural is a great thing. Society should accept it. We should adopt and enjoy other's good idea. The great poet Rabindranath Tagore said, "Whatever we understand and enjoy in human products instantly becomes ours, where ever they might have their origin. I am proud of my humanity when I can acknowledge the poets and artists of other countries as my own. Let me feel with unalloyed gladness that all the great glories of man are mine. " [125] In past, Aryabhata invented the mathematical formulas as "Sign" which travel to Arab countries and from there to Europe and England. We should not lose our ability to understand others culture in the name of purity and conversion of our own culture.

Universalist presumptions

Dr. Amartya Sen is trying to emphasise the belief in ability of different people from different cultures to share much common value and agree on some common commitments. The value of freedom should convert into organizational form into universal presumption. Tolerance is not hard to find in any culture. Against this, lots of violent incidents had taken place in past and in present in the name of freedom.

5.11 Social choice and individual behaviour

Introduction

Dr. Amartya Sen agreed that you cannot change past, but you can make your future. The behavioural norms and support of institution is necessary to prove the above with reasoning. Unintended events take place than it is futile to understand with reasons. The point is our behaviour will not go beyond our self interest. It means, it is within limit of market mechanism. The interest is in examining the relevance of values and reasoning in enhancing freedom and in achieving development.

Impossibility and informational bases

The Arrow theorem is not the impossibility of rational social choice but it base on limited information. Kenneth Arrow says that majority rule

---

[125]   Ibid, page no. 242.

has some inconsistency. Let us examine the voting paradox. If one person prefers X to Y and Y to Z, the second person prefers Y to Z and Z to X and third person prefers Z to X and X to Y. Now the parameter X, Y and Z are having majority. The decision based on some information will lead to inconsistency, unless we decide dictatorial solution, making one person preference final. Majority rule will not solve economic problem. Let us see the example. One cake is divided amongst three people equally. Now we take share of first person and distribute it to person two and three. The majority rule is applied here. In the name of majority improvement, the two persons will take benefit of share of cake and poorest of poor will suffer-the first person. Economics cannot make social judgment on little information.

Social justice and richer information

In social rule, we have to take into account other relevant facts. Who, whom, how and what are the important question to be asked. External facts are required to gather and then make economic decision. Arrow gave general approach regarding social decision based on individual conditions. Broadening of information gives the correct social assessment. Arrow's theorem is not impossibility theorem but conditional impossibility theorem.

Social Interaction and partial accord

The politics of social consensus calls require individual preference and sensitivity of social decision for development of individual preference and norms. Social ordering on the bases of public policy need not be complete, can be partial. Social justice does not require preciseness. Say tax rate should 39% or 39.5 %. There may be misunderstanding about social justice.

Intended changes and unintended consequences

Unintended consequences of Human action may bring big change in world. Example – the discovery of penicillin from fungus or destruction of Nazi party due to over confidence of Hitler. This had happened unexpected. The reasoned attempts in social change will get better result than unexpected events. Reasoned attempts to increase the literacy rate will bring good result. The Europe and North America as well as Japan are the precise examples. The disease of small pox eradicated. Europe is extending the health care program.

Adam smith believed that the action of rich in society gives benefit to poor. Adam Smith was doubtful about the morals of rich people. The theory of "unintended Event" was fully subscribed by him. This happens due to "an Invisible hand" and "Advance the interest of the society". A baker sale the bread for his benefit and consumer buy the bread for his benefit. Here consumer benefit is unintended event. Carl Manger and there after Friedrich Hayek contributed to this theory. Dr.Amartya Sen says that we have to look in to the emphasis in the unintended event. Something can be predictable. Economic and social reasoning may be the result of consequence by unintended event but it results from institutional arrangements.

Some illustrations from China

Some time consequence occurs which are not intended or anticipated. The human failure for this thing gives a chance to learn for future policy making. Chinese 1979 reforms had negative impact to economic reform. The social effects were seen in the field of rural health care. The introduction of "Responsibility system" of 1970 was replaced by cooperative system and financing of rural health care became difficult. Earlier health care system was getting finance through cooperative on non voluntary basis. Lately this effect came to the notice of Chinese authority. This could be avoided by making proper study earlier. Another example of "One child policy" was resulted in all together different results. The "one child policy" had given negative effect to child mortality and especially to female child. China could have studied the cause and effect properly for unintended and predictable events. This would help them to take preventive correction in policy. The favourable unintended events and predicated events had taken place in Chinese economy which has brought positive social and economical reforms.

The favourable unintended events in recent period in economic planning in China are land reforms, spread of education and literacy and health care programme. These were the social consequences. The economic reform was unintended event and market economy flourished. Mao in China was looking for social foundation and post reform resulted in good economic benefits as listed earlier. The social change had enhanced the human capability of Chinese people. Human capability reduced the vulnerability of life. The human capability is associated with improving the productivity and employability of people. The interdependence of human capability in general and human capital in particular is the result of reasonably predictable event. This proves that rational assessment of unintended or intended effects are necessary.

Social values and public interest

Individual is selfish. Self interest is important in economic and social fields. Our some actions are beyond selfishness because of value in our life. The social norms are communicative reason and evolutionary selection of behavioural modes. When people exercise freedom, they do not think of social reasoning or ideal of justice. The sense of judgment plays an important role in success of the various social events. Different people have different interpretation of the ethical ideas, which include social justice. The person does not think for himself but for family and surrounding of society and world.

The role of values in capitalism

Capitalism is not working on greed but on powerful system of value and norms. Capitalism has ethics. Capitalism is for achievements. Successful market operates upon basis of exchanges allowed on one side and effective legal system as institution and behavioural ethics on another side. Trust and promise are important ingredients for successful market operations. The concept of humanity is the part of ethical value.

Adam Smith considered economic, social and political values in his study. Montesquieu and James Stuart consider capitalism as "Passions" by "interest". Capitalism is the motivational improvement in capitalist ethics. The concept of humanity is the part of ethical value. The following of interest with rational and intelligence is the path of moral improvement. Capitalist ethics are limited in a sense of economic inequality, environmental protection and need for cooperation that operates outside market. Capitalism works in ethics which provides trust and vision for successful market operation and related institutions.

Business ethics trust and contracts

The mutual trust and norms make exchange operation successful. There were plenty of problems in pre-capitalist system in absence of development of capitalist virtue. Social scientist had considered capitalism as a profit maximization rather than motivational instrument which is more complex. None profit motives are also a part of capitalism. Good behaviour works as a catalyst in business. It is difficult to establish norms and institution in market economy in under developed countries. The corruption in Italy was a result of less development in some area and dynamic capitalism in some part of nation. Soviet Union and Eastern Europe experienced the absence of institutional structures and behavioural codes to develop the capitalism. Institutional development requires common behaviour pattern, mutual trust and confidence in other party ethics as this is like interpersonal relation. Mafia style operation requires to examine its' behavioural pattern. This is a negative side of capitalism.

Variations of norms and institutions within market economy

Behavioural codes are different in developed capitalist economy from country to country and resultant effects of them. The Japan is a capitalist country, a glaring example. The profit maximization and individual ownership of capital had turned in to rising output and generating income in Japan. Michio Morishima said that the "Japanese ethos" had worked because of rule based behaviour. Masahiko Aoki has given importance to cooperation and behaviour code. Kotaro Suzumura gave credit to commitment with competitive atmosphere and reasoned public policy. Wall street journal declared puzzling claim that Japan as "the only communist nation that works". The reason behind this is nonprofits motivation had worked in economy.

Institutions, behavioural norms and the mafia

The developing economy has to see that the ethical code is properly applied such as transparency, punitive legal action, trust and no corruption etc. These are the bases for success of capitalism. New challenge of capitalism is "Inequality" and "public goods". The institutional help and development of ethics will take us beyond capitalism to solve these problems. Behavioural code is necessary for economic corruption linked to organized crime. Public discussion and influencing public policy requires for this. The behaviour of trust is important here. You can put mafia to work for good of contract to be fulfilled by way of trust and assurance of each other without corruption or crime. This type of institutions requires where there is no behaviour code. Mafia gang can be eradicated by applying legal enforcement of contracts and behavioural code of trust and normative code.

Environment, regulations and values

Environmental protection is an important issue. This will not be solved by help, subsidy or incentive in tax given by government to anyone. The ethical behaviour has to change. Adam Smith had thought about this in his book "The theory of moral sentiments". Smith tried to control environmental disaster by rate of interest initially. The environment is a "Public good" enjoyed commonly. Unlimited use of Air, and water required to be checked. There are government rules for action and social provisioning. We have to develop social value and social sense of responsibility.

Prudence, sympathy and commitment

Rational choice is not limited for personal advantage but it has to extend up to consideration of ethics or justice or interest. The behaviour has to be defined as "Sympathy "and "Commitment". Self interest is our concern for well being for self as well as for others; therefore sympathy is the right behaviour. We sacrifice our commitment, which is beyond our value of social justice or nationalism or communal welfare. For example, if you help to a destitute than it is a sympathy. When you decide to remove the cause, it is commitment. As per Adam Smith said prudence remains with all virtue that which is most helpful to the individual. John Rawls calls them as moral powers – "A capacity for a sense of justice and for a conception of the good". [126] The power of reason allows us to do many things. This is the freedom in democracy.

Motivational choice and evolutionary survival

The rational choice theory expanded in term of formation of preference and evaluation of it. The rational choice theory has to be developed and examine in the interest of common men. It is better to have "direct" than "derived" reasoning. The direct is concern for justice and practical ethics. Justice can be direct as well as indirect. The value influence us, may emerge in quite different ways. (1) Value may come from reflection and analysis. (2) The value may arise from our willingness to follow convention. (3) The public discussion can have a strong influence on value formation. Frank Knight defines the value as an activity which is social, intellectual and creative. James Buchaman has defined democracy as government

---

[126]   Ibid, page no.272.

by discussion. Here the individual value can change in decision making process. (4) A crucial role played by evolutionary selection. Behavioural choice demand attention. All these four works jointly and alone in conceptualizing in human behaviour.

Ethical values and policy making

Ethics and norms have to reflect in public policy. There are two reasons for the value of social justice. The first reason is to identify the aims and objectives in public policy. The second reason is to find out proper instrument. Public policy is dependent on individual as well as social behaviour. The social behaviour influenced by social ethics. Thus making public policy requires value of public at large. We have to see the role that norms and ideas of justice play in the determination of behaviour and conduct, and how they can influence the direction of public policy.

Corruption, incentives and business ethics

Corruption makes public policy ineffective and productive activities will suffer. This may encourage violence and mafia activities. Asia and African countries are the worst suffer of this. In history, we get the examples of illegality and corruption. We have to learn the ways of stopping corruption.

The definition of corruption is personal gain and profit. You cannot tell them to sacrifice their personal interest but you can check corruption by way of organizational reform. First thing-are you having system of inspection and penalty? Kautilya had described 40 types of temptations to civil servants. He prescribed the spot checking and penalty and reward thereafter. Second, the discretionary power breeds corruption. This discretionary power should be made limited or removed. Third thing is, if a person is poor and has power than he becomes corrupt. These lines of corruption go upward and influence even the senior people. Above three investigative ideas have limitations. The code of behaviour, public awareness and organization should make effective.

Chanakya wrote that "It is possible that the water living fish may fly in sky but government servant do not make corruption is impossible".[127] As per Plato, a law, in which strong sense of duty would help to prevent corruption.

---

[127]   Acarya Mahapragnya, Mahavir ka Arthsastra, page no. 45.

It is important that how people look at the corruption. Financial incentive will help to some extent but behaviour mode is more effective. In case of corruption, inter cultural variation play an important role. The "Other does the same" tendency is responsible for corruption. If the person at the top is sincere; good people will work and bad will go in hiding. If the person at the top is dishonest; bad person will be in lime light and good person will disappear. But you can change the direction and make bad people good and see the effect.

5.12 Individual freedom as a social commitment

Introduction

The necked fact is, in this world there is a misery, hunger, below human condition lives, children died due to insufficient food, medicine and social care. Some argue that god has given intelligence to men to solve these problems. As per Indian philosophy, it is the KARMA of a person, which is responsible in past lives and in present life. According to Dr.Amartya Sen it is our responsibility. The solution of this kind of problems lies with us as a social responsibility. We cannot deny this; otherwise our social existence will vanish.

Interdependence between freedom and responsibility

The reply of above miseries is Self Help is the best help. The point is one should be independent. Dependence on others may be ethically problematic, disrespect to person for his ability and a loss of motivation. The individual efforts are productive. When we enjoy freedom then we have to fulfil responsibility. The non-educational facility, non-medical aid, bonded labour, landless labourer, subjugated girl child; these are the examples of deprivation of their freedom. Freedom and capability should fulfil responsibility. Freedom is necessary and should be sufficient to fulfil responsibility.

There is a link in between freedom and responsibility. At one time person may be responsible and at other time may not be responsible. Social individual freedom is not only the job of state but it should include other institutions and agencies. The institutions and agencies are of political, social, communal and non-government organization, media and other communication nature.

Justice, freedom and responsibility

An acceptable society is the result of evaluation and understanding of social justice.

(1) The substantive freedom checked in terms of individual advantage and social achievement and failures. This argued in terms of one's capability.

2) Freedom has two aspects-opportunity and process. Freedom oriented approach has relative claim of efficiency and equality. Freedom can be less unequal or freedom without restriction-even equality.

In the theory of justice, a solution is available for freedom and equality. Poverty, inequality and social preferences are neglected in public policy. The development requires the informational base of evaluation. The instrumental role of democracy is to protect the venerable section of the society.

In case of justice we see this example. When society is in a position to prevent the famine and even though does not take action is UNJUST. Extreme inequality in terms of race, gender and class is inevitable. The instrumental role of democracy and human rights are important but different at its own level. Justice and development are the factors in freedom which through light on agency as well judgement taken by individual. In a shared responsibility, society should solve the problem of bonded and child labour. Individual will decide to have employment or not. This is his freedom. All round progress of women is the responsibility of society and anticipated women development programme are announced.

What difference does freedom make? Why the difference?

Development in terms of GNP is old definition. Enhancement of freedom is the motivating factors to assess the economical and social change. The final definition of development is increasing the range of human choice. The growth of output per head is the centre of thought. This gives control on environment and more freedom.

We have to find out the difference between development and freedom. Development helps to expand freedom. Freedom is concerned with opportunity aspects and process aspects. The process of decision making and opportunity to achieve valued outcome are not working in political and social choice. You have to consider them as a part of constituent in achieving END of development. The opportunity in political, social and economic activities achieved will increase real income. Freedom can have importance only as it gives opportunity for actual use. Freedom gives us chance to choose which we may or may not choose. Person can reject it with strong option. This way freedom has many aspects.

Human capital and human capability

Human capability is expression of freedom. Now a day, to develop capability, human development is given importance in all respects. Human capital and human capability puts humanity in centre. Human capital is working as agency to increase production where as human capability is individual functional of ability. Human capability has reason to value. This can be direct as well as indirect. Human capital is considering both approach but more emphasis on indirect. Person gets education and his productivity increases. This way human capital and human capability are mutually helping each other. Adam smith had given importance to education and increased the scope of human capital in human capability. Human capital and human capability are means and end in freedom.

5.13 Welfare philosophy in development as freedom

In first chapter we show how the collective choice rule works for individual and technicality of it. Collective choices can be of few types but have its importance in its own way. Some accommodates something where as other accommodates other things. Pareto and Arrow are short for total agreement for collective choice. This is due to heterogeneity and diversity of man. Now we think about the freedom as an end of development.

Dr.Amartya Sen has taken development as freedom in right sense. It slowly opens up the subject to start with definition and expanding it to the horizon of freedom. The traditional definition of development is not up to the mark. Adam smith thought that the invisible hand will take care of problems of human because the seller and buyer, both are in win situation in market mechanism. The development and freedom are interdependent.

Freedom and unfreedom are the aspects of development in human life. According to Dr. Amartya Sen the income is not the end in chain but something more than that. Income is connected with many problems say-poverty, hunger, and famine; inequality, lack of education, good health and political liberty. The answer is CAPABILITY of human will solve these problems. The development of capability will give real freedom to human from varieties of problems. The human behaviour and his ethics with moral will play an important role to achieve freedom. Development can be 1) Primary end and 2) principle means. Japan made progress because of education. Again China had adopted economic reform in 1969 and India accepted economic reform in 1991.

Information has to evaluate in egalitarian, Libertarian and theory of justice concepts. Latest development is theory of justice in economical and political field. Dr. Amartya Sen gives importance to liberty as well as income.

Wellbeing is the result of income or bundle. Dr. Amartya Sen defines poverty as deprivation of basic capabilities and not low income. Information of deprivation is necessary for fairness in justice, for poverty and capability.

Adam smith and John Rawl had tried to solve the inequality. Given financial assistance for unemployment is reducing the persons' capability in many sense i.e. Motivation, psychological, physical, moral and social status. Extreme poverty and deprivation of capability in terms of life expectancy is different in India and Sub Saharan African countries.

Basic education is necessary for capability enhancement for individual. West, Japan and East Asian countries had made progress because of cheap basic education. Adam Smith is in favour of basic education as public good policy. Dr. Amartya Sen is against incentive and free distribution of public goods.

Few leaders in the world believe that poor countries cannot afford the luxury of democracy and political freedom. Dr. Amartya Sen said political freedom and economic need are interconnected. In democracy, the urgent matter is tackled immediately-example famine. China has suffered the loss of 30 million people in famine. At the same time public should exercise their political right. Democracy can successfully avoid famine by way of political parties, Multi party politics and press and media. People will get what they want in democracy. Indian democracy is stable and secure. In democracy, Gender inequality and basic education requires opposition support.

Women inequality and women well-being are points. Agency has helped women in case of education and employment, ownership right and say in family matters. The agency will help women to have endowment, to discuss fertility ratio and intra family food division along with health and child mortality problem. Child mortality rate is higher in India, Pakistan and many other countries compared to Europe and U.S.A. The literacy rate has made an impact on the situation.

In Human rights, national human right commission is important in the development. Some say human right is natural. Political liberty and civil rights are a part of human rights. Value and human right cannot be separated. Cultural value has to take in to account. Globalization has changed the scenario. You cannot stop the invasion of other culture. You have to preserve your own culture than to make compromise. Dr.Amartya Sen says you have to see at different culture and accept common values and commitments. Indian Philosophy believes in "VASUDHAIV KUTUMBKAM". It means that the whole world is my family.

Capitalism is working on system of values and norms. It is the motivational improvement in capitalist ethics. There are defects in capitalism such as inequality, environmental protection and cooperation outside market. The worst result of capitalist economy is it increases the gap in between rich and poor. Rich wants to become richer and richer as a result poor become poorer and poorer.

Environmental protection is an important issue. Unlimited use of water and natural resources required to check. We have to develop social value and social sense of responsibility. Behavioural code is important in any economy. Rational choice has to extend up to consideration of ethics or justice or interest. The behaviour has to define as "Sympathy "and "Commitment". Ethics and norms have to reflect in public policy. Dr.Amartya Sen says it is our social responsibility to remove non welfare elements from society. The solution is self help is the best help. We enjoy the freedom than we have to fulfil responsibility. Human capability expansion is freedom. Human capital increase production and human capability works for individual. Human capability and human capital helps each other.

Lord Mahavir accepted the development. Lord Mahavir strategy was with a view to keep all the natural resources intact and to give survival to human. Lord Mahavir agreed that nobody like to remain poor. Everyone wants to make progress. The selfishness is the key for development.

Lord Mahavir told for selfishness that the thing you like but thing may not be in your interest and thing you may not like but it is in your interest. The personal selfishness has created a lot of problem in society.

Lord Mahavir had three steps formula for development. (1) Non violence and purity of instrument (2) Moral and ethical principle should not be sacrificed. (3) Limit of selfishness. The limit will give you pleasure. The Religion will guide you about the right and wrong. Selfishness brings cruelty. This will result in to war, colonialism and ecstasy of power. The per capita income should be as such that everyone gets food, shelter and clothes as minimum requirement. Man can live with minimum wants. To reduce or decrease the want is the result of happiness. The minimum want is the key to mental and physical comfort.

Dr. Amartya Sen has given new direction to welfare economics by choosing few important aspects such as freedom through the route of development. Freedom is not in ordinary sense but very broad base on the foundation of social, economical and political consideration. He also speaks in the line of Lord Mahavir that you should honour others views, an anekantvada of Jain religion and behavioural norms are as vows and ethical rules in Jain religion.

Now from freedom, we move to inequality in society. The inequalities are of various kinds and various magnitudes. Dr. Amartya Sen has collected maximum information and established the importance to spread the equality in society for human being. This will take us to the third chapter.

6 The doctrine of Karma in Jain philosophy

6.1 Introduction

Universal philosophy of good and bad deeds

The Indian philosophy believes in karma. Semitic religions believe that one-day god will give judgment for good or bad deeds done by all human beings. The final day will be known as a "Day of Judgment" and /or "KAYAMAT" day for Muslim religion. They wait for an indefinite period for this. Semitic religions believe in angel and devil theory, Angel and Satan theory and good and evil theory. They do not believe in rebirth. The Semitic religions believe in god. Jain religion does not believe in the concept of creator.

We do not get the answers for the lots of unusual happenings in this universe. Most of Indian school of philosophy believes in karma. According to Jain religion, the soul will go in to four gaties, after death as per its karma. The supreme importance of the doctrine of karma lies in providing a rational and satisfying explanation to the apparently inexplicable phenomena of birth and death. It explains happiness and misery. It explains inequalities in mental and physical attainments and of the existence of different species of living beings.

The Karma theory can explain this. The karma theory is based on cause and effect. Jain philosopher maintains that neither sequence nor synchronism alone can account for the law of causation, but that both give us the correct estimate of the operation of causality. More or less you are convinced by it.

Comparison of Karma effects in two children

We see the difference in two children in a family. The parents will not give different treatment to them. They may be affected by outer atmosphere but the fundamental fact is that they carried the samskar from past birth. We have seen in the society that someone is rolling into luxury and someone is able to make both ends meet with great labour. The reason behind this is the past karma. You have done auspicious karma in past life and enjoying the fruit in the present life. Same way you experienced difficulties due to inauspicious karmas done in the past life which gives the fruit in present life. This proves that the karmas in present birth are the reason for future births. Scriptures tells us clearly that do not accumulate the wealth in the name of religion. You should earn income which is enough for maintenance of your life and your family. The hording of wealth is prohibited. The murderer, dacoits and rascals are not caught in the net of law because they have done auspicious karma in past life. They are moving freely in the society. The moral causation will teach them the proper lesson for their evil acts in future birth.

The difference in the position of different individuals can be explained only by the doctrine of rebirth. The accident or injustice without any fault can be explained by the doctrine of rebirth. The memory of past events of present life as well as past life can only be explained by the doctrine of rebirth. Doctrine of rebirth preserves and keeps intact man's moral responsibility. The rebirth doctrine helps us not to agitate or dishearten for unforeseen calamities.

Some people only think for the present birth. They think that let us enjoy the life. There is nothing after death. Who has seen the past or who will see the future? The body is going to be burned and ashes will fly in the sky. These types of ideas are not valid. Every cause has its effect. People should perform their duty and have feeling of benevolence. The belief of better reward in future birth and trust about eternality of soul makes man think that death is merely a change of body. The birth and death has nothing to do with soul.

The above types of people always think that to do evil to others is to do evil to one's own self. To hurt others is to hurt one self. Enmity breeds enmity. They always think good, act good and speak good. They see friendliness in all. This will increase the feeling of equanimity in them. They will not take pride in the name of family, wealth or intelligence.

Some people boast that they do not believe in god. They do all wicked acts without fear. As soon as misery comes to them, they start remembering the god. They take refuge in god. They want help form supreme power and want to get saved. The hardest misery is the fear of death. The strong atheist will remember the god and pray for mercy or help to get out of the difficult situation. In this way it is better to remember constantly about soul, god, auspicious and inauspicious karmas and finally rebirth. This will be a motivating force for spiritual progress. One who accepts the doctrine of karma, automatically accept the rebirth and god, auspicious and inauspicious karmas. The god is nothing but pure liberated soul. There are impure soul and partial pure soul. We can infer from this that pure soul is there as the impure soul is there. The pure soul is nothing but supreme soul which is considered as god.

From beginning less time, the world exists. It is not created at some point of time. It will not get destroyed. But it is subject to change. The Karma is material particles and has power due to assimilation with soul. The impression of the nature of diverse material particles are imprinted on the soul according to its mental state. This turns into karma. The auspicious and inauspicious karma gives their good and bad effects. This good or bad effect cannot escape from the eyes of karma. Karma rises at proper time and gives its effect to person. Law of karma is law of action and reaction.

Different theories for karma

The thinkers gave a thought to these unusual phenomena. They did penance, gone into solitude, stayed with nature. They try to get answer from their intuitions. They got answer in their soul and put before people in the form of sermon. They put forward the answers in the form of theories. The large number of people followed them. Jain religion puts this single theory in EKANTVADA-one sided view and NINHAV - a wrong belief.

The different intuitive answers were five in numbers. They were most prominent.

(1) Kala- Time
(2) Svabhav-nature

(3) Niyati - Destiny

(4) Purvakruit karma - past Karma

(5) Purushartha - Human efforts

I give brief account about them.

(1) Kala-Time: - Some philosophers gave total importance to time only. It is the time, which is the prime cause for unusual phenomena. Time brings existence and destruction. Time is the substance for the earth, water, air, fire to born. Universe is the creation of time. The child gets birth after nine months. The food gets cooked over a period of time. Birth and death are according to time. Time is the sole thing in the phenomena. Time is the only responsible factor in any event. This is not correct. This is EKANT- one sided view as per Jain religion.

(2) Svabhav-nature: - A few philosophers thought that nature is the only cause behind this unusual phenomenon. It is the nature of thing. Say the seed will turn in to tree. The mango seed will grow in form of mango tree and not apple tree. Sugar is sweet. The substance could not act independently. The nature of a thing is in centre. The nature of mango is to turn from unripe green to ripen yellow fruit. Some grains or pulses are as such that you cannot cook them even after soaking for number of days in water or keep it on fire for number of hours. The result will be negative. That was the nature of pulse. Again this is an Ekant-one sided view as per Jain religion. This is not only the reason for unusual things of happening in this universe.

(3) Niyati-Destiny: - Some philosopher thought that only the destiny is the cause for the happening of unusual thing in this universe. Look at a lot of sick people. Some are cured, some are suffering long illness, some had light sickness, where as some had multiple types of illness. In case of fatal accident of train or aeroplane, many people are dead, a few will have minor injury, and a few may have major injuries. The destiny works in its own way. The union of parent's gives birth to a child but child may have defect in body. This is one-sided view as per Jain religion. Only one cause is not responsible for unusual things to happen in this universe.

(4) Purvakruit karma-Past deeds: - you are suffering or enjoying your life today is due to your past bad or good karmas. Someone is high profile personality in the field of business, politics, corporate identity

where as someone is messenger or driver. People are suffering from poverty or starvation today. Some people are suffering without their fault. They attributed this to their past deed which is only the solely responsible thing for all this. The idea behind this is, in next birth he should not suffer. The rebirth theory is the root cause of this thought. Again, this is one-sided view as per Jain religion. This is not only the reason for unusual things to happen in the universe.

(5) Purushartha-to put heavy labour: - Person thinks that he can change his destiny. He thinks that he can have good fortune by way of hard labour. Person feels that by way of hard work he can win over any situation. Person does not believe in fortune or good luck. The human efforts are the only reasons to believe that anything is possible in the universe. He will resolve any difficulty. Person is having such a strong confidence. This is also not correct. This is one-sided view as per Jain religion.

The unusual things happening in this universe are the sum total of above all five theories of the great thinkers. The time is not only the factor to affect your birth or death. The nature of seed to grow in the form of tree and it is not the destiny to happen in that way. The past deed is not only responsible for the happening of good and bad in this world. Last but not the least; the struggle is not only the cause for unusual thing to happen in this universe. The child birth takes place due to nine months time limit for human being. It is the union of man and woman to give birth to child. It is destine that you will have birth and your past deed helps you to have human body rather than animal or plant body. You have to survive in the womb of your mother, than and then only your birth will take place. You have to put in labour for this. Simile of hand is the appropriate example for this. This is like a hand. Only one finger cannot do the required work. You do many activities with the unity of five fingers of hand which will prove the strength. We can infer from the above that some unknown element exists. This unknown element is the coordinating factor. This unknown element is nothing but "KARMA".

UNUSUAL BANK

First, I will explain you something about the UNUSUAL bank. The name of bank is KARMA BANK. This karma bank is universal. All are account holders in this bank from the beginning less time as per Jain philosophy. This is due to eternal relationship of karma with soul as a result of ignorance. You did not require any introduction to open an account with this bank. The passbook is with you. You have to make your own entry for credit and debit in your pass book. This should be done true to the spirit. If you make any wrong entry in the pass book then you will be caught. Another important thing is you can get any amount of loan, as you have kept your eternal bliss with the bank as collateral. You can get credit in your account from others; at the same time the credit in that person account will not decrease. This is due to your good thought for that act. The same thing is for debit. You will get debit from another person and that person debit will not decrease. This is due to your bad thought for that act. In few cases of new deposit, debit may turn into credit and credit can turn into debit. This is happening due to one uncommon rule of bank. The person stays calm during any good or bad effects of karma, and then this happens. Karma has the peculiar property of developing the effects of merit and demerit. You have to be extremely careful for this. Your soul is doing penance and meditation then debit will nullify to some extent. Karma bank is so liberal that if you repent for past bad deeds then it will nullify the debts in good quantity and will not insist for repayment. You always get loan to repay your previous debt and this way cycle goes on. You can wipe-out your entire loan before due date. If you do not pay your loan in time than the karma bank will start the recovery of loan only after due date. The karma bank is very cruel to get repayment on due date and you have to pay very heavily. If you pay all your debts by taking the advantage of liberal policy of bank, you are free forever.[128]

6.2 Definition and existence of Karma.

Definition of Karma

Karma is defined with many similar meaning of words. Sanskrit meaning of word karma is "Activity". Soul creates physical body with the help of Nama karma. Soul has to reside in that body. Karma comes into existence through a process. Karma is dynamic high energy fine particles of subtle matter that has ability to penetrate into the soul. The Soul attracts the karmic particles. The soul gets vibrations by way of Yoga (Action) of

---

[128] Written by Acarya Devendrasuriswar Maharaj, Edited by Sadhvji Ramgunashreeji, Karma Viapk, part 1, page no. 9 to 12.

body, speech and mind. The body action is the movement of your body. Speech action means what you speak and Mind action is what you think. Umaswatiji defined them as yog in Tattvarthasutradhigam. [129] The three vibration acts are divided in to two categories. The body and speech activities are DRAVYA karma and mind activities is BHAV karma. These activities may be benevolent or malevolent. The karma structure types are physical and psychic. The physical (Material particles) obscure the soul and pollute it, While psychic (mental states such as passions and perversions) cause imperfection. They mutually reinforce each other as cause and effect. Perfect souls such as the liberated one are free from physical karma, and hence they have no psychic karma or imperfection.

Jain philosophy had mentioned five classes of karmic conditions. They are (1) Rise (2) suppression (3) annihilation (4) mixed suppression (5) unconditioned thought. The soul has five bhavas or thought conditions. They are 1) Aupasamika bhav 2) Ksayika bhav 3) ksayopasamika bhav 4) audayika bhav 5) Parinyamik bhav. The last is unconditioned by karma while the four others are conditioned by changes on the physical side. We produce karmas every movement. Therefore innumerable karmas come into existence. There cannot be innumerable names for all these karmas.

The karma Pudgal-particles are infinite-anantanant and in subtle forms in this universe. These karma particles are categories in sixteen categories. They are known as vargana. Vargana means cluster. The eight karma varganas are useful and another eight karma vargana are not useful. Jain religion considers basic eight karmas. These basic eight karmas had 158 sub-types with their effects on soul.

Jain consciousness

Jain religion recognized the consciousness or chetna in two ways 1) Suddh consciousness or chetna and 2) asuddha-impure consciousness or chetna. Suddha–pure consciousness or chetna is Jnana chetna and impure type consciousness or chetna is (A) Karma Chetna (B) Karma - phala (Fruition) chetna.

---

[129]   Commentary- Umaswatiji, Tattvarthasutradhigam commentary by Pandit Sukhlalji on the book Tattvarthasutradhigam, Chapter no. 6 Stanza no.1 page no. 16.

Karma Chetna

Soul resides in body. Now body is having five senses. These five senses create flutter in soul. The person's activity and efforts to attain the desired object through five Senses with consciousness are karma chetna.

Karma – phala chetna

When your soul likes or dislikes the object through body then feeling of pleasure or pain arise out of it is known as KASAYAS – passions. This defines as a karma phala chetna.

Jnana chetna

Jnana chetna is pure consciousness. Here the soul has nothing to do with body or passions. This Pure consciousness is uncontaminated by any sense-passions and it does not get attracted towards any object.

Karma Formation

It is necessary to have detailed study of this karma theory. There are in all sixteen MAHA VARGANAS-big clusters of pudgal. When soul takes birth in any gati, out of four gaties, as per Jain religion, than soul will make use of ten prans to form body and to do related activities under Name karma. In this universe, as per Jain philosophy, there are six real elements. They are (1) Soul (2) Non-soul means Pudgal (3) Dharmastikaya (4) Adharmastikaya (5) Aakash-space (6) Kala-time. Out of this, Soul is conscious and Pudgal is unconscious. They are important to understand in relation to karma theory.

In this universe there are fourteen types of living beings as per Jain philosophy. They are from one sense to five senses. One sense living being is divided in to subtle and gross. Again this is divided in to sufficient and insufficient. This way, in one sense four types of living beings are there. In two, three and four senses living beings, there are sufficient and insufficient types, makes six types living beings. The five senses living being is divided into samanaska-with mind and amanaska-without mind. They are further divided into sufficient and insufficient types. These way five senses living beings are of four types. In all there are fourteen types of living beings in this universe.

Pudgals are of four types. (1) SKANDH-this is full thing (2) DESH-a part of skandh with a group of more than one atom. (3)PRADESH- The smallest part of skandh divided from skandh, which cannot be further divisible. (4) PARMANU- parmanu means AN INDEPENDENT ATOM, which cannot divide further. Parmanu is separate from skandh, desh and pradesh. The permutation and combination and assimilation and division process is going on in between parmanu and skandh.

Pudgal is having four characteristics. Pudgal is having (1) Colour (2) Smell (3) Taste and (4) Touch. Pudgal is having five colours- (1) Black (2) White (3) Green (4) Yellow and (5) Red. Pudgal is having two types of smell (1) Good smell (2) Bad Smell. Pudgal is having five types of taste. (1) Sweet (2) Sour (3) spices (4) Bitter (5) Astringent. Pudgal is having eight types of touch. They are in four pairs (1) Cold and Hot (2) Glossy and rough (3) Heavy and light (4) Soft and Hard. Every atom is having minimum five things, one colour, one smell, one taste and two touches.

There are eight RUCHAK PRADESH in soul. They are known as eight space points. These eight space points will never get attracted by karma pudgal. These eight space point are the real quality of soul. Soul does number of activities by way of body, speech and mind during day and night. As a result, number of karma will come in to existence. They do not allow soul to show its real quality. We have to see that which karma obstructs which quality of soul.

Uttradhyayn sutra, chapter no. 33 described the eight karma prakarati.[130]

SOUL QUALITY	Covering Pudgal Karma
(1) Infinite knowledge quality	Knowledge obstructive karma.
(2) Infinite Darsan-vision quality	Darsan-vision obstructive karma
(3) Infinite Character-conduct quality	Mohaniya karma (Delusion)
(4) Infinite strength quality	Antaraya karma (obstacle)
(5) Infinite shapelessness quality	Nama karma

---

[130] Edited; - Dhiraj Muni, Uttradhyayn Sutra, Ch.no.33, page no. 229 to 232, (Guajarati).

(6) Infinite heavy and light Quality	Gotra karma
(7) Infinite bliss quality	Vedaniya karma
(8) Infinite eternity-immortal quality	Aayush karma

Knowledge obstructive karma will not give you the right knowledge. Darsan obstructive karma will not allow soul to see the right things in proper perspective. Vedaniya karma will give the effect of honey coated sword experience. The honey coated sword will tempt you to lick and it will cut your tongue. Mohaniya karma is like a drunken man. The drunken man cannot judge anything. Mohaniya karma is divided into two, darsan mohaniya and character mohaniya. The Mohaniya (Delusion) karma is the king of all these karmas. This Mohaniya karma misguides the soul and gives illusion of all types. This illusion will create a lot of karmas and have effect on soul. Soul has to suffer or enjoy as per karma comes into existence. The soul will not be able to distinguish the right or wrong things. Soul has to complete the length of life in one birth which is known as aayush karma. Nama karma will give colour to skin, shape and size of body etc. Gotra karma will give you birth as high or low status in society. Antaraya karma is like treasures of treasury. The treasure asks first the account of amount given earlier and then will grant next amount.

Categories of Karma

These karmas fall into two broad categories (a) the ghatiya karma-the destructive karmas. Destructive means a veil that covers the right qualities of soul. Those have a negative effect upon the qualities of the soul. (b) The aghatiya karma the non-destructive karma. This has nothing to do with destructive activities. Those bring about the state and particular conditions of embodiment. Both the categories have four karmas each shown as under.

(A) The Ghatiya: -	I.e. destructive karmas.
1 Jnanavarniya	I.e. Knowledge – obscuring karma
2 Darsanavaraniya	I.e. Perception- obscuring karma
3 Mohaniya	I.e. The deluding karma and
4 Antaraya	I.e. the enjoyment obstructive karma.

Dr. K R Shah

B) The Aghatiya: - I.e. the non-destructive karmas

1   Vedaniya   I.e. the feeling karma

2   Aayush   I.e. the age karma

3   Nama   I.e. the body making karma and

4   Gotra.   I.e. The family determining karma

Only Aayush karma is not affected by any increase or decrease in the length of life span in one birth out of these eight karmas. The age fixed at the time of birth. Death is certain before birth in a sense that the length of life in one birth is decided.

Eight types of karma and its effect

Jain philosophy considers main eight types of karmas and their sub-divisions are mentioned here. Let us understand how the basic eight karmas and their sub-divisions get bind with the soul.

(1) A learned person is insulted, harassed, being ungrateful and do hatred, knowledge is disrespected, neglected, you stop others to gain knowledge, refusal to give knowledge, teaching wrong things, remain ideal are the causes of bondage of knowledge-obscuring karma-Jnanavarniya karma.

(2) When the above things are concern to darsan, a possessor of darsan, than it is the causes of bondage of darsan-obscuring karma-Darsanavaraniya karma.

(3) (A) Compassion, service, forgiveness, love, forbearance, donation, and self control are the causes of the bondage of Sata vedaniya karma. Child austerity causes the bondage of Sata vedaniya karma. This karma results into pleasant feeling.

(B) Pain, sorrow, heart-burning, crying, killing, etc to self as well to other are the causes of the binding of Asata vedaniya karma. This karma is the result of painful experience.

(4) (A) Preaching and propagating unwholesome path, denigrating the wholesome one, ill-treating the saints and good persons, and adopting

adverse attitude and behaviour towards the means of spiritual welfare-these are the causes of the bondage of darsan-mohaniya karma. (The karma which deludes our love for truth or our inclination towards truth)

(B) The acutely unwholesome some mental state resulting from the manifestation of passions are the causes of the bondage of conduct-deluding (charitra-mohaniya) karma.

(5) (A) Too much inclination for hurting, too much accumulation of possessions, and killing of the five sensed living being, cruel mental states are the causes of the bondage of narkaayush-karma. (Infernal-lifespan determining karma)

(B) Deceit is the cause of the bondage of tiryagaayush-karma. (Animal, bird-life span determining karma)

(C) Minimum infliction of injury, minimum accumulation of possessions, softness and simplicity of nature are the causes of the bondage of manusyaayush-karma. (Human-life span determining karma)

(D) Self-control of moderate degree, self-control accompanied with non-attachment, childish austerity, refraining from evil acts out of compulsion, are the causes of the bondage of Devaayush-karma. (Celestial-life span determining karma)

(6) (A) Straightforwardness, softness, truthfulness, healing dissensions, these are the causes of the bondage of auspicious personality-determining karma. (Subh-nama karma)

(B) The opposite of the just mentioned features-crookedness, hard heartedness, untruthfulness, creating and fostering dissensions, cunningness and treachery are the causes of the bondage of inauspicious personality-determining karma. (Asubh-nama karma)

(7) (A) Condemning one self, praising others, turning a blind eye towards one's own merits, displaying one's own shortcomings, humility and non-arrogance are the causes of the bondage of the high status determining karma. (Ucca-gotra karma)

(B) Condemning others, pressing one self, turning blind eye towards even the existing merits of others, displaying even the non-existing merits in one-self, pride of family are the causes of the bondage of the low status-determining karma. (Nica-gotra karma)

(8) To cause obstruction to others engaged in the task of donation, reception, enjoyment, etc, is the cause of the bondage of obstructive karma. (Antaraya karma) [131]

When you know full well and try to observe the law of karma, at some point of time, you may have to act against your will and to perform wrong thing; in that case person does bind the karma but the effect will be less in term of time, less bitterness of the fruit and of less intensity.

Karma theory in Jain philosophy

Lord Mahavir defined the man. What you see is not a real man. Man is having lots of animal senses. The first one is sex. The second one is desire of wealth. The third one is faith in religion. The fourth one is feelings. These are four known as DHARMA, ARTH, KAM, and MOKSHA. Chanakya wrote in 'Chanakya sutra' that Happiness is the root of Dharma, Money is the root of happiness, and State is the root of Money and Sense victory is the state. [132]

Jain religion believes that every living being is pure and has full capacity to develop his nature to the fullest extent. Jain religion is an atheistic. Jain religion foundation is on rational thoughts. It believes that every individual soul having attribute of divinity. Every soul has attributes to attain infinite knowledge, infinite perception, Infinite vigour and infinite bliss. The full development of all these will give him the status of Jina. Jina means conqueror of all his wishes, having no birth and death, but eternal bliss and peace. The Jain religion categorically states that soul is essentially free. Soul has infinite qualities.

When karma rises for fruition, at that time you must create equanimity. Here you will not generate new karma. Person enjoys the fruit with attachment and aversion then new karma will come into existence. When

---

[131]   Translated: - Nagin J.Shah, Jain philosophy and Religion, page no.281 to 283.

[132]   Acarya Mahapragnya, Mahavir ka Arthsastra, page no.16.

you are indifferent to the fruit of karma then it will be disassociated from the soul. Person with steady mind and resolves not to get disturbed is a wise man. This way all five senses will be unable to move man from his firm decision. The passion will not rise in person in spite of long experience of sense pleasure in this life. Person can do this with his internal spiritual power and strong will. The spiritual weakness will drag him in the transmigration and one need not to blame the karma.

Man is free to attain material, mental and spiritual wealth with acceptance of rule of ethics and justice. The ethics, justice and morality are essential for society. The rule of Stone Age is not applicable to day as the society has travelled long way on the road of civilization. It is stated in Bhagvati Sutra that "the past life action gives fruit in present life and present life action gives fruit in present birth" [133] therefore man should practice the truthfulness; self–control, give service which will bring auspicious karma. Practice of immoral activity, lie, theft, injustice and torture will bring inauspicious karma. Man is inspired by his experience to be virtuous, righteous in his life in the benefit of the society.

Karma works secretly and beyond your understanding. Human has two things-efforts and discretion. The efforts are for removing calamities happen to self as well as others and need not spend his life in high, fancy, imaginative state of living. He should aim to put his effort for social upliftment and progress. Person should not leave efforts thinking that he is transgressing the law of karma. On the contrary, when you put efforts, you are giving honour to law of karma. A person's effort goes in line with karma very well. Person is well within the nature of law by avoiding the flood by diverting the stream of river and saving human lives, animal lives and agricultural crop. Here person's efforts help for removing danger and doing the work of social upliftment. The fruit of such good act is the foundation of law of karma. Doctrine of karma teaches us not to remain inactive. One has to discriminate in the activities and always do and encourage the right and good activities which will be the cause of auspicious karma. The stoppage of bad activities will help to avoid inauspicious karma. The doctrine is encouraging and inspires to make efforts for human progress and wellbeing. The doctrine is conducive to progress.

---

[133] Translated by Nagin J.Shah, Jain philosophy and Religion, page no 273

Doctrine of karma is not fatalism but act with reality and cause of liberation. Soul is the sole cause of binding and liberation of karma. All karmas are not alterable but SOME can be altered by way of proper spiritual efforts. Upadhyaya Yasovijayaji wrote in the "Dvatrimsika", verse 24 that nikacita karma can be destroyed by tapas (Austerity). [134] But by tapas is here meant not external austerity or any such austerities, but only those highly spiritual and yogic practices that characterize the far advanced stage of spiritual development.

Donation used for gambling. One can give donation and earn inauspicious karma. The surgeon performs painful operation. This is auspicious activity. The crux of the thing is the intention of person is important. The intention is reason to person for the auspicious and inauspicious karma bandh. Again the activity of thoughtless person is the cause of bondage of inauspicious karma. Dharma means to be vigilant and careful in action.

We conclude that one must leave bad or evil activity. As the mind will not be inactive, one should keep mind active with good activities. This good activity will result into auspicious karma which should be transformed into PURE INTENTION. This is very difficult spiritual process and it is not easy to get liberation without putting hard labour. One cannot renounce the activity of his own but it gets renounced at proper time.

Four ways of karma binding:-The auspicious and inauspicious activity will bring the four types predictions as under.

1. Punyanubandhi punya(auspicious activity) and auspicious karma bandh

2. Papanubandhi punya(inauspicious activity) and auspicious karma bandh

3. Punyanubandhi papa(auspicious activity) and inauspicious karma bandh

4. Papanubandhi papa(inauspicious activity) and inauspicious karma bandh

I will give the brief detail of them.

---

[134]   Ibid, page no. 276.

(1) Punyanubandhi punya-auspicious karma related to auspicious activities and resulting into auspicious karma: - On account of fruition of auspicious karma, man gets health, wealth and happiness. Man becomes humble and engaged himself in religious activities. Person does the philanthropic activities, will remain away from sensual pleasure. This way the activity in present life will bind him in auspicious karma bandh for future birth.

(2) Papanubandhi punya-auspicious karmas related to inauspicious activities and resulting into inauspicious karma: - Man gets health, wealth and happiness. He uses them in wrong way. He indulges in all worldly things and remains engross in sensual pleasure, away from good activities. On the fruition of auspicious karma, he gets everything but in result he gets inauspicious karma bandh for future birth.

(3) Punyanubandhi papa-inauspicious karmas related to auspicious activities and resulting into auspicious karma: - On the fruition of inauspicious karma man is having low income, cannot enjoy the good thing in life. Man will pass the phase of time with patient and will do the religious activities and give donations as per his capacity. He will try to live simple life and will not harm others. Some good deeds will result in to auspicious karma bandh for future birth.

(4) Papanubandhi papa-inauspicious karmas related to inauspicious activities and resulting into inauspicious karma: - Man suffers due to his past karma on fruition. He will remain poor. He will have anger, speak lie, does all sorts of wrong activities. Man will not perform any religious activities, will not help others etc. The result of these activities will bind him with inauspicious karma bandh for future birth.[135]

EFFECTS OF KARMA

These karmas come in to existence at due date and gives its good and bad effects.

This effect will decide your future birth and determines the length of life in one birth as aayush karma. Other seven karmas will have effects to produce further karmas. You will go in any one of four gatis as per your karma. There are four GATIS in Jain philosophy (1) Celestial (2) Human (3) tiryag (4) Narki as explained earlier.

---

[135]   Ibid, page no.102 to 107.

Karmas are associated with soul from beginning less time. The soul had travelled number of times in all four gatis. The soul still enables to destroy all karmas and get emancipation. This happens because the soul is not conscious about to get out of the cycle of birth and death. The cycle of karma and movement in different gatis is continuing in this universe for every soul. The diversity in gatis and plurality of soul is in existence in this universal.

We show the working of karmas. It is necessary to find out and apply the break in cycle of transmigration. Person has to understand the karmas in three ways. The Jain philosophy described this as JYENYA, HEYA and UPADAYA. Jyenya is to know. Person should know the religion. Heya means to leave, the things which will bring bad karmas to soul. Upadeya means do good deed, which will bring good karmas to soul. These are the technical terms. At last, soul has to destroy all karmas. Ultimately, the soul has to obtained siddhatva-emancipation.

The reader will be anxious to know when there is a mention of causes for one particular karma the same cause will be effective in another type of karma or not. If the causes are applicable in more than one type of karmas then there is no necessity to give different set of causations. The scripture rule is that except aayush karma, all remaining karmas get bind at a time. The point is the one will be prominent and others will be in shadow. If this be the case, there is no necessity to mention separate set of causes. Here the answer is in respect of ras-anubagh = intensity is referred to the bondage.

The karma particles are attracted to the soul and these particles consist of all seven types of karma particles. At one time, particular karma and other karmas are also bound. This is understood as karma particles and not ras-anubagh = intensity. The different types of sets for causes are in respect of flavour. Scripture rule is just right in its own respect. The bondage is in respect of flavouring due to the passions and here yoga brings in karmic particles. The division of auspicious and inauspicious karma clearly tell us what type of activities to be undertaken and what type of activities is prohibitive.

The karma particles are sticking to the greasy surface named passion to the soul. When you remove grease like thing or clean the place, material particles will not remain there but slips from the surface. Man destroyed his passions than the above position is possible. At one place we say that soul is immaterial, how you can say that the passions are bringing the karmic particles. The answer is the soul is associated to passions through activity; karmic particles get attached to it. This cause is effective since begininglesss time. Mundane-house holder soul experiencing the pleasure and pain and has anger, deceitful nature, pride and greed. These are the causes of keeping soul together with karma. This results in cycle of birth and death.

Delusion-mohaniya karma (darsan and character) is the most powerful karma amongst all eight types of karmas. This karma controls and rules over whole karmic system. Human being is superior on the earth with intelligence and discretionary power. Human uses this power correctly than he can get the decrease bitterness of karmic bondage and sweetness increases. The spiritual power gets strengthened and karmic material particles does not stick but touch the soul and go away. The present karmic material particles fall off. This stage is the progress in getting nearer and nearer to the final target of liberation.

The consumption of liquor gives intoxication after some time, in the same way karma seed sprouting takes place after time passes as per activity. Similarly the karma gets attached to soul but gives proper fruits to the soul at the end of appropriate time after the bondage is affected. The karmas remains inactive not come to an age, till the time of fruition. Karmas are bound with soul; therefore they have to be disassociated from the soul at some time. Karma gives fruit which is fully experienced by soul and then karma gets disassociated automatically. The above process is technically known as "vipakodaya". Sometimes karmic particles only touch to the soul, do not give the experience of fruition and disassociates. This is technically known as "Pradesodaya". The pradesodaya is possible due to tremendous strength of spirituality and many aggregates disassociated from soul, makes process easy to get liberation.

According to Jain philosophy only the passions are the main cause of transmigration. The passions are classified as four in Jain philosophy (1) Krodh- anger (2) Man-pride (3) Maya-deceit and (4) Lobh-greed. The passions get bind with the soul in four ways. The first one is "anantanubandhi", second one is "apratyakhyanavarana", third one is "pratyakhyanavarana" and forth one is "samjvalana". The passions of Anantanubandhi are due to the association of unwholesome inclination or conviction. The passions of apratyakhyanavarana are due to partial abstinence from violence etc. The passions of pratyakhyanavarana are due to arrest only the total abstinence from violence etc. The passions of samjvalana are due to obstruct the conduct characterized by perfect non-attachment. Thus, the passions of first type are very intense, those of second type are intense, those of third type are moderate and those of fourth type are mild.[136]

There is a peculiarity in case of bondage of ras-anubagh = intensity to karmas. If the passions are intense than flavour of the bondage in respect of inauspicious karma is more intense and in respect of auspicious karma it is less intense. If the passions are mild then flavour of bondage in respect of auspicious karma is more intense and in respect of inauspicious karma is less intense. One can make out that in inauspicious karma the intensity of passions are in proportion to the strength of passions. In case of auspicious karma, it is in inverse proportion. The auspicious flavour causes the pleasure and inauspicious flavour causes the pain. Here the main culprit is rsa-anubagh = intensity which is the sole cause, not to get liberation of soul.

There are ten main stages of karma

(1) Bondage

Bondage is assimilation of karmic particles with worldly soul. The karmic particles interpenetrate to the space points of soul. The karmic bondage is not the same in all worldly soul due to different mental condition at the time of karmic bondage.

(2 and 3)Increased realization and decreased realization

The length of time and intensity of flavour is fixed. Human can make change in it. The increase in length of duration and intensity of fruition are called "udvartana" and decrease is called "apavartana". Earlier man had done wrong deeds and acted in all wrong ways, can repent and come back on the right path. The righteousness and truth will change his life. By doing this he can reduce the intensity and flavour of inauspicious karma. Man observes severe austerity can burn the major portion of karmas and go ahead on the spiritual path. He can be very near to the state of the supreme soul. Man who indulges in evil activities and do not want to reverse from that position than he increases the intensity and

---

[136]   Ibid, page no. 292 to 293.

flavour of inauspicious karmas of previously mild inauspicious karmas. The impure state of soul will reduce the intensity and flavour of auspicious karmas. In this process, some karmas rise before time and some karmas rise after time. Again some karmas gives in the fruit of higher intensity than the due intensity and some karma will give its fruit of less intensity than the due intensity.

(4) Endurance

Earlier we have stated that the karma binds soul. This karma does not give fruit immediately. They will in rest for some time. They will be in dormant position. This is known as abadhakala. When this period is over, karma becomes active and they start giving fruit.

(5) Rise (Uday)

Karma becomes ready to give fruit at due time. This moment is named as the rise of karma. This rise is the result of expiry of abadhakala. The rise is uninterrupted till the end of fruition. This means karma shows its actual activity and gives actual experience.

(6) Premature rise or udirana

Karma finishes his abadhakala and comes to rise. This is a normal process. Person with his pious efforts bring the karma fruition earlier than fixed time. The present karmic particles are mixed with the same type of earlier raised karma particles and fruition is experienced. This is called the premature rise of karma. There is a law that premature rise can possible only in same type of karmas and you cannot mix two different kinds of karmas.

(7) Transformation (Sankramana)

In this state, the sub-type of main karma can transform into another sub-type of main karma. Here the main karma cannot get transformed. You cannot transform your life span karma in to deluding-mohaniya karma. Again you cannot interchange the four types of life span karma say from Human life to Celestine life .You can transform you sub type karma of main karma say shrut-hearing knowledge to mati-intelligence knowledge and vice versa. Again there is restriction about mutual transfer in sub type of main karma. Example: - you cannot transform your right-conviction deluding karma to right-conduct-deluding karma.

(8) Subsidence (Upsama)

Here already risen karma is suppressed. You are putting pressure on it by will and do not allow them to come to fruition. This can happen in case of rise, premature rise, realization, the transformation, the increased realization and decrease realization as well as nidhatti and nikachita karmas.

(9) Nidhatti

Here karma state is as such that either transformation or premature rise or realization will not take place. The strength of karma is little strong. The karma position can be increased or decreased in terms of time factor and flavour of it.

(10) Nikachita

Here the karma position cannot be increased or decreased in terms of time factor and flavour of it. The karma position is unalterable. The karma rises at appropriate time and gives its fruit, which one has to experience it. In rare case some change can take place with exceptions.

Every birth is rebirth in terms of its past birth. This way it is connected from the beginning less time. The cycle of birth and death goes on till soul gets liberated, all karmas are annihilated. If we say it is liberated and gets birth after some time then the eternal liberation theory will be wrong. The meaning of liberation is annihilation of all karmas and only pure soul remains. When we say beginning less time birth can be stopped after liberation. In philosophy it is considered that in past the soul was with birth and same is the case for present. But in future soul can be without birth. When it is without body or birth than soul is perfect and liberated.

6.3   Different Stages of Karma

Earlier we have seen the process of karma coming into existence and other things. There are different stages.

(1) Origination of karma –Aasrav

(2) Bandh- assimilation of karmic matter with soul

(3) Samvar- Stoppage of origination of new karma

(4) Nirjara- annihilation of old karma

AASRAV

Aasrav: - Origination of Karma is known as Aasrav in Jain terminology. The karma originates and influx of karmic matter into the constitution of the soul. This karmic association with soul makes the transmigration in this universe. Person experiences the pleasure and pain in each and every birth. There is no end. The karma vargana can come to soul by 42 ways. They are, five through five senses (Sparsh-Touch, Swad-Taste, Gandh- Smell, Shrut-Hear and Drashya-see), not to observe five vows through (Act of violence, Speak lie, Make theft, Not to observe celibacy and Accumulation of worldly things), four types of KASAYAS-(a) Anger (b) Pride(c) Deceit (d) Greed, three activities, (a) body (b) speech (c) mind and twenty five types by way of other activities. Activities are a cause of influx and a cause of bondage as well. Both are interrelated. Total forty-two[137]. Aasrav will be for all eight types of karmas. This is like eight streams are coming in one direction and gets accumulated in a big lake. Like eight brooks meeting together at one pond. Aasrav is the reason for soul to have karmas and accumulation of karmas. Aasrav is the reason for existence. Aasrav is the jail to soul from where no soul can be freed.

The Aasrav is of two types. (A) Subh Aasrav (B) Asubh Aasrav.

(A) Subh (Meritorious) Aasrav: - Subh Aasrav is due to good karma and it gives PUNYA by which you have the happiness without any obstacle. You will have all of good things; like good body, enough wealth, good health and happiness. You can enjoy all things in the world, you can give donation, and you can have good feeling. Everything will happen in good sense. The meritorious deed will be the result of good thoughts by mind and good activities by way of body and speech. The meritorious deeds may result in to negative. This happens due to good deed with bad intention.

(B) Asubh (non-meritorious) Aasrav: - Asubh Aasrav is due to bad karma and it gives PAP-sin by which you have all bad things in your life. You will inspire to do all wrong things. You will think and act in a bad manner. These bad activities will bring bad karmas. The bad karma will bring to person unhappiness, shortage of required things in all manners and always in difficulties. Non-meritorious deed will be the result of bad thoughts by

---

[137]   Arunvijayji Maharaja, Karma tani gati nyari, part-1,page no.130

mind and bad activities by ways of body and speech. The bad deeds done with good intention will bring you the meritorious result.

BANDH

Bandh is assimilation of karmic particles with soul. Soul does the activities which attracts the karmic particles. Karmic matter enters into soul and gets mixed with. This assimilation process is known as karma bandh. This is like making dough. The water is mixed in flour and a combination is made. Like this, the karma bandh happens to the soul. The karma particles are divided in eight main karmas.

The activity can be with good OR bad intention. Sometimes, person does certain bad things compulsorily with a good intention. I.e. Mother gives medicine to a child for the improvement of the child's health. Doctor performs the operation for good of a patient. Sometimes, person does certain good things with bad intention then person attracts bad karmas. Give donation to have power as president of social organization.

Bandh Effects

These deeds will create four way effects.

(a) Good result but bad deed

(b) Bad result but good deed

(c) Good result and good deed

(d) Bad result and bad deed.

We can make out that there are two good results and two bad results. The good result will bring meritorious effect and bad result will bring non-meritorious effect.

(a) Good result but bad deed: - Mother gives medicine to child.

(b) Bad result but good deed: - Give donation with an intention of name & fame.

(c) Good result and good deed: - Give scholarship to needy student.

(d) Bad result and bad deed: - To do an act of violence to all six types of living being.

Reasons for Karma Bandh

Bandh means assimilation of karma particle with the soul. The reason for karma bandh are (a) Mithyathva- wrong belief, (b) Yog-Body, speech and mind activities, (c) Four types of passions, (d) Pramad-Idleness and (e) Avirati-non observation of twelve vows. These all five items makes soul not to perform the right thing and will be a strong force to stay in transmigration.

Types of Karma Bandh

The karma bandh is of four types (a) Prakarti bandh (b) Stithi bandh (c) Ras-anubagh bandh (d) Pradesh bandh.

(A) Prakarti bandh

Prakarti means NATURE. Pudgal is having its own nature. This nature creates veil on the soul. As a result soul does not act as per his original quality. The soul comes into the influence of karma and acts into opposite direction. This way it obscure the five types of knowledge, nine types of darsan, two types of vedaniya karma, twenty eight types of mohaniya karma, four types of aayush karma, one hundred and three types of nama karma, two types of Gotra karma and five types antray karma. In this way total one hundred and fifty eight types of veils will cover the original quality of soul. [138]

(B) Stithi bandh

Stithi means time limit. The karma pudgal will stay with the soul. This time limit is different for eight types of karmas.[139] They are as follows:-

Name of Karma	Minimum Time Limit	Maximum Time Limit
Knowledge	48 minutes	30 crodancrodi Sagaropam
Darsan	48 minutes	30 crodancrodi Sagaropam
Vedaniya	576 minutes	30 crodancrodi Sagaropam
Mohaniya	48 minutes	70 crodancrodi Sagaropam
Aayush	48 minutes	33 Sagaropam
Nama	384 minutes	20 crodancrodi Sagaropam
Gotra	384 minutes	20 crodancrodi Sagaropam
Antraya	48 minutes	30 crodancrodi Sagaropam

---

[138]   Ibid, page no.158.
[139]   Ibid, page no.159.

These eight karmas play a specific and significant role in your life. There are divisions and sub divisions. The effect calculated in mathematical terms and converted into time factor-number of years. The smallest time limit is of ANTAR MHURAT- means only forty-eight minutes and highest time limit is of 70 KRODANKRODI SAGAROPAM.

The Stithi bandh is of four types.

(1) Bandh (2) Satta (3) Uday- rising (4) Udirana – annihilation.

   (1) Bandh Stithi: - Bandh means karmaraj (Karma particles) come and attached to the soul. The karma gets bind with soul in other words.

   (2) Satta Stithi: - The karmas are in a dormant position till their time comes to rise. Karma will be lying idle till than time. One can say that karma is in hibernation.

   (3) Uday Stithi: - The karma will come into existence at appropriate time. This is the rising time of karma. The karma will give high and low good or bad effect as per intensity of passions at the time of karma bandh.

   (4) Udirana Stithi: - Here person experiences the effect of karma. Karma will expire as soon as the time limit is over. You can annihilate the karma, without experiencing real effect of it, by way of penance.

(C) Ras (Anubhag) Bandh

Ras bandh means the intensity of the mental condition of a person. Ras bandh is of four types. (1) Sprust (2) Baddha (3) Nighatt (4) Nikachita.

   (1) Sprust ras bandh: - Here karma will touch to the soul and go away. No real effect will be experienced. It is like to throw dry mud on wall. Here nothing will stick to wall.

   (2) Baddha ras bandh: - The karma will bind with soul mildly. The intensity will be mild because of passion was mild at the time of karma bandh. Here the dry mud particles will stick to cloth and as soon as you shake the cloth, many of them will fall out.

   (3) Nighatt ras bandh: - The karma will bind with soul firmly. The intensity will be firm because of passion was intense at the time of karma bandh. It is like the wet mud sticks to the cloths.

(4) Nikachita ras bandh: - Nikachita karma bandh is the result of repetition of thought or repetition of act. Person has to undergo the experience of nikachita karma. Person cannot escape of it. This cannot be taken ahead or sent back in the process of sankraman-a technical term. You cannot transform it in to other type of karma. Here the karma bandh will be most solid like a knot, which is made out of silk rope and some oil pour on it. In such a situation it is very difficult to open the silk rope knot.

(D) Pradesh Bandh

The karma pudgal particles quantity is attracted towards the soul. These particles will be divided in to eight karmas. [140] We presume that 64000 karma pudgal particles attracted to soul. These karma pudgal particles will be divided in to eight karmas. The likely quantities of karma pudgal particles for eight karmas are as follows.

1)	Vedaniya karma	48000
2)	Mohaniya Karma	12000
3)	Jnanavarniya Karma	1000
4)	Darsanavaraniya Karma	1000
5)	Antaraya Karma	1000
6)	Nama Karma	375
7)	Gotra Karma	375
8)	Aayush Karma	250
	Total	64,000

Karma bandh by way of Dravya (Speech, body) is of Prakarati-nature and Pradesh-quantity and by way of Bhav-(mental) is of Stithi-duration and ras bandh-intensity.

SAMVAR

When you are away from effective state of desire and aversion and your body, speech and mind activities are at rest than new karma will not originate. Samvar means stoppage of inflow of new karma. Samvar is like a tortoise hiding all parts of body and stay like dead. The soul repeats number of times the cycle of birth and death till it annihilated all karmas.

---

140   Edited by K.J.Gandhi and J.S.Shah, Shree Bruhad Thok Samgrah, page no. 34, (Gujarati).

You can put in efforts and make karma appear before time, you can dilute the heavy effect of it. Penance will act as stoppage of inflow of new karmas as well as shedding out of old karmas. Penance is the effective instrument for samvar and nirjara.

Ascetics and house holders have to make six fold attacks to stop for generating new karmas.

1. Gupti
   People have to control their body, mind and speech activities. People will act by body and speech whenever it is necessary. People will use mental capacity as and when necessary.

2. Samiti
   People have to follow the five samities to stop the incoming of new karmas.

Five samities are as follows.

(A) Irya samiti: - People will take care at the time of moving their body. People will take care that no violence takes place for one sense to six sense living beings while seating, sleeping, and walking.

(B) Bhasa samiti: - People will take care for every word to be spoken. The conversation will be true to fact and no word uttered to harm the all six types of living beings. Conversations are of seven types.

(C) Eesana samiti: – People require needful things day to day as well as in long term. They will take every care while collecting things. The act of collection will not be inconvenient to others as well as it is not hording.

(D) Adan Nikshepa samiti: – People make use of daily things. Here people will either pick up or put the thing with utmost care. People will avoid all type of carelessness.

(E) Utsarga samiti-Disposal of body waste. People will carefully dispose of faeces. People will take care for perspiration, cough, hair and nail grow and other body waste. People will see that it is not in any way an inconvenience to other six types of living beings.

3. Dharma

Here dharma is not in terms of religion. Dharma means day to day duties to be followed by people. Such duties are ten in numbers.

(A) Kshma - Forgiveness. People should pardon the opposite person on any act of violence, abuses, physical harm or feeling of dislike and any wrong doing. This act should be irrespective of age, gender, caste and creed, nationality and religion.

(B) Mardav - Politeness – egoless. People should be humble true to their nature. Politeness is not a weakness but strength.

(C) Aarjava- Straight forwardness People should be simple. People should be without and hypocrisy. People should be of mixing nature and without any grudge.

(D) Sauca - Purity. People should be pure in every respect. Purity requires in every sense. People should be morally faultless.

(E) Tyaga - cessation. People will try to terminate the material things one by one. People will be ready to leave the excessive needs of body. No excessive usages of material things for personal usages. People will try to leave as many things as possible and have no attachment for them.

(F) Truth - People will always speak truth. People will face any circumstance arising out of truthfulness. People are ready to die for the sake of truth. Truth will be the first and foremost essential virtue of their life.

(G) Sayama - Restraint. People will apply restrain in everything. People will try to cover them with modesty and stay away for any tempting offer. People will observe restrain in their vocal, physical and mental activities.

(H) Tapa - Penance. Every religion prescribes the penance in one or another form. Penance in Jain religion is two ways (1) Internal (2) External. Internal is the indication of mental stage and external is the indication of physical stage. The details are given in this chapter under heading nirjara.

(I) Akinchantvya - Non-possession:- People will not have any kind of attachment to material thing. People will not hold or stick to things unnecessarily. People will leave family wealth and have no sign of attachment. Person will not indulge in family affairs.

(J) Brahmacarya - chastity-Celibacy. Every religion prescribed certain rules and regulations for celibacy. Celibacy is a virtue and it requires nourishments for character building. Celibacy will give mental strength. Celibacy will benefit people in terms of physical and mental health.

4. Anupreksha
   Bhavna - Mental contemplations are twelve.

   (1) Anitya –People should think that in this world soul is permanent. All other things are perishable. According to Jain religion, in this universe only two things exists (1) Jiva – consciousness and (2) Ajiva-non conscious. One should think of consciousness only.

   (2) Asarana – People should have full faith in religion. People should refuge themselves in religion. All other things are not useful. People should develop this thinking in life. At the time of death; only religion comes to help soul.

   (3) Samsar – Concept of transmigration. People should always think that they have to get out of the cycle of birth and death. People had experienced this transmigration end number of times. Soul had not been free from the shackle of transmigration. Now, one wants to get relieved from this position. This type of thinking should be in people's mind.

   (4) Ekatva – I am alone in my transmigration. People should think that as he had come alone, he will go alone. No one is going to give him company. The wife for husband and husband for wife, children, relatives, and friends and near and dear will not accompany at the time of death. One has to go alone in transmigration. Person is alone and will remain alone till emancipation of soul.

   (5) Anyatva – I am the soul. I am conscious. All other things are non-conscious. The non living things are impermanent. The unconsciousness is different than conscious soul. Conscious has

nothing to do with unconscious. There is no match in these two things. Therefore one should concentrate on soul.

(6) Asuchi – The body is impure. This is in connection to soul as conscious and body as pudgal-non conscious. The soul resides in body. This body is creating a lot of unwanted things daily. The body is suffering from diseases. Body suffers cut, burn and decay. Body is the house of lot of impurities. Therefore person should think only of soul and not body.

(7) Aasrav - The inflow of karma. One should think that new karmas are due to Aasrav. One should make himself free from this situation and think of soul only. One should avoid the new karmas to make progress towards the path of emancipation.

(8) Samvar – Method of stoppage of karma. This is the effective tool to stop inflow of new karmas. Soul should always alert about stoppage of new karmas and apply effective measure to it. Samvar is the progress on the path of emancipation.

(9) Nirjara – Method of shedding of karmas. Nirjara is the important and useful thing to annihilate the old and new karmas. One has to apply effective technique for this by way of observing vows and character building with right knowledge and right faith. The soul will become lighter and lighter due to shedding of karmas. Soul will rapidly make its journey towards the siddhatva-emancipation.

(10) Lok svarup – Jain cosmology. As per Jain religion, universe exists from beginning less time. There is no god. God is neither the creator nor the destroyer of this universe. The universe constitutes of 14 Rajlok and having three parts Urdhva means - upper - lok, Middle lok and adho means – lower -lok. Urdhva lok is for celestial being residence, middle lok is for human, triyanch, and vegetation residence and adho lok is hellish being residence. On the top of Urdhva lok, there is a residing place for Siddha souls known as siddhsila. One should think about these things. One should always alert for not to transmigrate in this universe. One should think of making journey to siddhsila.

(11) Bodhi Durlabh – Importance of Three jewels. Umaswatiji had shown the way for attaining siddhatva. The process has three

spiritual steps to be followed. They are known as "Samyag jnana, Samyag darsan and Samyag charitra". One should try to get right knowledge, right faith and right conduct in life to move on the path of emancipation. This type of knowledge is very important for soul.

(12) Dharma Durlabh – Importance of faith. One has to put full faith in one's own religion. The solid foundation of religion will help person to be firm in his faith. Person should understand and accept the religious preaching. Person should put religious preaching into practice whole heartedly.

5. Parishajaya

There are 22 types of body, mind and speech suffering. One has to experience suffering for the upliftment of soul. The suffering will give strength to become firm in religion. This is a test of person to be away from devilish temptation. Ascetics have to follow these thoroughly in ascetic life.

6. Character

They are of five types of character.

(A) Samayika charitra – Attitude of equanimity to give up all impurities.

(B) Chedopasthan charitra - Monk carrier – To accept the monk hood for whole life.

(C) Parihara Visuddhi charitra – observe special type of penance for course of conduct.

(D) Suksmasamparaya charitra – The Passions is very negligible at this stage. No new passions will arise in soul.

(E) Yathakhyta charitra – No passions- Kevali stage.

The fourth stage will lead you for fifth stage in no time on burning of all traces of passions.

NIRJARA - annihilation of karma

Nirjara means falling off of karmic matter from the soul. Nirjara is the process to make karmic matter to decrease in terms of quantity. This happens when the karma ripens. Karma comes into existence at appropriate time. Person had experienced the effect of it, after that karma will be no more. Person can annihilate karmas by way of penance.

Nirjara is of two types

1. Savipaka Nirjara. Here karma comes into existence at appropriate time. Person experienced the effect of it. After this, karma is destroyed. The soul gets separated from that karma. This is the case of natural maturity of karma.

2. Avipaka Nirjara. We show earlier that one can change the time of karma to come into fruition. One can change the category of karma. Karma can be made heavier or lighter as per the intensity of passion. One who follows the ascetic practice and get karma raise early than maturity or can make karma effect from heaver to lighter. The soul gets separated from karma after following the ascetic practice.

All eight karmas are divided in two parts. They are known as Ghatiya and aghatiya karma. The explanation is given here for their quality and way to dismiss them from soul.

	Ghatiya(Hurting)karma	Aghatiya-non-hurting karma
A) Name of karma	1) Knowledge obscuring Karma	5)Feeling producing karma
	2)Vision obscuring karma	6)Longevity determining karma
	3)Obstruction producing karma	7) Body making karma
	4) Delusion producing karma	8) Status producing karma
B) Quality	Always inauspicious	Both auspicious and inauspicious
(C) Course	Subsidence, Subsidence cum destruction Or Complete destruction	

It is shown in table that ghatiya karma is always bad in nature. This ghatiya karma dismissal is (1) by way of subsiding their effect, (2) either removal or subsidence and (3) total removal of ghatiya karma. This depends upon which stage the soul has attained. The Jain religion prescribes the fourteen stages for evaluation of soul; from most active passion soul in first stage to the journey to Siddha soul, the fourteenth stage. The process of Subsidence, removal or subsidence and total removal of karma comes in between these fourteen stages. They are known as GUNASTHANAK - the stages of purity of soul. [141] The fourteenth stage is the siddhatva which is eternal.

In case of aghatiya karma, they are good or bad in nature. This karma is limited up to the auspicious or non auspicious in term of effect. They are removed at the time of Kevali samudghat.

3.   Importance of penance

In Jain religion, penance is the effective tool for stopping the arrival of new karmas and shedding of karmas. In Jain religion, penance means control of desires. Penance is of two types.

(A) External penance (B) Internal penance

(A) External: - External penance is having six sub divisions. [142]

>   (1) Ansana: – completely giving up of the food. Person decides not to take food. This is in terms of time. Say one day or up to any number of days as per his/her capacity. Again here person decides to fast with choice - to drink water or not to drink water.

>   (2) Unodari: - Person eats less food. Here he decides to eat less than full stomach. Person will eat two to three morsels less in his daily breakfast, meal and supper. This is a vow of partial giving up of food. This is good for health.

>   (3) Vrutisamkshepa: –Person should make limit of the items in use. Person voluntarily decides to make limit of consumable items I.e. food, cloths. Person voluntarily decides the limit of wealth. Person

---

[141]   Arunvijayji Maharaj, Karma tani gati nyari, part-1, page no.288.

[142]   Commentary by Pandit Sukhlalji, Tattvarthasutradhigam, ch.8,stanza no.19,page no.329 to 331

makes the limit of usage of luxury things. Person puts in to practice the limited use of items.

(4) Rasparityag: - Person should avoid the delicious items in food. Here person particularly avoid the delicious food. He will go without the most favourite items of foods say cake, butter, cheese, or sweets, Ice-cream and so on and so forth. He will decide to have only few things to eat and that to without taste. This will strengthen his will to take away his sense from worldly things.

(5) Kayaklesa: – To make body fit for spirituality. Person will observe voluntarily all types of control. Person will go away from worldly things and concentrate on inner most self - the soul.

(6) Samlinta – The act of living lonely. Second meaning is to prepare body for various postures for meditation. Here person does the meditation and observe silence to get mental strength. Person resides in lonely place and prepares himself for upliftment of his soul. Person will be away from passions and moving fast to annihilate his karmas.

(B) Internal penance is having six sub divisions [143]

(1) Prayascitta - Repentance:-. This is a mental stage. Person has to prepare himself for regret of any bad act. Person will feel sorrow at the end of the day for his unpleasant deeds. In Jain religion, there is a one daily act, known as Pratikraman. In this act, person remembers daily, his sinful activities of day, before retiring at night, repent for it and decides not to repeat it again. Person feels that he should pardon all living beings and all living being should pardon him. Person has the friendly feeling with all living beings and there should not be any enemy.

(2) Person should respect the elderly people: - Person should respect virtuous people. This people will guide him on the path of religion and helpful to get emancipation.

(3) Vaiyavacha – To help needy monks for their requirements:-The male and female ascetics are growing older and sometimes suffering from diseases. They need medical and physical help. Apart from this, young ascetics need various things for education and they

---

[143]   Ibid, page no.331.

have other requirements. It is a duty of householder to help them in all respect.

(4) Svadhyaya- studying scripture for self: - Person is studying the scripture to get in depth knowledge of religion. This in - depth knowledge will help him to follow religion precisely. This will help him to climb the ladder of purification of conscious.

(5) Dhyana – Meditation: - The meditations are of four types. Each one is having further four sub - divisions in it. The first two types of meditation are not useful for person to attain emancipation. Looking to the present circumstance, it is difficult to have the fourth type of meditation. Therefore person should concentrate on DHARMA DHYAN. Person should do maximum possible religious practices with utmost care for purity of soul.

(6) Kayotsarga – to leave selfish feelings: - Another meaning is to stand in a meditative posture and meditate on self to have inner vision of soul. This will help to establish self in to soul and away from karmas.

In External penance, first four types of penance will help to have conduct purity and last two types of penance will help to have body purity.

In Internal penance, first four types of penance will have mental purity and last two types of penance will have SOUL purity.

Liberation of Soul

Soul has to get out of the cycle of birth and death. Soul has to attain the eternal position. Soul is mundane means impure. The impure state of soul has to be removed and pure state of soul has to attain like crystal clear, totally pure form of soul. Jain religion gives a magical formula for liberation. It is known as "RATNATRYI". The formula of three jewels A) Samyag Jnana B) Samyag darsan C) Samyag charitra - character. The sum total of three and application of them will definitely give the liberation to soul. This is possible by two ways. (1) Annihilation of all karmas. (2) To attain pure state of soul.

Jain religion considered eight main karmas and has sub divisions of them. The bondage of all types of karmas makes soul impure and result is transmigration. The attachment and aversion are the causes for karma.

Attachment is selfishness and partiality is the result of it. This is a reason for bondage of karma. One who always has auspicious karma bandh may have the highest auspicious karma bandh known as "Tirthankar nama karma". One has to keep himself away from passions which are the main causes of karma bandh. The delusion is the most important amongst them. You have to gather the spiritual courage slowly. Make the soul's condition indifferent and be in the state of equanimity. This will help to make spiritual progress rapidly. At one state soul will leave all karmas way behind and attain the non-karma position. Now when soul attains this stage, soul will be destroy the accumulated bunch of past karmas and make rapid progress in spiritual behaviour. A stage will come where there are no new karmas and old stocks of karmas are also exhausted. Then there is no trace of any karmic particles and soul will be totally pure. At this stage soul will get liberation.

6.4   Limitations of Karma theory

According to Jain religion, the present period is counted as fifth AARA - Time frame. In this period no one can get liberation or emancipation of soul.

The reasons are 1) the body is not capable to withstand the changes taking place due to fast and meditation. 2) The Details of procedure prescribed in Karma Granth is not possible to follow thoroughly in this period by house holder or ascetics. 3) The time limit of passion - anger karma is maximum of 70 crodancrodi sagaropam years, which is how far reliable is a matter of individual belief. 4) The matter regarding transmigration is rests on individual belief, knowledge, experience and faith in the religion. 5) An average life span is of eighty years. Out of this first ten to fifteen years man will not be able to understand religion and last fifteen years will give him maximum trouble in the sense of physical and mental health. The remaining period will not be suitable for religious activities as man is pre occupied with other matters of life.

6.5   Philosophy of Welfare in Karma theory:

Indian philosophy believes in Karma. This is the sole cause in the life of human to come up in every respect in his life. The poor has to work hard to come up economically. The poor understands the pain of progress, therefore he helps other poor to come up in the life. The rich does not need to suffer for coming up in the life nor did they realize the trouble of other human. Karma gives an explanation for this. Person has done good deeds in past, Person is enjoying the fruits in this life. Whereas other person did bad deeds in past as a result he is suffering in this life. Jain religion says that you should pass the phase of happiness as well as sorrow without extreme joy or extreme grief. Human should be calm and quite in both the positions. Human should not condemn the bad time nor praise good time. Human should be simply onlooker and be witness of good and bad deeds. Human should remain in senses and do not go away from the charted path for religious life.

The present economic situation can be defined in terminology of karma as under.

The universe is soul, UNO help is good karma, and all types of negative activities are bad karmas in broad sense.

The list the good karmas

(1) UNO resolution for making the under developed countries to come up economically. They should make Debt free countries.

(2) Undeveloped and underdeveloped country should have a share in import and export trade.

(3) Undeveloped and underdeveloped countries should join in main stream of economy of the world to avail benefits.

(4) Undeveloped and underdeveloped countries should be able to use resources to fullest extent for betterment of their people.

(5) Undeveloped and underdeveloped countries should have economic buffer for famine, earthquake, flood and Tsunami and other natural calamities. The rich countries should extend all help in such calamities.

(6) The developed countries should help Undeveloped and underdeveloped countries to establish necessary industries, infra structure without their literal exploitation.

(7) The developed countries should not expand their war industry and do not instigate Undeveloped and underdeveloped countries for war amongst each other on some false ground or pretext.

(8) The developed countries should protect their interest reasonably but not at the cost of Underdeveloped or undeveloped countries.

(9) The developed countries should take responsibility to make underdeveloped and undeveloped countries to flourish and create brotherhood with them.

(10) The developed countries should not exploit the underdeveloped and undeveloped countries' natural resources in the name of trade and commerce and political support.

(11) The undeveloped and underdeveloped countries should be able to give employment to their people, food and shelter, better medical and educational facilities and political freedom to have wellbeing and improved standard of living.

The list of bad karmas

(1) The developed countries make consortium for their economies and political interest.

(2) The developed countries ask other countries to follow WTO, GATT like other agreement. This is another form of slavery.

(3) The one developed country through U.N.O. and with support of other developed countries ask other countries of world to sign an agreement which curbs their freedom and right I.E. Nuclear non proliferation treaty.

(4) The developed countries, through politics, established their right by agreement to have economic benefits.

(5) The developed countries put ban, restriction, apply quota system to number of items to import or put heavy import duty to protect their industries and agriculture.

(6) The developed countries import highly skilled man power for their benefit and under developed countries suffers for export of skilled

man power. Underdeveloped countries spent money on education and cannot get benefits of it for their own countries.

(7) The highly skilled men power exported from under developed countries are not paid standard wage in the receiving countries. They are victim of colour, race, language and culture. They are exploited by local firms and industries unrestrictive.

(8) The developed countries in the name of globalization promote industries in underdeveloped countries and make huge profit from it. They take away money by way of profit, consultancy fee and dividend in the name of consumerism and fashion and better life style.

(9) The developed countries give asylum to the political leaders as refuge, who had followed developed countries policy in their countries, in past.

(10) The developed countries do not care for betterment of human on this universe even in their own countries.

Good results

(1) The small and underdeveloped countries are allowing an inflow of foreign capital. This has resulted in export oriented industrialization, created employment and export. This had contributed into high revenue to state, high G.D.P. This resulted in high standard of living. World population does good things. This is possible due to auspicious time of earth. This is due to increase in Sata vedaniya karma.

(2) The globalization had made the speedy movement of people from one country to another country. Skilled manpower is going abroad for better opportunities rather than decaying in their own countries. The Jnanavarniya karma increases knowledge in low profile and less intelligent people. The movement is the reason of diluting effect of darsan mohaniya karma. People can think right thing and take right decision without delusion. This is due to subsidence of Jnanavarniya and darsan mohaniya karma.

(3) The globalization has increase brotherhood. The feelings for fellow brothers awakened and are eager to meet and exchange the ideas

for betterment. This is due to decreasing effect of darsanavaraniya karma.

(4) The globalization has increased the understanding to know and understand others' view. People listen and understand each other ideas, thought and working with patience and try to accommodate each other with the let go attitude. This is due to subsidence of Jnanavarniya karma. This is an ANEKANTVADA of Jain religion.

(5) The globalization will bring the power of tolerance. This will make intelligent person to join in the main stream of world. The intellect will meet and work for betterment of earth and down trodden people. This is due to subsidence of Jnanavarniya karma.

(6) The globalization has improved the productivity due to specialization. Number of innovation has come into existence. The veil on the sun of knowledge will go away and knowledge will luminous with full capacity. The peace and prosperity will be there due to Sata vedaniya karma. This is due to subsidence of Jnanavarniya and Sata vedaniya karma.

Bad results

(1) The lender countries are getting lion share in profit, charges heavy royalty, hefty service charges to the public and private sector industries. This will happen because the wicked people will only believe in materialistic gain. This is due to increase intensity of asata vedaniya and character mohaniya karma.

(2) The speedy movement of highly skilled man power had made them vulnerable for exploitation. The employer will look at maximization of profit; as a result exploitation of labour will be there. This is due to increasing veil of character mohaniya karma.

(3) The group of countries such as rich G8 countries, OPAC, European Union, and GATT, SARC or pacific union is taking advantage of globalization. These countries will look into their interest with narrow selfish view. This is due to increase in delusion of darsan mohaniya karma.

(4) The specialization and innovation have made human selfish. Mohaniya karma will show you wrong path as a result you will leave your good and adopt bad with maximum limit. This is due to rise in effect of Mohaniya karma.

(5) One highly developed country's inflationary and recessionary business cycle will effect to other related countries. The related countries will suffer the consequence. This is due to high power of Mohaniya karma.

Which is biggest immoral act? The answer is to take away the employment. This is done by big industries by way of mechanisation of jobs, to have the work done by ROBOTS, retrenchment in the name of profit maximising etc. One who does this is incurring heavy Antraya karma. Dr. Amartya SEN has rightly said that ENTITLEMNT APPROACH is the answer for basic need of man. Lord Mahavir told that each one should get the earning as per his requirement. The person who gets the minimum earning will not indulge in any immoral activities.

Jain religion and Indian philosophy show the way to detach from the union of soul and karma. Soul desires to have eternal peace. This is possible due to the immense strength of soul. Human puts whole hearted efforts to break the union and succeed. This is the free position of soul known as emancipation of soul. Here the body is no more. This welfare is forever and for each one, who so desire.

In Jain religion we show the importance of Ahimsa in life. The next thing is action - karma. You show the illusion of karma and in - depth analysis of it. We move now on the third doctrine of Jain religion known as Anekantvada. We will see that it is useful in life in the coming chapter.

7 Dr. Amartya Sen's idea on Inequality Re-examined

7.1 Inequality

Equality of what and why has to be defined in ethical term. The terms are interdependent.

Dictionary meaning of equality is, as noun, the equality or state of being equal. We have to find out equality in economic terms.

Ethically, equality analysis should know by way of asking the question (1) Why and (2) What. The both parameters are separate in its' own nature but interdependent of each other. Equality of what is income, wealth, opportunities, achievements, freedom, rights etc. Why will be answered automatically in examination of the above parameters. Equality will be examined by way of standard of comparison. The poor man is considered for this examination. Equality of something requires the norms in theory for social arrangements. The subject matter of theory may be diverse and may clash with each other but it remains common in all theories I.e. equality.

Many economists gave thought on equality in political philosophy say John Rawls, Ronald Dworkin, Thomas Nagel etc. Some economists have disputed the case of equality on the other grounds. Robert Nozick, demands equality for libertarian rights, James Buchanan, thinks of equal legal and political treatment. Harsanyi gave same weight to all individual's interest. Hare thought giving equal weight to the equal interest of all the parties. [144]

Utilitarian considers equality as maximization of the sum-total of the utilities of all the people taken together. This means that the gain or loss in utility will be equal to all people. Here the equal weight meant for everyone in terms of utility. Egalitarian believes in social, economical and political equality among human being. Utilitarian means the aims of actions or social policy should be the greatest happiness of the greatest number. Here the interest of both approaches coincides in to each other. In particular case, when we define equality in terms of some space then it is different to each other.

William Letwin argued against equal distribution of income as "In as much as people are unequal, it is rational to presume that they ought to be treated unequally-which might mean larger shares for the needy or larger shares for worthy".[145] Here the "need" and "worth" are in definition. Need is understood. Dr. Amartya Sen explains the worth as 'equal treatment for equal worth'. Indirectly the equality is there in terms of equal treatment for equal worth.

Harry Frankfurt speaks about 'equality as a moral ideal'.[146] He disputed the claims of economic egalitarianism that it is desirable for everyone to have same amounts of income and wealth. According to him (1) equality is of no great intrinsic interest and 2) it leads to the violation of important values.

Impartiality and equality

The point of equality of what and equality of why are equally important. It is worthwhile to discuss the above thing even the theory may be vague. You may not get precise results. One may not be partial for equality on this very reason. The theory needs to be explained and defended for each case.

So many different theories of the ethics of social arrangements gives the answer for why and what. Ethical theories of social arrangement demand the equality of something. This equality can be discussed at different

---

[144]   Amartya Sen, inequality re-examined page.13·
[145]   Ibid, page no.14.
[146]   Ibid, page no.15

levels. Dr. Amartya Sen argues that at some level, reasoning of equal consideration for all is critical. In the absence of equality; theories will become discriminative which will be difficult to defend. It is better to discuss about many variables in terms of inequality. Ethical reasoning of social arrangements is a Kantian view in a sense personal obligations or commitments but not necessarily structure.

Thomas Scanlon had analyzed the power of requirement and relevance. According to him "One should be able to justify one's action to others on grounds that they could not reasonably reject". This gives us the basis of fairness of justice. This is a matter of equality in between two individuals. This implies condition of acceptance. The impartiality and universalizability are the general requirement in foundations of ethics on reasoning. Dr.Amartya Sen says John Rawls (1971) has build up the theory of justice on the preposition of fairness.[147]

"Impartiality" is the demand of universal. Here the impartiality is in a sense of equality. The point is the plausibility of equal consideration at some level is important in political or social circumstances. Equality has to be considered at some level to defend theory, judgment and claims. Now it is to be decided that it is a logical requirement or a substantive demand. This type of reasoning is the foundation of ethics. The point is equality proves for inequality. This is more important in the case of space. This may be former in equality and later in inequality but within same circle.

Human diversity and basic equality

One human being is different from another human being. We have different external appearances and endowments. Let us start the discussion with his wealth and liabilities. We live in a hostile environment than other; different opportunity in society and community as well as health is prime concern. We differ from natural, social and environmental characteristics and in personal characteristics say age, sex, physical and mental ability. These are the factors help us to examine inequality. Say two people are having the same income. One is disable person and another is able. In such case, the disable person will not be in a position to compete the able person. This is a matter of inequality. The variable of income takes us to another variable of functioning ability which gives the idea of advantage and disadvantage.

---

[147]   Ibid, page no.18

The plurality of variables takes us to the interpersonal inequality. The choice of evaluative space will be a problem. Human diversity takes us from equality to another inequality such as from income to health, well-being and happiness.

Dr. Amartya Sen says Author Nozick is in favour of liberation right than inequality. We accept this than we cannot talk about welfare equality. We accept equal right than we cannot think of income, utilities, wellbeing and positive freedom. We try to prove the inequality through equality. We should select such a "base" that can give us the equality and impartiality between individuals. Equality of what will endorse the equality in space which will have far reaching consequences on distribution pattern of other space.

Equality verses liberty?

We can put liberty against equality. The conflict is in between equality and liberty is nature of political philosophy and political economy. Robert Nozick is considered as anti-egalitarian because he emphasis liberty than equality. Dalton, Meade and Tawney are egalitarian because they thought for demands of equality.[148] You cannot distinguish the equality and liberty in above manner. The next thought is who, how much, how distributed and how equal. Here the distribution of right is important. The equality of liberty comes in picture. Equality and liberty are not two opposite things but one can see as supplementary to each other. The possibility is you think one variable as income and another person think a variable as liberty. Income and liberty requires equality. Liberty may be possible field of application in equality and equality can be a possible pattern of distribution of liberty.

We have to select "SPACE" and to fix item say income. We include other things with income than 'space' becomes broader. The diversity of spaces will give different views. These different views will help us to assess amongst each other's space. This assessment will give different views of equality. Now we can say about inequality of income; on one side liberty and on other side equality in terms of achievement and freedom to achieve. The study will have many fold consequences.

---

[148]   Ibid, page no.21.

Plurality and alleged emptiness

Plurality of spaces generates doubt about the idea of equality. This should not reduce equality as the political force of idea at the same time. Can demand be considered as serious as many voices speak for equality? Douglas Rae said 'one idea that is more powerful than order or efficiency or freedom in resisting equality'.[149] The equality is itself so powerful that it resists itself.

Weston said equality is empty. Equality has many interpretations. Equality cannot be taken as truly substantive demand. Equality of what will remove emptiness. The general requirement of the need of the value in some space is not empty. This relates impartiality and equality. This will help in evaluative system and in basal equality.

Dalton was in favour of transfer of income. This is known as "Dalton principle of transfer".[150] He thought for distribution of income in poor people collected from rich. Small portion of income transferred from a richer person to a poorer one will help. Equality is imposed in the form of ranking pattern. Here the total amount remains unchanged. The transfer of portion of income is a distributive improvement in society. This is a general requirement of equality without disturbing other space index or measure.

After deciding the space, if space may have broader choice than it will demand equality. The choice of space has motivation to demand equality say for example-evaluating justice or social welfare or living standard or quality of life will not be formal but substantive discrimination.

In equality, diversity of space will give different solution of different variable in the advantage of individual. This will show how it is advantageous to different people in each other context of spaces. The plurality shows different views with equality and information base. The plurality of choice of space is equally applicable to 'efficiency' also. Efficiency as individual utility in welfare economics gets converted into "Pareto optimality", [151] Efficiency can be considered for liberty and any other item of space. Efficiency is comparable with other variable. This is polarity of notion of efficiency. The plurality of space really reflects diversity to individual advantage and on informational base for interpersonal comparison.

---

149   Ibid, page no.23.
150   Ibid, page no.24
151   Ibid, page no.25

Means and freedoms

In case of demand, based on norms and social arrangement equality requires in one or other space. This is a 'Basel equality' which has effects on other spaces in distributive system. Basel equality in one space will be directly responsible for inequality in other space. In modern political philosophy and economics, the most prominent name is "John Rawls", who talks about choice of space and its' consequences in theory of justice. Individual is holding the primary goods as here the efficiency and equality are analyzed. This is known as the "difference of principle".[152]

According to Nozick, Inherited wealth and talent would not generate income in egalitarian approach and Rawls, in difference principle, considers the Basel equality. The primary goods and wellbeing vary due to the personal diversity. This will be a hurdle to convert into achievement. Example-Pregnant woman will be uncomfortable compared to man of same age and same income and other primary goods. The efficiency of pregnant woman will differ to a person having other things as equal. Similarly the primary goods and freedom will differ in achieving objectives. The relation between primary goods and freedom may vary in interpersonal and intergroup variations.

Apart from individual diversity, the group as men and women is having contrasts. The pregnant woman has less freedom and wellbeing even though same primary goods. These differences are visible in case of interpersonal and inter-group variation of specific characteristics. Inequality differs in interpersonal relations with different spices even though it is interconnected.

Human diversity gives scope to examine the inequality. Egalitarianism is due to inequality in different spaces. The same different spaces are the ethical point of inequality in human diversity.

Income distribution, wellbeing and freedom

Human is diverse due to physical features and social things in many ways. It is difficult to accommodate this diversity in evaluative frame work of inequality. The analysis of inequality is mainly in relation to Income. Now what we can and cannot do and to get or not to get our achievement

---

[152]   Ibid, page no.26.

depends, apart from income, in physical and social characteristics. The deprivation of physically handicap person is more than able person in spite of equal income. The real inequality is in opportunity and not income. The handicap person is not in a position to convert his income in to achievement. This will happen due to 1) there are other means available and 2) interpersonal variation in means and ends.

Atkinson proposed social loss of equivalent income in his "inequality indices".[153] This is very broad assumption. This is not possible for practical purposes as we agree about heterogeneity of human in society. This approach is useful in integrating income inequality considerations for overall evaluation of social welfare. The negative point is it does not take into account the difficulties of some people to convert the income in well-being and freedom. The positive point is to consider the inequality in distribution of income and not level of well-being.

7.2   Freedom, Achievement And Resources

Freedom and choice

A position of a person in society can be seen in two ways (1) The actual achievement (2) freedom to achieve. Actual Achievement is past. Freedom to achieve is future. You have to achieve something in coming time. Inequality has to be examined from achievement and freedom to achieve point of view. This is applicable to efficiency also.

Freedom achieved and freedom to achieve is for social evaluation. You can judge the achievement in terms of utility, or opulence or quality of life. Further it is important to know difference between 1) extent of achievement and 2) the freedom to achieve. Individual advantage and good social order are concern for achievement only and freedom to achieve is mean. Utilitarian believes only in interpersonal comparison and utility achievement.

Bergson-Samuelson social welfare function draws the attention toward the achievement and that too in individual freedom as an achievement. [154]

---

[153]   ibid, page no.29
[154]   ibid, page no.32.

Arrowian social-choice frame work thinks in term of individual preference over state of affairs and not the freedom to choose the affairs.[155]

Achievement and to achieve are two different things. To achieve indicates the lot of happening in future for freedom. Achievement shows the past and no future prospective to improve upon it. This both approaches are partial. It has definite connection to combine for welfare of individual and society. The past will show us the way and future will show to achieve it. Recent development in social choice theory emphasizes on freedom in specific value of liberty.

Primary goods give us the ownership idea and resources give the idea about future achievement. This will make a difference for equality. It will be an assessment of freedom. Dr. Amartya Sen is of the opinion that the primary goods or resources are the cause towards freedom but if you look in term of utility it is freedom away from achievement.

The point is to equalize the freedom to all is not correct as conversion of these things have variations. Variation can be simply due to physical condition and of complex nature-say under nourishment may not solve, even though the same primary goods and resources with two persons, one may be free to avoid under nourishment and another may not. These people think in different ways. One thinks for present where as another person thinks for his future wellbeing.

Real income, opportunities and selection

The real income interpreted in two ways 1) Achievement 2) freedom. Real income can be defined as a person receives benefit from particular bundle of commodity. "Is X a better bundle for this person than Y bundle?"[156] You have comparison amongst bundles can be called as 'selection'. Now person can buy budget set A or budget set B than it is 'options view'. Person has liberty to buy more than one bundle from his income. In comparison to 'selection view', 'optimal view' is superior in a sense that it gives possibility to choose from budget set A as well as budget set B inter alias. This is known as 'revelled preference' in real income. The reason thought gives you freedom to choose whether from A one could choose what was chosen

---

155   Ibid, page no.32.
156   Ibid, page no.34.

from B. The standard assumption in real income gives the above result. We drop the standard assumption than the result will be different as strategy changed. The optional and revelled preference logically extended up to the choice of freedom.

Freedom distinguished from resources

Freedom and means of freedom are different things. The budget set gives freedom of space and it derives on person's resources. The attention shifted from achievements to resources, commodity bundle to income and to freedom. You can differentiate the means and extent of freedom in the resources on which budget set depend and budget set itself. The shift from achievement to resources is in direction to greater freedom.

Political and moral philosophy partly motivated to freedom interpreted as interpersonal comparison of individual advantage. The freedom to achieve and extent of freedom itself is important in principle but difficult in practice. When you convert resources into budget than standard assumption will change and it becomes powerful interpersonal variation. The resources or primary good with a person is imperfect freedom. Resources get converted into budget set. There can be great difference in case of conversion of resources or primary goods into freedom. Freedom does not get bind with anything. Person can have 'selection' or 'option' or not to use the resources.

7.3   Functioning and Capability

Capability sets

Capability defines in terms of 1) well-being and 2) the freedom to pursue well-being. Well-being is a quality of a person's being. Living is functioning. The functioning can be of (1) being (2) doing - Functioning means achieving. Functioning can be elementary as well as complex. Functioning is a constitutive of a person being and evaluation of well-being is the assessment of function. The functioning is closely related to capability. The functioning is various combinations which man can achieve. Capability gives freedom to live life any way. Capability set reflects the person's freedom. Well-being of a person is depending on nature of person. Person is well nourished or in good health is important for well-being of a person. How does capability related to well-being is a point. Here nature and functioning are tied together.

Person's capability of well-being is interrelated on two considerations. The achieved functioning is person's well-being and the freedom is to have well-being. The ethical and political analysis has relevance to well-being freedom. For example, people consider freedom enjoyed to achieve well-being is the goodness of social state. Some may take individual goodness of social state as 'right'.

Freedom is opportunity of well-being in other words. It is instrumental in the process. The indicator of goodness of state is the degree of freedom. The degree of freedom decides the goodness of social state. A good society reflects in to society of freedom. The indicator of 'rightness' is the degree of freedom.

The achieved well-being depends upon the function of capability. Choosing is living but the genuine choice with option is much richer in a sense. Specific types of capability directly contribute to well-being. When freedom is considered as an instrument than capability function is a social evaluation. Capability set gives us information of functions within reach of person and no matter how well-being defined. Capability approach is new, compare to primary goods, resources and income which are traditional. They are only instrumental to achieve well-being. They have limited function. They are in fixed boundaries. The traditional things are objective and only means to instrumental achievement in well-being. Capability reflects the freedom for constituents which help to get well-being. This is a direct route. Capability is in much broader term. Traditional approach works in the boundary. It does not allow the person to move anywhere.

Value objects and Evaluative spaces

One can ask two questions for evaluative exercise.1) what are the objects of value? 2) How valuable are the respective objects. The first object makes the second object working. You apply the weight to object for valuation to distinguish the thing. When you apply weight, it becomes "Dominance ranking ". (X is higher than Y, if it yields more of at least one of the valued object and at least as much of each).[157] When you

---

[157]   ibid, page no.42-43.

apply dominance ranking, it converts into some standard regulation-transitivity. The standard regularity properties will show difference in evaluative process. This will give us an idea about the comparison. In case of utilitarianism approach—information constraints are there. In utilitarian approach all people are taken together and sum total of all is taken into account.

In capability approach primarily the value object identified and functioning of capability in evaluative term. You will not get the particular answer regarding their relative value. Selection of space can discriminate in positive sense as inclusion of potentially valuable and negative sense list of weighted object. The capability approach is more deeply evaluative but cannot give particular answer to the question and their relative values.

A variety of doings and beings is a part of capability approach. This gives fuller recognition and enrichment to lives. Capability approach differs from personal functioning say wealth, opulence, resources, liberties and primary goods. In capability approach evaluation—being and doing are important. Capability has to be judged from both the point of views.

Being is static state and doing is continuous state. Both are important in terms of freedom. The capability is a person's strength and it has to be used in past as being and will be used in future as doing. This gives a variety of ways to enrich and improve the life. This is the real essence of well-being of a person. The capability is the heart of the thing. Capability approach is the real solution for welfare of person.

Selection and weighting

Real choice element exists in the list of relevant functioning and capability. You can add 'achievement' in the list of 'doing' and 'being.' There are certain function easy to describe but do not carry importance. There will be problem in selecting a class of functioning and capability. In terms of value, some function may be important and others are not of that importance. The functioning and capability is easy to conceptualize in the sense of selection and discrimination. In the welfare analysis of poverty in developing countries, we have to go along with relatively small and important functioning. In case of more general economic development problems, we have to go longer with diverse subjects.

Dr.Amartya Sen says, according to Charles Beitz, in interpersonal comparison, there may not be the same footing for capability approach. [158] The capability approach may be of little interest. You have to select and weight the things properly in capability approach. Real income framework and capability framework has varying importance in their respective fields-say commodity for income and capability for capability framework. In both the cases equal valuation is necessary. In evaluation of well-being, capability and functioning are value objects. In case of assessment of person's well-being, all types of capabilities are not valuable at the same time single remote capability should not be neglected. On one side the value of functioning and capability requires to be examined, on other side attention is required for means as achievement and freedom in capability approach.

Incompleteness: fundamental and pragmatic

Capability approach gives definite answer in the circumstances of not having total agreement in uniform weight attached to different functioning. Without specification of weight, a particular value object has 'dominance partial order.' Relative weights are in agreements for improvement of different capability and functions. Dominance partial order can work without full agreement for relative values.

Dr. Amartya Sen gives an example "If there are four conflicting views claiming respectively that the relative weight to be attached to X vis-à-vis should be 1/2 ,1/3 ,1/4, and 1/5, there is, then, an implicit agreement that the relative weight on X should not exceed 1/2, nor fall below 1/5".[159] This general agreement permits us to have many pairs not covered in the dominance ranking.

Let us examine the dominance and intersection in the figure.[160]

---

[158]   ibid, page no.45.

[159]   ibid, page no.46.

[160]   Ibid, page no.47.

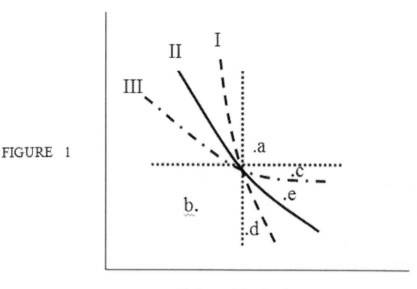

Value object --1

FIGURE 1

FIGURE 1

The intersection approach only takes us to a distance for all alternative weights on shared implications. The interpretations of the intersection approach are as under. A is superior to B. Dominance ranking is incomplete and cannot rank as C, D, or E. When there are more than two value objects, more indifferent curves are possible without giving idea about which one is correct.

1) Since A lies below C according to all of them, the intersection approach declares A *to* be inferior to C.

2) Similarly, since a lies above D according to all of them, A can be declared to be better than D.

3) Here the result is still partial because A is above E according to some indifference curve and below it according to another, so that A and E cannot be ranked in this case.

Capability approach exercise is not for all or nothing. Interpersonal comparison of well-being and inequality evaluation admits this incompleteness. Well-being and inequality cannot be taken as total ordering. Incompleteness in relative weights reflects in incompleteness in value of well-being. The partial ordering has two different justifications in interpersonal comparison and inequality 1) well-being and inequality may look like complete ordering due to ambiguity. This is due to fundamental reason. 2) The pragmatic reason for incompleteness is there. There are certain areas, which are clear, should be presented without waiting for complete ordering.

Capability or functioning

Capability is freedom to achieve valuable functioning. Capability concentrates on freedom rather than means to achieve freedom. Capability is the person's freedom to achieve well-being. Capability can be a level of well-being achieved. Achievement of well-being is the process in which various functions, choice of decision associated. This line of thinking over wide domain is the case of capability to achieve well-being which includes the freedom to achieve well-being. Function goes to well-being and capability goes for freedom.

Capability defined as functioning. "N" is a point in this space of functioning. The functioning combination is a point in a space, where as capability is a set of such points. Well-being approach is income, utility etc. and capability approach is constitutive elements of living, does not make any difference as far as space is concern. Capability set contains inter alias information of functioning and we can evaluate the capability set on these chosen combination of functioning.

In elementary evaluation, only freedom of choice is considered. The capability set of evaluation can be used for achievement. Chosen combination gives limited information. We examine the theory of evaluation of well-being in terms of capability than chosen combination is preserved and others are omitted.

Freedom of choice has importance in person's life and well being quality. Acting freely and able to choose are useful to well-being. In standard consumer theory, the value of the best element is available. You can remove the other parts than chosen part in set will not make any difference as freedom is out.

Now choosing is considered as part of living than 'doing x' is distinguished form 'choosing to do x and doing it. This achievement in well-being is influenced by freedom in capability set. Functioning has various aspects. Let us discuss the functioning of "Fasting". You can interpret the fasting in more than one way (1) Fasting is religious thing (2) Fasting is a case of starvation. Again we can analyze second alternate in two ways (a) Fasting due to insufficient food (b) Fasting voluntarily.

The achieved well-being is a list of items. This requires bigger and better information. Therefore well-being to achieve should be a functioning and need not to bring in capability set.

In statistics, the data are prime important thing. After that right technique is important. The social situation is liquid .This will hamper the data availability which will result into not proper procedure. The information on the part of data and information about procedure are practical difficulties. Here we have to take into account our ultimate interest and circumstance of informational availability. The work of information is to give analysis of quality of life and economic progress rather than individual utility and commodity holding. The capability approach should take note of full freedom in choosing bundle but in practice we have to satisfy with analyzing the achieved functioning.

Utility Vis-a-Vis capability

Capability approach as utility will be seen as personal well-being and social ethics. The value of utility is in welfare economics as individual satisfaction in physical and mental stage. Desire fulfilling is the existence of utility and not mental state. Intensities of desire would have to be compared with desire fulfilment than it is a right approach. One can say that why mental metric in not taken in to consideration for capability approach. This is not possible due to motivational problems. Utility-based valuation is indirect and only pleasure and happiness will affect the other functioning. The desire fulfilment is taken as criteria in evaluation of capability functioning than it is disputable due to no proper mechanical metric of desire available. The inequality can be considered as one thing and deprived person is another thing. Both can be interpreted as desire fulfilment or in mental metric. The problem of deprivation is intense in inequality. Inequality is socially generated differences in capability than some capability will be wasted due to utility metric.

7.4   Freedom, Agency and well-being

Well - being Vis-a-Vis agency

Person is working for self with plan for well-being as well as pursues value and goal for others. This is known as 'the agency aspect' and 'well-being aspect'. In agency aspect person's success is in totality for the considered goals and objectives. This may not be connected with his personal well-being. Person's aim is to have community development, or to start educational institute for downtrodden children, or general goal as agency achievement in social state.

There is a difference between 'agency freedom' and 'well-being freedom'. Agency freedom is one's freedom to achieve value which one attempts to produce. Well-being freedom is the constituents of well-being of one's freedom to achieve those things. Well-being freedom reflects in capability set. The agency and well-being are thoroughly interdependent. The non achievement of well-being goals leads to frustration.

Agency, instrumentality and realization

Agency objectives are further divided into two. 1) Incidence takes place for those things that one values and one aim at achieving 2) Incidence takes place through one's own efforts. Goals realized without one's own role is the first type objective. In second case, the agent has to put in efforts to get realized his goals. The agency objective includes the elimination of famine which fulfils with or without my efforts. Here the comparison is in between the objectives and actual realization of those objectives. In second view, I have to promote elimination of famine objectives. My agency success depends on my own role to promote them. The above two cases are of 'realized agency success' and 'instrumental agency success'. Two things can happen in person's agency aspect, the achievement is valued irrespective of instrumental help or value has great importance in our result. Now happening of an incident "A" is direct or through our own effort is like an 'instrumental agency success', coincide in 'realized agency success'. The control of instrument in realization of outcome is important. Person should be free to have control on instrument to bring out the achievement.

Can freedom conflict with well-being?

Let us look at freedom as another aspect. It is seen that in evaluation limit of freedom is proper. More freedom is harmful due to cost of decision. The more freedom may make person less happy and less fulfilled in his well being. Here freedom is in conflict with well being. Conflict in freedom and well-being will not move in the same way or same direction. Here we have to distinguish well-being freedom and agency freedom. The agency freedom can reduce the well-being freedom. The example is regarding the prevention of crime. Here your presence on the spot of crime will increase your agency freedom; well-being goes down.

Well-being achievement and well-being freedom goes in opposite direction in case of agency freedom. I am at the place of crime and unable to move out of the situation than my well-being and freedom to achieve well-being will reduce. We see the situation in enhanced way. I leave the place and decide not to fight. In that case my mental peace will be disturbed. The act of my leaving the place and my mental disturbance will decrease my well-being and freedom. My well-being achievement is there in term of well-being and freedom. Here the agency freedom goes in opposite direction in term of well-being freedom and well-being achievement. If we take this as well-being freedom than achievement and well-being will increase. In case of well-being freedom, if you change the objective than achievement will go down and freedom will go up. An interesting example of a doctor's wished to serve in remote place. Here the Doctor sacrifices his Well-being but the means and opportunity are lacking. The rise in income will result in increase of well-being freedom and agency freedom and less well-being achievement. This proves that freedom and well-being achievement moves in opposite direction even in the case of interpretation as agency freedom or well-being freedom. We can assess inequality in both the perspective.

Freedom and disadvantageous choices

Freedom might be disadvantageous due to time and energy to be wasted. The more choices can result in hassle and inconvenience and far from advantageous. The point is can we consider increase in our choice is expansion of freedom. This concept plays an important role in assessment of social structure and public policy in relation to enhancing freedom.

More alternative does not mean expansion of freedom. The peaceful life is equally important. The small choice is not that important for freedom. You have to decide which option is important and which is not. Choice is both way opportunity and burden. Under the circumstances, choice is made but it is up to you to say NO. This is a case of no value expansion of freedom. Sometimes the choice is a worth part of living and sometimes we are force to do, as obligatory, which we may not like. This will bring a negative result on our ability.

Control and effective freedom

Freedom is to get what we value and what we want without control. This is in relation to our decisions. This gives us more power and more freedom to live our life. Example: - The proof reader checks the spelling mistake and errors from my book which is going to get printed. The freedom to print the book rests with me. The control is in other hands but the proof-reader is doing the job which I am supposed to do. The point is proof-reader will take instruction from me or he will work as per my desired instruction. Here the control is in my hand till proof-reader does the job and my freedom is uncompromised though my freedom as control is limited or absent. It is difficult that you have all control of your life in your hand. Some body may exercise control on you. As a matter of fact how the control exercised is important.

Freedom as control on self is the instrumental and realized control is in boarder perspective. Person, if given choice to live in epidemic-free atmosphere, will choose the same. Here the control of epidemic free atmosphere is in others hand. Here you cannot say anything for freedom as control. In broader sense public policy to prevent epidemic is more freedom to us. Now instead of elimination, somebody is promoting than our freedom as control will not affected but our effective freedom will be compromised badly. The elimination of epidemic is enhancement of our well-being.

The freedom we enjoy and inequality has to be assessed with the help of informational evaluation. This is in light of our counterfactual choices and relation to the freedom. Only control on freedom will not work. Elimination of unwanted or unlinked thing by people can be done by the way of public policy. People will get what they want .This will be a case of freedom enjoyed.

Freedom from hunger, malaria and other melodies

We wish not to have diseases or hunger. This will add to our well-being. This is a misunderstanding of the concept of freedom. It is not the case of more freedom and in reality, it is nothing. The control on actual choice is an idea only in terms of liberty and freedom. Isaiah Berlin (1969) Author said "Man's or people's liberty to choose to live as they desire."[161] The signification of this is it directs to the ability to choose and live as one's desire. Hunger free life through public policy is an enhancement of liberty to choose live as they desire. Hunger free living through public policy does not increase the range of freedom that one has. Freedom is a social idea. Freedom as social idea is very strong thing in analysis of well-being and freedom. We are not examining the difference in well-being and freedom but we rejoice the freedom.

The relevance of well-being

A person's agency aspect is wider than well-being aspect. Person will promote his own well-being and weight of this objective will be in balance with agency aspects. The relative advantage of different people can be a comparison in between their respective agency freedom. The information on agency aspect will speak about each person's own well-being. The agency aspect will tell all about a person. An intelligent person will choose one out of two things. Say perfection of life or perfection of work. The first one is chosen, in such case the second one do not loose importance. Both the things are important to all. Well-being and agency aspect have different role in interpersonal comparison for diverse exercises. Example: - society might accept some responsibility for person's well-being that does not mean that society is promoting person's other agency objectives. On one side society takes responsibility about no one starves, at the same time society cannot take responsibility to erect a statue in honour of hero.

Interpersonal comparison is in term of agency achievement and agency freedom. We did wish to know that who has how much power to purse his goals. Some people may successful in this type of functioning. Others may fail. In society some people are successful having political and ethical views and some are not. The agency aspect and well-being aspect gets prominence in light of the requirement of any one. In interpersonal comparison both

---

[161]   Ibid, page no.67.

are important. The evaluation of inequality depends on 1) purpose and 2) choice of information. Social security, poverty alleviation, removal of gross economic inequality is important in well-being aspect. Social justice is for general. An idealist sacrifice his well-being for some cause does not mean that he is sacrificing other causes for his well-being. Well-being aspect is important in analyses of social inequality and assessment of public policy. In different class and different group, inequality and social injustice is having strong disparities in well-being. The agency aspect is broad and important.

7.5 Justice and capability

The informational bases of justice

Any Judgment depends on truth of information and independent of other truth or falsity. Specified variables are directly involved in assessing the justice of alternative system or arrangement.

Example: - In utilitarian justice, utility is only the information base and it relates to individual for evaluation in state of affairs. Most of the theories analyzed the information. Information can be used in two different ways.

1) Selection of relevant personal features

2) The choice in combining characteristics.

In utilitarian theory the relevant personal features are utility and combining characteristic is total utility. In welfare theory the personal features remain as utility but combining characteristics are other things. Relevant personal features are utility along with liberty, primary goods, rights, resources, commodity bundles and various mixed spaces. Personal features are considered as opportunity in other theories. Personal features can be supplemented with choice in combining formula. The informational variation is plurality of focal variables. 'Basel equality' in turn influences the choice of focal variable for assessing inequality. Justice has close relevance to equality.

Rawlins justice and the political conception

John Rawls theory of "Justice as fairness" is most distinctive discovery of century. This theory is widely accepted. John Rawls device –"the original position" is the hypothetical state of equality in which people choose alternative principles that would govern the basic structure of society. The alternative principles are (1) each person has an equal right for equal basic liberty, which is compatible with all other's scheme of liberty for all. (2) Social and economic inequality has to satisfy two things. (A) An open position should be for all under fair equality of opportunity. (B) They should be to the great benefit of the least advantage members of society.

The first one is coming in the way of liberty as it makes the condition weak. Second is "difference principle" in which greatest benefit of the least advantaged. Dr. Amartya Sen see that the person and society's liberty should be compatible is a matter of thought. Dr. Amartya Sen agrees with the proposal of benefit should passed on to least advantageous people in the society.

We have to examine this in light of politics. We can make out two distinct things from Rawls political conception of justice.

(1) Political conception means, it is political, social and economical institutions as moral conception.

(2) "Constitutional democracy" in which concept of justice is independent of philosophical and religious doctrine. The tolerance, which is metaphysical, has no place in this political conception.

Earlier we had rejected the idea of tolerance on the ground of metaphysics. Tolerance has to be included in political conceptions of justice due to two different opposite sides. The first one is inequality and second one is injustice. There can be justice and injustice in choosing the political, social and economical institutions. The judgment is difficult without these political conceptions. Tolerance is one of the most important aspects in politics in living society. It is difficult to judge the Right and Wrong of politics. The theory of justice should address these things. Therefore scope of political conception limits the concept of justice.

In absence of tolerance, it is difficult to resolve the issue like inequality, injustice and deprivation. The court is the right place and no political party is able to solve this of their own by way of tolerance. This will limit the domain of political conception of justice.

In 1973, there was a famine in Ethiopia. The emperor HAILE SELASSIE said, "We have said wealth has to be gained through hard work. We have said those who do not work - STARVE".[162] This is no-nonsense principle and might have support from Bible. This is purely in economical term. The concept of welfare is far away. The emperor was not in a mood to apply the ethical thought for his people. Here the question of inequality in capability of famine affected people and rest of the society is important. There was inequality in holding of primary-goods. Emperor and opponent did not put the principle of tolerance in political solution for desire of living together. There was absence of institutional famine relief and principle of social choice was outside the domain of political conception of justice. The theory of justice should not embrace for 'overlapping consensus' of philosophical and religious doctrines.

The social circumstances are important factor in political justice. In this world, under the social circumstances, lots of injustice is prevailing. In such society, the 'political liberalism' and 'principle of tolerance' application, is not easy and not helpful. This reduces the scope of political conception of justice.

Primary goods and capabilities

Lots of people have thought about the equality of opportunities in literature of justice. Rawls thought of 'primary goods' in 'differential principle' is a move in that direction. Primary goods include right, liberty, opportunity, Income and wealth as well as self respect. This is in direction of outcome of freedom enjoyed in equality and justice. Primary goods are not constitutive of freedom but means of freedom. Ronald Dworkin theory of 'equality of resources' broadly accounts for means of freedom.[163] Now the means has to convert into value. John Roemer had a formula in mathematical term. In this formula he interpreted "equality of resources implies equality of welfare".[164] Here the value of resourced is considered as resourced yield. You can say that equality of resources yield in equality of welfare. Ultimately it is the valuation of means into valuation of ends. Primary goods into freedom of choice will tell us the inequality in actual freedom enjoyed by different people due to different functioning from person to person.

---

[162] Ibid, page no.77.
[163] Ibid, page no.80.
[164] Ibid, page no.80.

In capability base assessment of justice actual freedom enjoyed is important. The freedom is the capability of a person to achieve the result of various alternative functioning. Capability as actual freedom is in two ways 1) Primary goods and 2) achievements. The point is a disable person has more primary goods but less capability. Another example: - in poverty study you come across such an illustration that a person may have more income and more nutritious intake but less freedom to live healthy life due to many reasons. In richer country a person may have less income and primary goods - characteristics of age, disability; susceptible of diseases then it is difficult for him to convert basic primary goods into capability. Now let us look in terms of achievements. One person has same capability as other person but choose the different functions to reach the goal. Two persons having same capability and goals end up in different outcome due to different strategies. It is a fact that disadvantageous people will get less from primary goods than others.

Diversities: Ends and personal characteristics.

There are two variations in primary goods as means and as achievement in the end.

1) Inter-end variation in the form of different conceptions of goods that different people have.

2) Inter-individual, in this, relation between resources and freedom to pursue end.

Rawls believes in first one with the understanding that same primary goods serve all different ends. The first variation is the cause of second one. Person's actual freedom works for his end. Now what end and what power to convert primary good in to ends is to be seen.

The human beings are diverse and have different mean and different end. The ethical and political consideration is more important in respect of justice of fairness. Diversity is our ability to convert resources into actual freedoms. The theory is most significant in relation to divert our attention from only inequality in outcome and achievement to opportunity and freedom. In Dr. Amartya Sen opinion freedom can distinguish from means that sustain it and achievements that it sustains.

Rawls in fact concerns with importance of liberal institutions and processes need to restrain public policy when personal liberty threatened. Theory of justice cannot ignore the difference in capability of space. Over all freedom to achieve cannot ignore negative freedom. Genuinely, we think in a sense of equality of freedom than it is equality of results and not equality of means. Freedom relates both.

7.6   Welfare economics and inequality

Space choice and evaluative purpose

Evaluation of inequality lies in polarity of spaces and diversity of individuals.

Inequality in different space is related to each other, diversity of human divides them apart. In the exercise of evaluation of inequality measurement for purpose, motivation is the factor in different spaces.

Interpersonal comparison and inequality assessment is with some purpose. It is a matter of interest to know how different level of well-being of different people.

Income distribution gives us little idea about inequality of welfare. The study of income distribution is having other motivation than well-being comparison. The study is useful to know about crime in society, social discontent by way of income inequality. We can check the primary goods distribution through public policy by a state or political system.

Short falls, attainments and potentials

An interesting point is in judging individual advantage, should advantage position of a person is positive as level of achievement or negative as shortfall is to be known. The assessment of achievement can be in two approaches. It is possible that result can be different for two distinct reasons.

1) The shortfall in maximum value varied between persons is due to ordering of absolute attainment can differ from respective shortfalls. 2) When we take maximum value for all then comparison is done in 'proportionate' attainments and shortfalls term and not in absolute term.

The first issue is important in assessment of inequality after acceptance of human diversity. Equality has two features1) attainment and 2) shortfall. Attainment equality is actual level of achievement and the definition for short fall in equality is of an actual achievement level minus from maximum achievement level.

In interpersonal inequality, achievement in proportionate is remote. Interpersonal inequality is clear in human diversity in terms of maximal.

Attainment equality is compared in terms and actual level of achievement. Shortfall in equality is the difference between actual achievement and maximal achievement. Human diversity is the cause of not allowing using potential equality than it is an uncertainty in assessing achievement, judging equality of achievement or freedom to achieve. Only circumstances are the answer to it.

A disable person is not in a position to attain equality then he should be given a chance, "on the base of fairness", to maximize his below par functioning ability rather than make him to accept shortfall.

John Rawls believed in "maxim" can be further taken up to 'to make the worst off to well-off as possible'. John Rawls 'differential principal' comes in way for maximum in primary goods; deprivation comes in field of "capability". A policy of attainment will lead to 'low level equality'. This is not true in sense that equality of many types such as aggregates inclusive of efficiency. Attainment equality, to achieve fully, will be difficult in a sense that it is unfeasible and inefficient.

Inequality, welfare and justice

The evaluative process for inequality is important. Analytical process motivated with many purposes. Inequality and social welfare has definite connection. An argument for social welfare will decide the connection in between them. Social welfare can be a function of individual utility at the same time it can be argued direct function as vector of income. Social welfare can be a function of individual distributing each commodity. The social welfare function can be termed as interpersonal comparison.

The question of "Equality of what" requires knowing the purpose and motivation behind it. Inequality evaluation is for analyzing social justice, basic structure in general political and social ethics. "Justice based inequality evaluation" is used in welfare economics. Here it is assumed that vector of income determines the level of social welfare in Dalton, Atkinson literature. In Indian philosophy, "Mimansa" is the word. The meaning of Mimansa is general good of people, in interest of public. The judgement should be delivered taking in to account this aspect.

Welfare - based inequality evaluation

HUGH DALTON (1920) found out a way to measure inequality in term of social welfare loss.[165]The formula is, given total income with the percentage shortfall of the actual sum-total of utilities from the maximal level. This formula is very useful for measurement and in interpersonal comparability of individual utilities. It is not easy to talk in percentage.

ATKINSON"S index of inequality operates on income and measures social loss involved in unequal income distribution in terms of short falls of equivalent incomes. It measures the inequality of a distribution of incomes by the percentage reduction of total income that can be sustained without reducing social welfare by distributing new reduced total exactly equally. This is known as 'equally distributed equivalent income' concept. Here the difference in actual income gives us the measurement of inequality. Atkinson index is widely used in public economic in general. This is useful for public policy making.

Inequality had descriptive and normative content. In normative approach inequality can go against an institutional. Example: - individual utility is liner function of individual income than in utilitarian social welfare function actual income is the same. Here the inequality level will be zero in social welfare concept. Atkinson measure shows how bad the income inequality is.

Dr.Amartya Sen has truly explained the ATKINSON measurement of inequality. "When there is slowly diminishing marginal utility, there is less inefficiency from unequal distribution of incomes, and it is this inefficiency in generating social welfare that the ATKINSON index really measures". [166] The social welfare function is additive in Atkinson concept can be dropped as the matter is related for inequality. When you consider social welfare function as individual well-being than variable relationship

---

[165] Ibid, page no.95.
[166] Ibid, page no.99.

between income on one side and function and capability on other side has to be taken in to account.

7.7   Poverty and Affluence

Inequality and poverty

Poverty means the number of people below poverty line. Poverty line is a level of income below which people are designated as 'poor.' Poverty index means proportion of the total population that happens to be below poverty line. This called HEAD COUNT THEORY. This theory is widely used in empirical literature on poverty and deprivation.

In measurement of poverty, two things are interrelated (1) Identification of poor (2) aggregation of statistics.

In traditional approach of identification is done by using 'poverty line' income as cut off. Aggregates are total number of poor person in proportion in population below poverty line. This is known as head count ratio. The possibility of little people below the poverty line or a lot and distribution of income among poor may or may not be unequal. An alternate theory in literature is "income gap". Here additional income needed to bring poor near to poverty line. The gap can be considered as per capita. Both are different approach for poverty.

In head count theory only the people below poverty line will be counted. Income gap theory does not take in to account number of poor but only average income gap of poor from poverty line. The transfer of income from one person, who is below poverty line, is transfer to another person, who is also below poverty line than it will not reflect in the changes either Head count or Income theory. The net effect will be poor person will be poorer. The aggregate poverty increased. Here deprivation will be more in case of poorer.

We have to measure the poverty. Let us say it by "P". P will be a function of Head count-"p"- and income distribution-"I". This will reflect into GINI coefficient as "G". Dr. Amartya Sen suggested "D" as deprivation in poverty should be taken into account for poverty measure. Poverty measure P depends upon "H", "I" and "G". Here head count and income theory taken together than the rank of nth person, given rank order weighting, is to be measured in terms of poverty. The richest poor have the least weight;

the poorest poor would have the highest weight. In head count theory, government will concentrate on richest poor to bring them above poverty line; in that case, poorer amongst poor will be more sufferers.

Ordinal approach used in Rank order weighting in social choice theory. This is BURDA (1781) theory.[167] This helps in Gini coefficient for inequality measurement. This successfully used in India, Bangladesh, Iran, Malaysia, United States, Brazil and several other countries. This approach used to measure income inequality.

The deprivation theory is based on income. So income is important in poverty. Dr.Amartya Sen is of the opinion that all the three should be taken in to account.

The nature of poverty

There is person 1 and person 2. Person 1 has slightly lower income than person 2. Now person 2 is having kidney problem and needs dialysis machine. We have to judge, who is poor? Person 1 is because of low income and person 2 because of capability restriction.

Poverty exists in society and it is recognized at a particular movement in context of question poses. Poverty evaluation is necessary. Poverty can be described and poverty can be of a policy matter. Poverty is due to deprivation. Deprivation will lead to policy recommendation. Now the question is society has to judge who is deprived in which way. Society has to decide in policy, how to remove poverty deficiencies. In the first case of poverty, description is primary and policy conclusion derivative. In second case, primarily focus of public action and description is derivative.

Poverty from descriptive to public action is the correct way to follow. Public fund should be available to implement the policy for deprivation. The negation of this will make us to redefine the poverty. It is reasoned that the economic hardship has to be eliminated than policy recommendation for fund, which should be available. One should not think that poverty is not there as we took action. Any recommendation should be feasible as we are having fund.

Next step is change in policy. Poverty and society are not independent. Social variances are an objective of study. Social variances are in agreement

---

[167]   Ibid, page no.104.

to deprivation. Basic general functioning and capability are in agreement. Example: - there may be intercultural agreement to avoid acute hunger in the society. Poverty is better seen as capability failure than failure of basic needs in the form of commodities. The motivation is in direction of achieving functioning and acquiring capability.

Lowness vis-à-vis inequality of incomes

We established poverty as failure of capability. The functioning analysis can be of elementary nature and complex nature. These are general functions. The specific functions vary from society to society due to fundamentals.

Poverty is as capability deprivation in two senses.

1) Low utility   2) Low income

One may think that why low income, low utility is not related to well-being. The poverty has link with deprivation and deprivation is in economic sense. Low income is important concept in poverty. Poverty is due to low income and not due to low well-being. Mr. Ramchandran has high income even though he failed in utilizing opportunity does not mean that he is poor. Adequate income is not the answer. The answer is income and resources can be converted into capability to function.

An inadequate capability results into inadequate income. Example: - a person with high metabolic conversion rate, parasitic disease requires more nutrient than normal man. He is unable to have same quantity of nutrient against normal person in term of income. Even though same income, first person capability is failure compare to normal person. So capability is important against achievement. We cannot consider resources as freedom.

Do concepts matter?

The idea of 'income inadequacy' is more important in the analysis of poverty than low income. The first one is more sensitive to convert income into capability. The income conversion into capability is in relation to the relative advantage in the opposite direction. As the income is only the criteria, ordering of poverty and identification of poor will be different in terms of size of income.

Now we define poverty as specific type of deprivation. This deprivation can be in1) biological reasons and 2) social factors.

Women have disadvantage to convert income into particular functioning. There are number of examples of such types. Income may not give the proper judgment in deprivation but capability failure is the right judgment.

The relation between income and capability affects to age, location, epidemiological atmosphere and many more parameters. Only Income in study of poverty will lose the importance as deprivation. The above factors reduce the ability to earn more and hard to convert into capability. The poor in advanced countries are facing this problem. Advanced countries underestimate such poverty. The disable person's income earning and income using will be different in generating capability. The aged person has number of limitations and it is -difficult to make income use in many areas.

Poverty in rich countries

In U.S.A., low income is not only the parameter to measure poverty. Other social environment and many more varieties of parameters are also associated. Capability deprivation is remarkably high in affluent countries. Studies have been conducted and found that U.S.A. person and Bangladeshi person are not at par in age. Bangladeshi can go beyond the age of 40 where as a citizen of New York may not cross this limit. This is due to crime; less medical help and other factors. The intense inequality of non-income in different group is there. The same way a black of U.S.A. in age group of 35 to 55 is having 2.3 times mortality than white of U.S.A. [168] The low income reason may be 50%; other parameters are of rest 50%. The rest 50% may be due to inadequacy of health care, violent mode of inter-city living, absence of social care and other factors.

Food deprivation in U.S.A. exists, compared to poor countries, even after adjusting the price difference. This is also a reason for hunger in spite of higher income compared to middle-income group of developing countries. Capability approach can help us to solve this paradox. The hunger is due to food intake and to make use of nutrient. The general health care is another important factor in capability. Relative deprivation in the space of income can yield absolute deprivation in the space of capability. The

---

[168]   Ibid, page no.114.

statistics proves the poverty, other than economic factor, at the same time the view of life is important.

The affluent people are having more diverse space basket and therefore they need more income compared to rural Indian native. Here the standard of living comes in picture. The moderate life style will help to spend more for other commodity and man can live in society with due status. The bigger basket of commodity variations takes the much of income. He is left for less for health care and nutrition.

7.8   Class, Gender and other groups

Class and classification

Inequality in space is due to the nature of human diversity. Equality in one space leads inequality in different spaces. Basically human is diverse in age, in gender, physical and mental ability and disability, epidemiological effects and social and economic bases. Equality of what can be proved by way of study of empirical data. The data is huge. We have to select one and decide priority about diversities. After that we have to ask in which context inequality is.

In general analysis, it is between groups rather than individuals. In this classification of groups, mostly the recent trend is to consider the economic class only. They are either the Marxist type or Wealth categories or income groups. This type of class base classification is useful in context of general political, social and economic analysis. This class will guide us for analysis in libertarian right for well-being or freedom to live life for some value. The inequality in wealth and income is considered as 'inequality of opportunity'.

In the theory of Marx – exploitation is the main theme. Here the hard working person gets little income and little toil person enjoy higher income.[169] Dr.Amartya Sen says-PROUDHON-economists contention was that Property is THEFT.[170] Marx had not accepted his views. Max gave proper account of time of labour and explains the contrast of poor and rich. The theory of exploitation is identifying who is producing what.

---

[169]   Ibid, page no.118.
[170]   Ibid, page no.118.

Male-Female ratio

South Asia, West Asia, China	0.93
North Africa	0.96
North America and Europe	1.05

An enjoyment of one person is a fruits of another person's labour, known as exploitation.

It is difficult to decide which factor of production has what share in product. PETER BAUER is of the opinion that one who produce has right to enjoy it.[171] He did not believe in theory of equality. Production is interdependent process. Many resources work at one time and it is not correct to decide arbitrarily. The marginal product concept is not thinking who has produced. The guiding factor is if one more unit of resources is used than what will happen. Here the rest of resources has very limited role than labour. Marx was also not clear about this.

The theory of exploitation is not sufficient in regard to economic opportunity and freedom. Class base analysis does not help to explain equality and freedom. Even if you remove the inequality in property then also lots of questions are unanswered about productive ability, needs and personal variations. Marx had understood the diversity of human and only said equal reward for equal work in connection of 'bourgeois Right'. Marx had agreed that equality in reward for work would not conflict with equality in satisfying needs. He distinctly understood the needs of workers. Marx noted the fact that different workers have different family size.

The income base approach will help after normalization and 'equivalence scale'. The argument of control of number of children is in parents hand has little importance. Primary goods or resources satisfy need. In equality the need will be different. This is a case of interpersonal comparison.

The resource distribution to satisfy need will be different. Now the wellbeing or equality thus goes beyond income theory and for that matter beyond Marx.

---

[171]   Ibid, page no.119.

We agreed with the variety of things. For freedom we have to go beyond the income theory. We have to take into account other diversities for life we live and freedom to enjoy. In case of class base analysis, disparity will be a part of it, race and colour of human as example. This definitely effects to human for employment, day-to-day living, medical assistance and assistance from police. These types of far reaching influences are there.

Gender and inequality

There is a systematic disparity for freedom of man and woman in the society. The freedom will not make man and woman equal in terms of higher income OR resources. Apart from income, in house, the division of labour, care, education and liberty will differ amongst the family members. In house inequality may be due to different need of members. Now the resource used and transformation into capability aspect has not studied in income distribution within the family. There is a differential treatment in men and women in the world and particularly in family in between boys and girls. In rural area of Asia and North Africa, the morbidity and mortality rate shows the difference in deprivation of female. This is in extra ordinary proportionate.

Higher death ratio of men in rich countries like North America and Europe is due to social reasons.[172] In South Asia, West Asia, China and North Africa women mortality is high, not due to biological disadvantage but it is due to 'attainment inequality' and 'shortfall of inequality'. In developing country, it is a case of general inequality and not the income inequality in family. Here the functional difference and disparity reflected into elementary capability to avoid the mortality and morbidity. The sub-Saharan Africa, anti-female nutrition results in morbidity and mortality is less, but there is big gender difference in terms of education, body mutilation, free to pursue independent career and leadership in capability. This affects to their freedom. Social capability difference is seen in female of rich countries. They have less mortality. Ultimately, this is a case of gender deprivation in terms of capability and freedom than income or primary resources.

Interregional contrasts

The empirical examples study show in term of interregional comparison between the inequality by way of income and inequality in achieving

---

[172]   Ibid, page no.123.

capability in basic functions. A factor of long live in standard of living is having impressive difference in case of income per head.   This will be compared in terms of GNP and income per head and life expectancy in birth. [173]

Interregional contrasts

	G.N.P	Premature mortality
South Africa	$2470	53 to 60 years
Brazil	$ 2540	53 to 60 years
Gabon	$2960	53 to 60 years
Oman	$5220	53 to 60 years
China	$350	70 years
Sri Lanka	$430	70 years

Some time life expectancy of rich country and poorer country may be nearly same. [174]

	GNP per heard	life expectancy
U.S.A.	GNP-per head is $20910	75 years
Costa Rica	GNP-per head is $1780	75 years

We divert our attention from income to functioning and capability than picture will change drastically.   The comparison is regarding social, educational and epidemiological. Here the public policy comes in a picture.

In China, Sri Lanka and Costa Rica, the communal health services and medical care, basic education has played a great role. Here is a distinction in income deprivation and capability functioning in public policy.

In large country like India, one state may be way ahead than other state. [175]

	Literacy ratio	Female literacy ratio	life expectancy
Kerala	91%	87%	70 years
All India	52%	39%	57 years

In China and India, male female ratio is 0.93 where as Europe, North America and sub-Sahara Africa is excess in female than male. The male female ratio in Kerala is 1.04 is equal to 1.05 of Europe and North American

---

[173] ibid, page no.125-126.

[174] Ibid, page no.126.

[175] bid, page no.127.

rich countries. [176] Kerala GNP is lower in India compared to other countries but it is failed to explain high capability level to premature mortality. Kerala capability achievement is due to public policy in education and health care, food distribution in comparison to rest of India. The women property right in particular and politics in general had played a great role.

7.9   The demands of equality

Questions of   Equality

We should ask to egalitarianism that why equality and of what equality? Equality can judge by (1) Diversity of human being in personal characteristics and external circumstances (2) Plurality of spaces–income, wealth, utilities, liberty, primary goods, capability. These can be compared.

We have seen that due to diversity of human, equality of one space do not coincide with each other. Equality at one space may be inequality at another space. Second approach is dealing with real approach to equality in connection of freedom to achieve and actual achievement. This was discussed in terms of capability to functions. Capability approach is freedom to achieve in general and capability to function in particular.

Equality, space and diversity

Any ethical theory of social arrangements will demand equality in space, equal treatment in human respect. The space will differ from one theory to other theory say-libertarians for liberty, egalitarians for equal income and wealth and utilitarian for equal weight in everyone utility. The difference in approach will give different answer. Equality of what is the distinction between diverse ETHICAL approaches to social arrangements.

Therefore it is important that all theories should have some common thing. Each theory should defend and found out why equality. The why takes us to what equality? We have to take basic equality as in individual feature in conception of social justice and political ethics. If you take one space and examine the concept of equality then other spaces will dispute the equality. This is a conflict of principle.   Therefore "BASAL EQUALITY" concept

---

[176]   Ibid, page no.127.

is necessary. BASAL EQUALITY will explain the claim and denial of claim. The need of basal demand including equality requires tolerance of inequality. The thought of basic equality is very broad. Dr.Amartya Sen has tried to give all to gather new thing in welfare economics.

Plurality, incompleteness and evaluation

Basal equality has certain amount of plurality with demand of equality in various forms. The inequality will be ambiguous here in terms of ranking compared to full equality. We have to find out inequality to what extent is in the ranking. This "Internal plurality" related to (1) Heterogeneity of space and (2) the measurement of distance and distributional inequality in homogeneous variable. The examples of heterogeneities are (1) Liberty for different rights (2) Primary goods of different types (3) different capability and (4) diverse utility.

In Basel categories, ethical theory is including more than one variable-Liberty and well-being, well-being and agency, freedom and achievement. This is ethical in practice where as Heterogeneity looks like moral philosophy.

There are different ways to evaluate the equality in homogeneous space by using distinct method to measure inequality. The variation of inequality can measure in terms of coefficient of variance, Gini effect, standard deviation etc. in given space. We use the different measurements to measure inequality having good reasons behind it. The different measurement may conflict with each other.

In measurement, we may use different ranking and combining and uniting the space in terms of weight. By applying all ways and means as discussed above, some ambiguities will remain in the ordering of equality and inequality. The ambiguities are creating problems in decision theory and social choice theory. Analysis of theories has asked for reasoned decision in spite of ambiguity. In inequality, when you use shared partial ranking in which all desirable features move together. The intersection partial ordering places X above Y if and only if X is better than Y accordingly to all the desirable features. [177]

---

[177]   Ibid, page no.133.

Intersection requires scrutiny of desirable features. The different criteria are conflicting in ranking two alternatives than that pair should be left unranked. When more information required then plurality should exclude and extension of partial ordering should allow. Some time incompleteness in inequality may be in concept itself or because of lack of information or in respect of the disagreement amongst parties. Arbitrarily to complete the partial ordering will be misleading step. It is difficult to judge in partial ranking view of interpersonal comparison and assessment of inequality that whether we have more equality in situation "A" than situation "B". In social and political dispute, clear equality is unattractive.

Data, observations and effective freedoms

Data problem can restrict our calculation. It will be difficult in such a situation to represent capability set. In absence of data, in capability set, one has to take functioning combination as base and judge the actual opportunity enjoyed. In such situation, one has to accept partial capability set. The data limitation makes our motivation lower to accept lower capability set in practical position. Freedom can assess in terms of "Effective freedom" and "Freedom as control". There may be limited comparison in freedom as an outcome. In particular circumstances, observed functioning can tell us about well-being achieved as well as freedom enjoyed. Available data can give us more precise picture of freedom and inequality.

Aggregation, egalitarianism and efficiency

Internal plurality has to be supplemented by recognizing claims of spaces in Basel equality. The aggregative and distributive consideration will raise conflict in basal equality no matter which space is chosen. "Efficiency" is the common element in aggregation. Efficiency is a part of our moral sentiments. Efficiency considered in economy in "PARETO OPTIMALITY" in space of utility. This is a weak condition in a sense that it cannot raise the utility of all. This used in welfare economic vary widely without any controversy. Pareto optimality is priority of space of utility then the claim of liberties, freedoms.

Aggregation takes us in different direction in case of equality in general. When we consider the case of basal equality, we should not forget the plurality of ethics, which takes us beyond equality. The aggregate and distribution will differentiate on the bases of assessment in terms of result. Example:-conflict between increasing total income and reducing distributional inequalities in incomes, or between rising aggregate utility and decreasing interpersonal utility difference. The other space may be in contrast but not in result. Say promoting some rights in general and these rights seeking equal distribution is a conflicting thing. The aggregate and distribution is necessary in social evaluation. Aggregate requires thinking for what to include and what weight to be given. We are giving equal weight to each person in utilitarian than it becomes egalitarian stand. The demand of equality may come in many distinct contexts, in quite different ways. The equality may influence the aggregative objectives, the demand of maximize the aggregative object is not the demand of equity.

Alternative defences of inequality

The equality of social arrangements can be argued in three ways (1) The wrong space argument (2) incentive argument (3) operational asymmetry argument. This will not dispute the equality in social arrangements.

The wrong space argument: - The variable is not right one in terms of equality required. Here the equality in other space is inter alia therefore equality in particular space is in dispute. Equality in terms of capability is itself an argument on equality in other space.

The next two arguments are showing the conflict between equality and efficiency in the same space. It is a fact that inequality is a bad thing but removal of inequality will result in worst thing.

Efficiency based critics of equality has two arguments. The first one is 'incentive argument' and second one is 'operational argument.'

Incentive argument is much discussed in literature. Incentive should be given to people to do right things and promote the objectives. Inequality will work for investment, enterprise and more work. It is understood that objectives are aggregate type. The efficiency is in any type of objective say-aggregate and distributive. The incentive argument is in individual term.

Egalitarian policy was criticized on the ground of social goals including equality. This went wrong in recent period-say Maoist china or redistribution in welfare state policy.

The operational asymmetry is about aggregates only. This is encouraged by inequality due to operational asymmetry. People's skill and ability difference requires asymmetry. Inequality will be there, if more power given to capable man. The asymmetry requires because of social role. The person requires more power or authority to help everyone. The indivisibility in economic operation and technology nature will help for asymmetry on the ground of aggregate objectives. Here a personal incentive problem is not the reason but social role of asymmetry is important.

Incentives, diversity and egalitarianism

Incentive argument is most famous in economic literature. Incentive explains deep rooted human diversity. The inequality evaluation is the reason for incentive argument. In this sense, incentive argument is different than popular understanding. In welfare economic model, mainly the difference between different persons achievement comes from disparity in efforts and decision variable and not from diversity in productive ability. This difference is in relation to motivation and opportunity in incentive argument.

If you say that incentive argument is only the result of human diversity and not the difference in decision than it is wrong. Incentive argument is in relation to inequality and freedom. It is solely not the diversity. Example: - You say that only gender or age is responsible for inequality in capability then a policy decision can be taken that the special help will be provided to such gender or aged member of society. Now the point is age is not in your control and it is very hard to change gender, the incentive to this type of problem may not help. People may speak lie about age or gender but not of much help to convince.

Here the incentive argument will help little to egalitarian than standard economic model as individual future is changing due to own chosen level of application. Incentive argument has less stand in light of special medical help because no one wish to have disease and not for longer period. Look at other way as the medical relief is free or heavily subsidies than they will take less precaution and negligent about illness. This is also not true that treatment is free to you to invite diseases. In policy you can decide the medical help could be free in special genetic and or environmental risk of illness.

In egalitarian theory the inequality is related with human diversity which is not a problem due to incentive policy or inequality due to difference in effort and application. An incentive argument is focusing much on effort and application. The factor behind unequal freedom is gender, age and class which are of much concern.

On equality as a social concern

Capability approach is the base to judge the individual advantage. This capability approach is for evaluating the equality and can be use for assessing efficiency also. You think that capability is economic efficiency. It will reflect as no one's capability can be further enhanced while maintaining the capability of everyone else at least at the same level. You can accept aggregate in social evaluation, which will make difference in equality assessment. Efficiency will help in understanding the demand of equality. The equality interpretation depends on other considerations. These considerations are internalising. These will help to understand equality in much lighter way.

The attainment equality and short fall equality are there. The attainment equality is useful due to weight given to aggregate consideration. Example: - Person A is in a position to achieve X as his potential; whereas general achievement is 2X of all others. The A's achievement is hampered due to some reason. The argument is we should lower others' achievement to achieve X for person A. This does not mean that in equality we should bring down the 2X level to X level. Here shortfall equality has some merit. In such cases, the achievement of all others should be proportional to their maximal value. This will be a liberal view. Person A will be given preferential treatment to achieve higher efficiency. Here the efficiency is included in equality in aggregate terms. These two terms, aggregate and efficiency come to the help of equality. In such circumstances it is the case of attainment equality.

Rawls used the difference principle as primary goods in 'justice of fairness'. He is supporting the claim of capability in judging individual advantage. Rawls was equating the capability in the interest of public policy. Rawls asserted that the public post should be filled by open competition for fairness. This is put into practice than it will end up in unequal capability. Rawls was of the opinion that greater skilled person should be employed rather than people differ in moral, intellectual capacity and skill. This is an example of operational asymmetry argument.

Dr. Amartya Sen agreed with Rawls argument for higher skilled person appointment. Here the question is "why" one should agree with Rawls. The efficiency is the right point for the answer. The merit base selection of person and influential position relates to efficiency. Dr.Amartya Sen says the person with lower mental skilled is not his/her fault and such people should not penalized. In influential position and officers are not working with efficiency than the argument of Rawls acceptable. The inequality is there for indifference in capability in influential position and officer's appointment. The inequality should consider as efficiency and not inequality as everyone had opportunity to compete. This is justified in terms of aggregative consideration. This proves that the primary goods in individual advantage are not proper against capability approach. The demand of equality should be supplemented with efficiency.

Rawls had given importance to efficiency consideration in the interest of worst off people. Rawls maxim formula is accommodated in individual advantage which does not record inequality but readily record the space of capability. Here political scrutiny is poorer in information sense. Here capability should be replaced by efficiency for examination.

In case of open competition, it creates a "Meritocracy" which treats less favoured group, unequally treated. The argument should be granted for freedom to appear for competition. The system should absorb the impact of aggregative and distributive aspect in freedom and capability in the name of justice.

Responsibility and fairness

Rawls and Ronald Dworkin were thinking that a person is responsible for matters, which are in his control. Responsibility is not attributes of a person. Person can change his responsibility. Rawls theory of justice as fairness criticized in capability perspective due to person's difficulty to convert primary goods into actual freedom achieved. A person is less able to use the primary goods to secure freedom is disadvantage, compared to the person–placed in favourable position; even though both are having the same bundle of primary goods. This difference has to take note in the theory of justice as fairness.

Person's position can be judged in given choice between achievement and freedom. The individual can claim on society that he should be given freedom to achieve. If individual is wasting the opportunity given to him than he is responsible. This has direct relevance to capability. The person has no control over adversity of event, than he is not responsible. A person gambles incurred loss than he cannot go out of responsibility.

Person must have adequate information so he can take correct decision in risky position. An insurance company OR bank becomes bankrupt and person is not compensated. Here an account holder has freedom to chose, which a case of freedom to choose is a case of freedom achieved. The Person's knowledge, ability to understand, and ability to choose in alternative is a case of actual achievement.

The capability should be accounted in real freedom enjoyed by person. Now a person is not showing courage in social condition to choose then it does not come under ethical assessment. One should not say that person had not effective choice. This is a case of real freedom enjoyed after taking in to account all barriers and social discipline.

There is a difference in a person who manages his desire and a person who do not courage to achieve desire. "Manage to desire" is one of limiting aspects of utilitarian ethics. In capability account, this is a negative point. People do have the capability. In entrenched inequality, person chooses the comparative deprivation and accepts victimized condition.

Capability, freedom and motivations

The 'capability approach' has to offer for evaluation of well being and assessment of freedom. Capability to well-being differs in two ways. Well-being is a shift of commodity and resources to functioning. This is a constitute elements of well-being. Second, the set of alternative functioning vector is available for person's choice. Here the capability set is a freedom which person enjoyed for well-being. If ability to choose in alternate is worthwhile to live life than capability set has further role in determining the person's well-being. The set "S" is having number of function. A person chooses "X" functioning from "S" set in which "X" belongs, than the well-being of person is dependent on his doing. The well-being of a person is not dependent on "X" but on the choice of "X" from that set of "S".[178]

Capability approach is much broader than well-being. In well-being freedom is important either instrumental or actual. Apart from instrumental freedom, for good society, freedom enjoyed is important. Therefore, society should prefer individual freedom. Equality of freedom can be a one of the evaluative foundations. Capability approach should be used to assess and analyzed the equality of freedom in each motivation.

The poverty is seen as capability failure. This may be due to various factors. The poverty analysis from low income to insufficient basic capability is important. This related to the foundation of equality of freedom. This provides guideline

---

[178] Ibid, page no.150.

for proprieties for elimination of poverty in rich countries like Europe and America.

7.10 Philosophy of welfare in inequality:-

The first chapter was regarding basic thing that how the collective choice rules works in human life and economics. The second chapter was about development. Earlier development means everything. Now welfare is the meaning of development. In this chapter, freedom of individual is most important. We show freedom can be achieved and what different aspects of freedom are. Ultimately freedom is in Rawls thinking as political fairness and justice. Now we talk regarding inequality.

One can see inequality in society. Equality is necessary for economical and political philosophy. Equality can be defined in Utilitarian, Libertarian and egalitarian concepts. Equality of why and how is important. Equality is as impartiality, liberty of space in turn income and many variables. Income reflects in standard of living and freedom to achieve. Utilitarian and libertarian both believed in achievement.

Political and moral philosophy is in favour of freedom. The heterogeneity of society is the reason for inequality of converting resources and primary goods in to achievement. Capability works two ways. It works for well-being and freedom to pursue well-being. Achieved functioning is well-being and freedom to achieve well-being is capability. Well-being and inequality are recent subjects.

Evaluative approach has information constrain. Welfare analysis of poverty in developing country, you have short list of items and in case of economic development a long list of items. The agency aspect and well-being aspect is interdependent. Inequality can be assessed in well-being and agency aspect. A well-being aspect has importance in analysis of social inequality and assessment of public policy.

Theory of justice demands basal equality. Rawls' theory of Justice as fairness is important in economics. Disable person will be looser in case of primary goods conversion into capability and in terms of achievement due to different strategies and different functioning. Human beings are diverse and their goals, function and strategies are different therefore inequality in capability will affects for freedom to achieve and freedom to enjoy.

Deprivation is intense in inequality. Inequality and social welfare has definitive relation. Inequality analysed social justice, structure of general politics and social ethics. Justice based evaluation is used in welfare economics.

Measurement of poverty in society is important for policy matter. Functioning can be of general as well as complex nature. Poverty as deprivation has low utility and low income. Poverty in terms of deprivation can be biological as well as social factor. Pregnant woman need more income. Old age person need more income due to deprivation of opportunity to earn more. Income earning and income using will be different in case of handicap person. Poor cannot convert their capability in earning of income in rich countries. People are facing the problem of deprivation of food and other social requirements in rich countries.

Human is diverse in gender, age, physique, mental ability and social and economic bases. This creates inequality and it is analysed in intergroup variations. Female members in the family does not get that importance compares to man. They are deprived in case of food, education, health and liberty. In South Asia, West Asia, China and North Africa male female ratio is different than Europe or North America. Female of rich country has social capability difference.

The equality in space gives requirement for inequality. All three concepts will create inequality1) incentive 2) competition 3) Efficiency. In operational asymmetry argument, capable person is given power with a view to help to all but this will not fulfil. Incentive policy is in reducing inequality due to diversity. The open competition for filling the job is the test of efficiency, capability and moral.

Rawls and Ronald Dworkin thought that person is responsible for the responsibility which in his control. A person not showing courage and not choosing space than ethically person is not responsible. Commitment is related to responsibility. The tolerance is necessary in society.

Individual well-being and freedom is the good sign of the society. Poverty is seen as capability failure. Various underlying concerns can help to improve capability in policy. The rich countries are using this concept for poverty elimination.

Inequality is thought in various ways in every quarter of life and society. In any regards, Inequality is not accepted by all. This will spoil the social and economical health of any country. This is the real welfare of human.

Now we go to the last chapter. In this chapter we are examining and analysing the crucial question of hunger, starvation and famine.

8 The doctrine of Anekantvada in Jain philosophy

8.1 The doctrine of Anekantvada

One, who understood anekantvada, will understand the Jain philosophy. In nut shell, the entire philosophy of anekantvada is to accommodate the different views.

Definitions

(1) To view a thing not only from a single point of view, but to examine it from all possible points of views is the simple meaning of the doctrine of anekantvada.

(2) Anekantvada proves the existence of apparently contradictory properties like eternal and perishable in the same thing.

(3) Anekantvada is speculative method of looking at a thing, where as Syadvad is the way of its expression. Syadvad is called KATHANCHIDVADA. Syadvad is helpful in understanding the viewpoint of others.

(4) Anything is neither eternal nor transitory but is both eternal as well as transitory. To admit this is anekantvada.

(5) To examine a thing from every possible point of view, to have frame of mind favourable for such examination and try to examine in that manner is called the ANEKANTVADA.

(6) The meaning of anekantvada is to look at, to think over and to test everything from different point of view. If person wants to understand its real meaning, then person calls it APEKSHAVADA. The term apeksha means the stand point or intention of thinker.

(7) The anekant doctrine of the Jain has for its province all the fundamental things, sentient as well as non-sentient.

(8) Our wisdom is quite limited, so without possessing infinite knowledge, we cannot know about the endless properties of a thing. Nevertheless, we can definitely know, according to the power of our intellect, many of its properties clearly visible.

(9) The "Un manifested" and the "Manifested" real should be recognized as possess of different characteristic and to strictly speaking as not entirely identical. They are identical and different both-identical in so far as it is the same substance and different in so far as it under goes a change of characteristic. This is the Jain position of non-absolutism.

The entire lot of definitions give some specific angle and talks about anekantvada. It gives the different alternative names for anekantvada. It talks about plurality of things. At the same time, it talks about two things which can be opposite in nature and sustains in one thing. This is highly logical. In fact it has many sides and as our intellect is limited; we can have partial truth of the matter. Anekantvada is a thought principle of friendship. In anekantvada, person is talking from his own point of view. The absence of VIVEK – the judgment of good and bad becomes the boiling point and then it goes out of control. One should be tolerant to others' view. One should have patience to hear the other person.

8.2   History Of Anekantvada

The systematic exposition of this doctrine found only in Jain scriptures that embody the preaching of lord Mahavir.

The development of the doctrine first found in the commentary of TATTAVARTHADHIGAMA SUTRA written by Shri UMASWATIJI - a well-known Jain scholar.

The full-fledged discussions of the doctrine of Anekantvada is found in the works written from 5ᵗʰ century to 10ᵗʰ century by such great Jain scholars as Siddhsen, and Samantbhadra, Mallavadi, Pujyapada, Simhaksamasramana, Haribhadra, vidyanandi, Prabhacand and Abhayadeva. Samantbhadra introduced a new style to discuss the philosophical problems based on Anekantvada. We could clearly see the contribution given for Anekantvada doctrine from 10ᵗʰ century to 18ᵗʰ century by Vadidevsuri, Acarya Hemchandra and Yasovijayaji. [179]

This synthesis found first in a slight degree, in discussion of syadvad, found in the work of Siddhsen and Samantbhadra. However, latter on, this same synthesis of Anekantvada with the doctrine of monism and other system of philosophy is found clearly on a larger scale in the discussion of Nayas, found in the work of Haribhadra, Aklanka, Vidyananad and Abhaydeva. Commentator like Abhayadeva was very fond of discussing Anekantvada doctrine on an extensive scale. [180] Looking to the wonderful power of assimilation and synthesis of this doctrine of Anekantvada, the historical tendency of the Jain acarya were in giving a place to different doctrines in their discussion of naya.

We can see a great resemblance found to the Anekantvada in the system of Ishavashya Upanishad. Ishavashya Upanishad describes "ATMAN" as a substance, which moves and does not move, which is near and far, which is inside and outside. Later on, this reflected in Vedanta and in writing of Nimbarkar, Ramanuja and Vallabhacarya along with Buddhist. Some said it is a thought of VIBHAJYAVADA – division. QURAN suggests 'to you your religion and to me mine'.[181]

Development of Anekantvada

The Nasdak sutra-Rg Ved declared two things. (1) Positive-affirmation, (2) Negative –negation, this is described as (1) neither a being or (2) nor non-being. There was neither air nor sky above, But something different.[182]

---

[179]   Muni shri Jina Vijay and Rashiklal C.Parikh, Sanmati Tarka, Page no.133-134

[180]   Ibid, page no.134.

[181]   Editor Tara Sethia, Ahimsha, Anekant and Jainism, Essay of Kamla Jain, page no. 122

[182]   Surendranath Dasgupta, A history of Indian Philosophy, Vol.no.1. page no.33

It seems that origination of seven fold prediction lies in SANJAY BELATIPUTTA's agnosticism. Sanjay develop fivefold formula to answer metaphysics and moral question as reported in SAMANNAPHALA SUTRA of Dighanikaya-1. All the five answers are negation only. [183]

Question-"Is it this (or so)?" Answer "NO".

Question- "Is it that (or thus)?" Answer "NO".

Question- "Is it otherwise (different from both above)?" Answer "NO."

Question- "IS IT NO (at all there)?" Answer "NO".

Question "IS it not, that it is not (at all there)?" Answer "NO".

Historically it seems that SANJAY BELATIPUTTA period was either earlier or similar to Lord Mahavir's period.

Lord Mahavir and his treatment to Anekantvada

Lord Mahavir preferred a conditional affirmation to the answers of questions about after life. I think this is perfectly in line with a theory of transmigration of JIVA from one gati to another gati, in relation to time- past, present and future. Lord Mahavir put the answer in affirmative "YES" and used the word "SYAT". The insertion of qualifying phrase "SYAT" which emphasise the relative truth of the predication, is dictated by a twofold necessity of, firstly, furnishing a necessary proviso and, secondly, a corrective against the absolutist ways of thought and evolution of reality. Syat is consisting at least one part of truth in it.

Lord Mahavir put the principle of TOLERANCE in anekantvada. The beautiful expression of anekantvada is the importance we give to our thought, the same importance we should give to other person's thought too. Every person expresses his views as per circumstances, in relation to his mental condition and experience. Human knowledge is limited therefore it express the truth partly and it is one sided.

---

[183]   Bimal Krishna Matilal, The central philosophy of Jainism, (Anekantvada) page no.47.

Makhali Gosala and others thought

Another learned personality, Makhali Gosala of Ajivaka was contemporary of Lord Mahavir. Gosala developed a "TRAIRASIKA"[184] three-termed formula. Gosala declared that everything has three characters. (1) Existent –sat (2) not existent-asat (3) Both–living and non- living-sadasat. BUDDHA put it in a little different way. Buddha said four-fold alternative. This is in Madhyamika of Buddhist literature.[185] The fourth one is "Neither …Nor…." The answer is negative given by Nagarjurna.[186]

In Bhagvati Sutra, there are three dialogues of which the first one says that a certain thing is eternal from the stand point of dravya and non eternal from that of bhav. The second is that a certain thing is eternal from the stand point of dravya and non eternal from that of paryaya. The third is that the certain thing is eternal from the stand point of avyuchittinaya, non eternal from that of vyuchittinaya. [187]

In terms of an atom as self, the possibilities are (1) It is (2) it is not. In terms of more than two, three, four, up to six atoms aggregates, there are in all 23 possibilities. Bhagvati sutra disallowed three possibilities out of total 26 possibilities. [188] Therefore a loose atom has three possibilities and aggregates made up from two atoms onward describable through six possibilities. Jinbhadra gave this definition in his book "VISESAVASYAKABHASYA."

Samantbhadra in Aptamimasa stated that there are four points of views. (1) It is. (2) It is not (3) it is and it is not (4) it is inexpressible.

Positive and negative in the same substance

We have seen in definition the characteristics of anekantvada.

We see contradictory elements in the same thing. Say- a person can be a father, son, father in law and son in law and uncle. A person is father in the eyes of his son and same person as father-in-law in the eyes of daughter-in-

---

184   Ibid, page no.49.
185   Ibid, page no. 48.
186   Ibid, page no.49.
187   K.K.Dixit, Jain Ontology, page no.24
188   Ibid, page no.26.

law. We accept opposite attribute from different stand points in one and the same person.

We can accept the permanence and impermanence in the same thing. When we talk about a pot made out of clay. The clay has changed in the form of pot. Here the pot is paryaya-mode. One can say that the pot is paryaya-(mode) not absolutely different than clay. Clay itself is known as pot. We break pot and make bowl than the mode or form or appearance will change but clay remains as it is. Here the question is whether it is permanent or impermanent. Clay assumes the mode first as pot and thereafter bowl. Here the pot and bowl were made out of clay. One can say that clay is permanent and the pot-mode is impermanent but pot is made out of clay therefore it is permanent and impermanent. This two different stand points are anekantvada. Here you reconcile the thing with another from different stand points. Different stand points are synthesized in a coherent whole in syadvad.

Three characteristics of substance

Jain philosophy says that the substance has ORIGINATION, DESTRUCTION, and PERMANENCE nature. Take an example of golden necklace. The Necklace is made out of gold. Now we break the necklace and make the bangles out of this. In that case the earlier necklace was origination and when broken, it is destruction and again it turns in to bangle than it is origination. Now the necklace and bangle were made out of GOLD. The substance of gold remains as it is. Here gold has permanent nature. The whole process proves the origination, destruction and permanent nature of substance. Such instances are present everywhere.

The substance persists in this world in gross or subtle form and ultimately in the form of atom. The atom, independently or jointly combines in the form of aggregate gives the new effect. The aggregate persists in world and gets changing in to various modes. This proves that atom is not ceased but changed. The atom is not destroyed. This is unalterable universal law.

The substance changes the mode is called PARYAYA and the substance, which is eternal, called DRAVYA. The method of describing a thing as neither absolutely permanent nor absolutely impermanent but as permanence-cum-impermanence is known as syadvad.

Now if the soul does not have a changing effect then it is absolutely permanent. In this state soul cannot experience happiness and unhappiness. The happiness and unhappiness is always with soul. This is the result of meritorious karma and non-meritorious karma. This influences the soul. This is impossible in the state of eternal permanence. The bondage and liberation of soul comes in the question. Bondage is due to conjunction of karma with soul. Here the thing was previously absent and later it becomes present. This does not fit in the formula of unchanging nature of soul. Therefore the liberation is the totally free stage from karma which is permanent nature of soul and not free from karma is impermanent nature of soul-that is bondage. Soul goes through changes even though the soul remains as eternal. Soul goes in change from one birth to another birth and gradually gathers the excellence of spirituality.

We take soul as impermanent; than it is purely momentary. The moment coming into being and pass away in nothingness. In such cases, the soul cannot be an author of deeds which gives good and bad effects in the form of karma. The doer and enjoyer position is zero. The soul cannot experience happiness and unhappiness due to momentariness. The question of Punya and Pap does not arise. As a result the bondage and liberation has no meaning. Now the sole is momentary, over many births, soul cannot enjoy the fruits of good deeds. We take soul as eternal than the change of happiness and unhappiness will not affect. The sentient soul cannot be considered as absolutely permanent or impermanent.

The reality in Jain philosophy is considered as origination, destruction and permanence. From modes point of view, it is origination and destruction and substance point of view, it is permanent.

General and particular characteristics

The substance has both, general and particular qualities. When an owner of elephant says "this is an elephant" "this is an elephant" in the group of elephants. The owner in general said about elephant and in particular that particular elephant belongs to him. Here owner cognate the identity. The general and particular are independent and the thing is having both the nature. This is possible due to syadvad as it synthesise two view points.

Particular are of two types (1) Quality (2) Mode. One can say that particular is either quality or mode. Material is with quality and the quality exists in substance. They co-exist. The mode is change in substance. The modes come one after another. The modes are non co-existent in substance. Thus quality is different from mode. Quality is embedded in substance; therefore it is "sahabhavi". Mode is appearing at one moment and disappearing at another moment there for "krambhavi". Here one mode gives place to another mode. The substance gets change due to quality. One can understand that the quality is cause and mode is effect. The quality in terms of capacity resides in substance in position of infinite numbers. The same way infinite numbers of modes are manifest in three phase of time. Now the different modes can appear simultaneously due to different qualities in the substances but different modes belonging to same class cannot appear in the substance due to one quality. Substance is having one quality, but it can produce only one mode at one time and not more than one modes at the same time.

A shield is made out of gold on front side and back with silver. Now a person facing front side of shield will say it is made out of gold. The person looks from back side of shield will say it is made out of silver. Both persons are right in their respective standpoints. Only third person inspects the shield both the side and declared that it is made out of gold as well as silver. The first and second person is right in their judgment partially. They show only one side of shield. The third person is having total knowledge of shield therefore he is completely true. One sided view never gives complete truth. Third person observes all possible aspects of thing, knows all possible attributes of it from various standpoints.

The true function of anekantvada is to give effect. The synthesis of different opposite view points to make them consistent with one another from different stand points. These will help to achieve harmony in society, reduce the conflicts and quarrels by way of liberal view and noble thoughts. Anekantvada will create friendly atmosphere and universal brotherhood. The world will turn into blissful and welfare state.

Anekantvada reconcile the conflicting views. The partial truths are synthesis and co-ordinate them in one final grand truth as Anekantvada. The opposite view teaches us to understand the stand point. Here the tolerance of intellectual level will increase to respect the same.

Someone may say that anekantvada is the doctrine of doubt. It describes permanence and impermanence, existent and non-existent at one and the same time. Anekantvada tells us to ascertain the different standpoints from particular attributes from particular standpoint.

8.3   Syadvad

The other significant corollary of Anekantvada is Syadvad, which takes note of these numbers of possibilities of thought and gives a logical and verbal expression to it in its predication form of SAPTABHANGI (seven-fold prediction) incorporating affirmation, negation and inexpressibility along with their combinations. Someone asks the question is the pot impermanent? The answer is "yes". Here the statement is untrue or incomplete. The person who gives answer is wrong. He thinks that he has taken after full consideration all the aspects of a thing in to account. Logically it is proved that pot is permanent as well as impermanent. If you say it from ONE particular point of view then it should make clear in the answer, it is from one particular standpoint only. If this is so then the statement should be said in such a way that it does not avoid the negative standpoint in the answer. One should use the word "syat" in the statement to avoid the confusion about permanence and impermanence. Syat means from a particular point of view. There is another word "KATHANCIT". The meaning is from "certain stand point". These predictions are complementary because affirmation implies the negation of its opposite and negation implies the affirmation of its opposite. Every proposition is true, but only under certain conditions, i.e. hypothetically. Naya is not false though. It is partial knowledge, provided it takes stock of a real attribute without asserting or implying the negation of other attributes.

Our worldly dealing is the result of one standpoint which is in presence and useful to the purpose. Due to this any one property comes in to highlight. In our worldly dealing we avoid the word syat due to determine aspects in predicating thing.

The question can be answered in two way basically-"yes" and "no". This way mode of answer is called "bhanga". Mathematically there are maximum seven bhanga-possibilities. Anything can be examined from these seven points of view. There can be maximum seven questions about the property of a thing. It can be answered in any one particular possibility. It is used in seven different ways of judgments which affirm, negate, severally and jointly, without, self-contradiction, thus discriminating the several qualities of a thing. From seven-fold predication, the knowledge of mutually consistent predicates, affirmative, or negative in respect of one subject derived. All seven-fold assertions understood as subject to the conditions with objectively demarcate the attributes.

Substance and infinite aspects

A thing is having innumerable dharma – aspects. For Example: - Table- it has Height, length, breadth and made out of what type of material and with or without colour, used for writing, eating, computer etc. There can be any number of qualities and any number of modes. The doubt comes in to existence due to your curiosity. You can raise the doubts in seven ways only. Seven possibilities cover everything. When we say table made out of wood than other aspects are not in limelight. It highlights one aspect and it keeps other aspects on low profile. Lord Mahavir applied the word 'Syat' and decided a limit of it. A person with his knowledge and by using word 'syat' can see a limit. The very word cannot rule over other aspects and it does not deny the other aspects of a thing at the same time. By applying this technique, you are not opposing others. This is a very good way of accommodating all different views. The view called Syadvada, since it holds all knowledge to be only probable. This is anekantvada. Anekantvada is not the whole truth but it takes us near to the truth. A person believes in anekant will never say that particular view is right or wrong.

Role of Seven predications

The final form of seven predictions is as follows.

(1) The pot certainly exists (It is).

(2) The pot certainly does not exist. (It is not).

(3) From certain point of view pot exists, and from another point of view certainly it does not exist (It is and it is not).

(4) The pot is certainly inexpressible (It is indescribable).

(5) From certain point of view, the pot, exist and from another point of view certainly inexpressible (It is and it is indescribable).

(6) From certain point of view, the pot does not exist and from another point of view is inexpressible (It is not and it is indescribable).

(7) From certain point of view, the pot, exist, from another point of view it does not exist and from a third point of view it is inexpressible (It is and it is not and it is indescribable).

(1) Syat Asti- The first proposition is '"it is". From the certain point of view it exists. It exists from the stand point of its own material, place, time and nature, a thing is, i.e. exists it-self. The jar exists as made out of clay, in my room at the present moment, of such and such a shape and size. Here the existence affirms from the intrinsic character of a thing. This is not in absolute term but in relative term.

(2) Syat Nasti- The second proposition is "it is not". From the certain point of view of it is not. It does not exist from the stand point of view of its own material, place, time and nature of another thing, a thing is not, i.e. it is not no-thing. The jar does not exist of clay-as made of metal, not in my room-at a different place or time-at this time but some other time, and of not the previous shape and size but of a different shape and size. Here the non-existence affirms from alien character. This is not in absolute, unrestricted and unconditional term but it is in relative, restricted and conditional term.

The self existence is of A is identical with non-existence of non-A. This is not true. Both are different. To say that I have a coin of a rupee in my hand and to say that there is not a coin of pound in my hand is another thing. Here the knowledge is of two types. Both are independent. So we have to employ both the modes-affirmative and negative. Here they are not contradictory but complementary. Here it is due to the relative value and not absolute value. The critique does not understand the fine line of logic. They understood that "the pot does not exist" equivalent to "the pot does not exist as pot". The true interpretation of it should be "the pot does not exist as the jar". The eminent philosophers of Hindu philosophy have missed this point.

(3) Syat Asti Nasti- The third proposition is "it is and it is not". From a certain point of view of it exist and from certain point of view it does not exists. The mode shows the succession of thing. From the point of view of the same quaternary, relating to itself and another thing, it may be said that a thing is and is not. In a certain sense the pot exist and in a certain sense, it does not. We say here what a thing is as well as what it is not. This is a compound situation. The requirement of comprehensive view of positive and negative is necessary in compound character of an object.

(4) Syat Avaktavya- While in fourth propitiations, we make statements that a thing is in its own self and is not as another successively. From a certain point a thing is inexpressible. This is due to infinite characters. All seven fold standpoint is applicable to one character only. When we take a pair of permanence and impermanence from infinite qualities as opposite pair then how it can be indescribable? You cannot express both the things at a time. It becomes impossible to make these statements at once. In this sense, a thing is unpredictable. Though the presence of its own nature and the absence of other-nature are both together in the pot, still we cannot express them.

Words are limited to characters. Supreme knowledge cannot express all the qualities in language. The substance has either positive or negative qualities. First you describe positive qualities, second time negative quality and third time positive and negative co-jointly even than the description will be incomplete. This is due to infinite characters those which are not describable cannot be described. We cannot express human experience fully in language. Say how sweet the sugar is? You have experience of sweetness of sugar. You are unable to put in to language. Therefore it is inexpressible or indescribable.

(5) Syat Asti avaktavya- In the fifth proposition we make a statement that it exists and it is inexpressible. We note here both the existence of a thing and its indescribability. Thus by combining the first and fourth modes, we get fifth mode successively.

(6) Syat nasti avaktavya- In the sixth proposition we make a statement that it does not exist and it is inexpressible. We note here non-existence and inexpressibility. We note here what a thing is not as well as it is indescribable. Thus by combining the second and fourth mode, we get the sixth mode.

(7) Syat Asti nasti avaktavya-In the seventh propositions, we make a statement that it exists, it does not exist and it is indescribable. We bring out the inexpressibility of a thing as well as what it is and what it is not. Thus by combining third and fourth modes, we get seventh mode.

A thing is having infinite characters. It is called anantdharmatmkam in Jain philosophy. The substance has infinite qualities and transformation of the same in infinite modes. Example: - You take photographs of your house from four sides. All four different directions will have different photos. They are not identical. Ultimately all four pictures represent the house. We make different statement about thing taking into consideration different condition. We consider affirmation and negation at the same time. Example: - Mango is smaller than pumpkin and bigger than berry. Here we speak about big and small in the same statement from different standpoints. No one objects to it. These examples are of doctrine of many-sidedness-anekantvada.

Free from contradiction

An interesting point, when two characters at same time reside in a substance then it is not contradiction. If a thing is regarded as existent from the stand point of its own substance, place, time and quality and as non- existent from the standpoint of alien substance, etc, it involves no contradiction. Syadvada is free from defect of contradiction and free from defects arises out of contradiction.

Example of seven predications

Person replies question in any one predication out of the seven predications. Look at this illustration. A patient is on death bed. His relatives are asking the doctor, "How is his condition?" In reply doctor gives answer in following seven ways.

1. His bodily condition is good. (is)
2. His bodily condition is not good. (is not)
3. Compared to what it was yesterday, to-day it is good, but it is not so good that we may hope for his survival or cure.(is and is not)
4. We cannot say as to whether it is good or bad.(Inexpressible)
5. Compared to what it was yesterday, to-day it is good, still we cannot say as to what will happen (is and inexpressible)
6. Compared to what it was yesterday, to-day it is not good, still we cannot say as to what will happen.(is not and inexpressible)
7. Generally it is not good, but compared to what it was yesterday, to-day it is good, still we cannot say what turn it will take (is, is not, and inexpressible) [189]

---

[189] Translator-Nagin J.Shah, Jain Philosophy and religion, page no.355 & 356

People understand and apply these seven fold judgment then it will create the atmosphere of peace. It is accepted as code of conduct then there will be a harmony in different community as they know the facts. You cannot force upon your ideas on other community as they belong to different religion and cast. The seven fold judgment requires the discretion on the part of a person. The absence of discretion will not be useful to men or society, but it may cause harm.

8.4 Development By Jain Ascetics

Bhagvati sutra mentions only three primary modes - "sia atthi, sia natthi, sia avattavvam". (Existent, nonexistent and inexpressible) The seven fold judgment is the development from this threefold predication. [190] The agamic proposition of naya is in the form of (1) Dravyarthika (2) Paryayrthika. They are further express as

(a) Vyavharnaya and Nishyanaya

(b) Arpita naya and Anarpita naya   (Particular and general)

(c) Jnana naya and Kriya naya

(d) Samanya and Visesa.

Samantbhadra examined ten pairs of contradictions, like above, and draw conclusion that it is applicable universally.

Aklanka had derived six pairs.

(1) Cause and Effect

(2) Substance and Property.

(3) Parts and Whole

(4) Existence and Non-existence

(5) Oneness and Separateness

(6) Permanence and Transience

---

[190]   Ibid, page no.355

Haribhadra had derived four pairs.

(1) Existence and Non existence

(2) Permanent and Transience

(3) General and Particular

(4) Describable and Indescribable.

"Existence" by itself is not capable of being understood in a uniform sense. Existence may be absolute or relative and, as such, there is room for misconception.

In anekantvada, the various modes of substance cannot match. The same substance assumes various forms from various standpoints. Sometimes this has to be put under the title "indescribable".

Accommodation of infinite aspects in seven numbers

According to the anekant doctrine, a thing or entity is supposed to possess infinite aspect but seven fold formula will applicable to each attribution of a property. Vidyanandi said the Jain anekant doctrine of reality only welcomes such attributes. It maintained that the sevenfold predication as generated ontological situation and further that the predicates, in their different combinations are also understood in reference to the same context and not different contexts.

In Jain literature, the province of anekantvada is to examine the fundamental nature of a thing. In the province of the philosophy of anekantvada, for instance, rules of conduct came to be added later on. If we look at the discussion of Naya, Saptabhangi and others, they are resulting from anekantvada. One, who does not welcome different thoughts, will not reach to the truth. Anekantvada is the foundation stone of successful life in day-to-day affairs. Siddhsen Divakar said "Salutation to the revered doctrine of Anekant which is the preceptor of this whole Universe and without which the daily intercourse of human being is not at all possible".[191]

As per Jain philosophy "KEVALJNANA" is absolute reality (SAT).It is self-illuminating. In Syadvada, you have knowledge one after another but

---

[191]   Muni Shri Jina Vijay and Rashiklal C.Parikh, Sanmati Tarka, page no.126

in keval jnana you know all substances and its all-infinite modes at a time. Syadvada is due to senses and it is indirect, where as keval jnana is direct knowledge and it gives knowledge of all three phase of time- past, present and future. Therefore Syadvada shows us the way for absolute knowledge through partial truth way. Syadvada do not compel us to accept the partial-truth but shows the different ways to reach to absolute truth as the man is having limited capacity. First we reconcile the Vyavahar truth and then we can achieve absolute truth. The Jain philosophy says you can attain the keval jnana on attempts.

8.5 Western Logic

When we say that a thing "S" is characterized by property "P" is, the thing characterized by this property in certain condition. When you place the thing outside of this then the property condition does not apply. This means that the thing characterized by property only order certain specific conditions. When this condition applied then very well one can say that it is negative in opposite conditions. This means that both the statements are true. It is not identical. Therefore "S is P "and "S is not P" both are true. Here the anekantvada proves that neither something self contradictory nor something self repetitive.[192]

HEGEL Dialectic

HEGEL made familiar idea that in ways numerous things of the world harbour within their bosom elements that are mutually contradictions. This is the root thesis of the celebrated Hegelian dialectics. In his logic, Hegel sought to demonstrate how all the basic categories of human thought involve a synthesis of mutually contradictory aspects. [193]

Hegel's treatment of the following categories is worth noting.

1) Being (Which comprises 'being', 'not-being' and 'becoming').

2) Determinate Being.

3) Being-for-self.

---

[192]   K.K.Dixit, Jaina Ontology, page no. 168
[193]   Ibid, page no.170

4) Identity and difference. (Includes likeness and unlikeness)

5) Existence

6) Thing (Which include the thing and its properties)

7) Relation (Which includes the whole and the parts)

8) Substance and accidents

9) Cause and effects

10) Reciprocity.

Interpretation in Jain philosophical term

One can interpret these ten statements in terms of Jain philosophy as under.

The first statement of "Being" is in three categories. The first 'being' is as per Jain philosophy all six types of living beings. Jiva is the very first dravya in six dravyas. The second 'non-being' is in relation to pudgal. This is non-living dravya in six dravyas. This is second dravya in Jain philosophy. 'Becoming' is the last position of jiva as a liberated soul. They are known as Siddha jivas. The principle in Jain philosophy is to become from 'being' to 'becoming'.

The second "determinate being "is as per Jain philosophy the category of ASCETIC. The ascetics, who have left worldly affairs and are, progressing on the path of emancipation, observe certain vows physically and mentally. Ascetic will reach to such a stage where he does not have any trace of karma and by annihilation of all karmas, he will be transforming from being into becoming.

The third one is being for self. This is a category of house holder- laity. In Jain philosophy, who is interested to annihilate karma but he cannot do so in this life. He makes spiritual progress on the path of liberation and in future birth he will get liberated due to old Samskar.

The forth statement is Identity and difference. Liking and non-liking can be compared in Jain philosophy for Samyag charitra-character. This is the vedaniya karma. The Sata vedaniya karma is the effect of liking and asata vedaniya is the effect of non-liking.

The fifth statement is existence. The Jain philosophy divides all living beings in six broad categories with moving and non moving types. Now non moving category is further divided in to gross and subtle. They are known as EKENDRIYA (one sense) with fully developed and partly developed. The moving categories include dvindriya, trindriya, caturindriya and pancendriya (two, three, four and five sense). In case of five sense living beings, they are with mind and without mind. All two, three, four and five senses are fully developed and partially developed. This way it becomes totally fourteen types of living beings.

The sixth statement is "thing" with its property. Jain philosophy says that there are in all SIX dravyas. The dravya has quality and mode. The first one is jiva and the second dravya is Pudgal. In ajiva categories, there are five dravyas including pudgal. In all six dravyas, kala-time does not have body.

The seventh statement is "relation (Which includes 'the whole and the parts'). In the Jain philosophy it is the dravya having quality and modes. The quality is inseparable from dravya. The whole is dravya, whereas modes are the modification of substance due to time factor. Modes are different, coming in to existence at different time and in succession. Mode can consider as part.

The eighth statement is substance and accidents. In Jain philosophy, this is the function of PUDGAL, non-living entity. Pudgal is substance. Pudgal is aggregate of atoms. The atoms gets combined and separated. This process of integration and disintegration goes on. This can be defined as accident. This is from two atoms to end number of atoms. The aggregates are known as skandh.

The ninth statement is cause and effect. In Jain philosophy, cause and effect is in relation of karma and it's binding with the soul. Soul does the yoga as result karma comes into existence and gets bind with the soul. In Jain philosophy, yoga means activity by body, speech and mind. This binding will appear immediately or may appear at later stage. Karma will come into fruition over a period of time. When this karma comes into existence, the person experienced its good and bad effects. Here the cause is the karma and effect is pleasure or pain experienced by soul through body.

The tenth statement is reciprocity. Reciprocity means mutual dependence. In Jain philosophy it is "PAROSPOPGRHOJIVANAM".[194] Here from one sense to six senses living beings are dependent on each other. One sense includes earth, water, fire, air and vegetation. Two, three, four and five senses being are in a position to move where as one sense cannot move. The violence to them will affect all. The protection to them will help all. In this way interdependence is the cause of existence. All six senses living beings are the result of transmigration. Jiva gets birth, death and birth, like this cycle goes on. As per Jain philosophy, jiva travels in four gatis. This includes the celestial, hellish, human being and triyanch. The cycle starts from NIGOD-the very first existence of jiva till the last position siddhatva-liberation of jiva (Soul).

Hegel philosophy had lots of similarities with Jain philosophy.

Views of other scholar

Hanumant Rao said that "The Jaina philosophy of Relativity" as "refreshingly modern" and as "a happy blend of naturalistic and spiritualistic, realistic and idealistic tendencies", observes:"'just the philosophy' is perhaps what many contemporary philosophers would say. But on close scrutiny, it fails to satisfy some of the deepest metaphysical and religious aspiration of mankind. Its fascination is the fascination of eclecticism- a philosophy of compromise". This is said to be "the central defect" arising from the relativism of syadvad and further said "We see the tendency to please everybody and to compromise and in trying to compromise it involves itself in self-contradiction; the saviour of all systems is committing suicide". [195]

8.6   Naya System.

Pramana is an all round knowledge where as naya is partial knowledge. Both are form of knowledge but pramana disclose the thing as a whole and naya reveals a part of it. You see a cow in the market. You see it in totality. You describe the cow to your child with certain salient features

---

[194]   Commentary :- Pandit Sukhlalji on book Tattvarthasutradhigam of Umaswatiji, ch.5, stanza no.21, Sanskrit text page no.15

[195]   Y.J.Padmarajiah, A comparative study of the Jaina theories of reality and knowledge, page no.364 to367

and subtract a lot of things from abstract detail of cow. This intellectual analysis represents some character of object. This object is having partial knowledge known as naya. Naya is part of pramana. Different nayas are originating from pramana. Nayas are the point of view which says only partial view. Pramana is whole truth which syntheses all the partial views. Pramana is considered as synthesis of the aspects, parts or attributes or analyzed by nayas. Naya is the method of analysis and pramana is the method of synthesis.

One person understands one character in X way and second person understand the same character in Y way. There are different opinions for one and the same character from different people. A standpoint of an object may be different. Even if other standpoint is known than it is only in the limit of that object. This is the way of dealing, communication to the world.

Naya is different standpoint about the same thing comes out due to different opinions. One and the same person is son and father, son-in-law and father-in-law, uncle and nephew etc. Certain standpoint related to knowledge is achieved as knowledge standpoint, known as Jnan naya. Certain standpoint related to practice is achieved as action standpoint, known as kriyanaya.

Jain philosophy of metaphysics bases on quality and modes of a substance. This is known as Dravyarthika and Paryayrthika views. Substance and quality are coincide each other, where as modes are the result of time factor. Agamas are the base of the doctrine of Anekant. The Dravyartika view is the view point of Universal and general. The paryayrtika view is the viewpoint of specific and particular. Lord Mahavir discussed all philosophical doctrine in the order of their greater and greater subtlety and assigned a place to them in his Anekant doctrine.

Naya is knowledge of a thing in its relation. A naya is a standpoint from which we make a statement about a thing. We define and separate our standpoints by abstraction. This is a relative knowledge. What is true from one standpoint may not be true from another stand point. A particular aspect is never adequate to the whole reality. Jainism makes basic and fundamental principle that truth is relative to our standpoint. You can know the whole truth only on attainment of Keval Jnana.

Naya is a particular view point and does not rule out other view points. Nayas don't interfere with one another or enter into conflict with one another. Nayas stick to their own objects and do not reject others' objects.

Nayas becomes fallacy when they refuse to accept all other standpoints, exclude them and contradicts them absolutely; insist that the partial truth is the whole truth.

Man is full of ego and pride. Whatever little intelligence is with him is limited knowledge. When he makes some favour then it is considered as final and complete. Here he forgot patiently to consider others view point. He thinks mistakenly that his partial knowledge is complete knowledge. Man do not respect others different view point due to the fancy of knowing full truth of something.

Different viewpoints of one and the same thing establish the different systems. This is known as naya. Knowledge touches upon all its aspect is pramana and naya is one aspect of knowledge of a thing. Naya cannot say independently as pramana, but at the same time it is not a no-pramana. Example: - A drop of an ocean cannot be called an ocean nor can it be called no-ocean but can be called a part of ocean. Person acquires the knowledge of a thing by part to part and makes a whole thing. This is pramana. In practice person uses this knowledge in part. This is naya. Pramana grasps the knowledge in totality and naya grasps the knowledge part wise.

The interpretation of doctrine of naya is it harbours the views which appear to be mutually contradictory in synthesis form. Example: - In Agamas it is stated that "the Soul is one" at one place and at another place as "the souls are many".

This raises a question that whether it is real or not? The answer is negative then why? The answer is in compatibility of contradictory things. It is the intention of speaker or writer from which view point he talks or writes. Now the above example is true in one philosopher's thinking where as other philosopher will consider it untrustworthy and third philosopher will have altogether different view. These will create conflict. To resolve such conflict, the system of naya is very essential.

Siddhsen Divakara said that there are many standpoints (naya) to express in many ways. It means (1) stand points are many an (2) it can be express in verbal form. Nayas can be divided into two (1) Bhava naya (2) Dravya naya. Bhava naya is the state of conception and dravya naya is expressed in verbal form.[196] Vidyanandsvami explained it in this way. All the nayas are verbal when they are employed to convey their partial truths to OTHERS. On the other hand, those very nayas are cognitional or conceptual when they reveal their partial truths to SELF. This is bhava naya. Cognitional or conceptual means the partial view discovered through own experience by man without help of other. When he gives this partial view to other, through language, than it is dravya naya or verbal.

Dravyarthika and Paryayrtika naya

There are infinite view-standpoints. The nayas are infinite. The definition of doctrine of naya is investigation of views. Originally there are two types of nayas (1) Dravyarthika-naya and (2) paryayrtika-naya. Dravya means substance, say clay and paryaya is modes, transformation of substance-say a pot made out of clay. This transformation may be subtle or gross. Gross is visible but subtle is not. We can know the subtle transformation through inference. Dravyarthika-naya means a standpoint concentrates on substance in generic and permanent aspect. Paryayrtika-naya means a standpoint concentrates on modes. Dravyarthika-naya considers all things as eternal, where as Paryayrtika-naya considers all things impermanent or momentary as they go into transformation-change.

Human thought about the aspects of substance is sometimes in generic term and sometimes in specific term. Now Dravyarthika-naya grasps the modes some time and Paryayrtika-naya grapes the generic term. But they do not grasp exclusively. Dravyarthika-naya has the substance in predominant and mode subordinate and in Paryayrtika-naya, mode is predominant and substance subordinate. Example:-You are seating at the shore of ocean. When you see the vastness of water than it is Dravyarthika-naya and when you think about the colour, taste and other thing of water than it is Paryayrtika-naya. The water is in all places all over the world carries the same aspects of nayas. Therefore every substance has generic as well as specific aspects. Though the substance is different from its one particular mode, it is identical from the standpoint of continuation of modes.

Seven nayas

Jain texts give a list of seven nayas covering the possible ways of understanding substance. These nayas are (1) Naigama naya (2) Sangraha

---

[196]   Najin J. Shah, Jain Philosophy and religion, page no.357.

naya (3) Vyavahara naya (4) Rjusutra naya (5) Sabda naya (6) Samabhirudha naya and (7) Evambhuta naya.

1) Naigama naya: - Naigama means resolve or imagination. There are three divisions of naigama naya.

   (A) Sankalpa–naigama: - Sankalpa means intention, resolve etc. Sankalpa-naigama means concentrates on resolve. Example: - You are putting the clothes in your travelling bag. Your friend arrives and asks "what are you doing?" your answer is "I am going to London". Here your resolution is for travelling to London and your friend accepts the talk. Another example: - A person is carrying the fuel. On enquiry he replies that he is cooking. His intention to convey is that he is carrying fuel for the purpose of cooking.

   (B) Amsa-naigama: - Amsa means part. Here the standpoint takes a part for the whole. Example: - A spark falls on sari put on by a lady. Sari is a part of woman dress in Indian culture. She will cry and say that her dress is burnt.

   (C) Aropa-naigama: - aropa means superimposition. This stand point superimposes one time-division on another, one state on another." Example:- Today is, the Deepavali day, is the day of lord Mahavir's nirvana". Here past is imposed on present. Upachara-naigama is included in this. Upachara is metaphorical words Example- to Say about beautiful lady- "She is a beauty incarnate".

Naigamanaya subordinates substance and quality, any one, out of two.

(2) Sangraha naya: - Sangraha means collection. Here the method is applied to collect things or individuals in one class on the bases of common features. The physical and conscious existence on the earth comes in this category. The particular features will be overlooked and treating that all features is reflecting in one. The generic feature is taken into account, treating the things in one class. Example: - a shopkeeper is showing varieties of shirting clothes to you and the shopkeeper will say common name "cloth". The larger use of generic feature will result in to large sangraha naya and lesser use of generic will result in to less of sangraha naya.

(3) Vyavahara naya: - Vyavahara naya is the popular conventional point of view based on empirical knowledge. The generic term has to make

more specific. The specific features attract attention. Example: - Cloth should be spell out as mill cloth, hand spun or silk cloth etc. You have to distinguish in the category of physical and conscious. In case of conscious, it is of two types (1) mundane soul-worldly soul and (2) Siddha-liberated soul. It deals with particularity and focuses on diversity. It is the empirical and practical approach. The analytic operation of intellect is Vyavahara naya. The distinction is the cognitive and therefore it is dravyarthika naya.

(4) Rjusutra naya: - Rju means straight. This does not take in to account past or future. Rjusutra naya is narrower than the vyavahar naya. It takes into account the state of a thing at a particular point of time. It overlooks all continuity and identity. It aims at presenting the aspect of reality from the point of view of momentary present. Example: - Happiness. Happiness is in current situation and it is not experienced in future or in past. Human cannot ignore the past or future but here the present is most important. Again pleasure and pain are recognized in the present state, condition or a mode of thing, which is real. Rjusutra naya has two sub-types (1) suksma (subtle) and (2) sthula (gross). Suksma is a one fine moment and sthula means it continues for more than one moment- many moments. The example of life span of hundred years falls under sthula Rjusutra-naya.

According to ancient tradition the range of the view of Dravyartika naya was up to Rjusutra naya. The first four nayas are in the categories of dravyarthika naya and rest three nayas are in the categories of Paryayrthika-naya. The first four of cognitive type and it gives meaning of the word. They are known as Arthya naya. Paryayrthika-naya covers sabda-naya, samabhirudha-naya and evambhuta-naya. These are called sabda naya. They chiefly consider the word expressing a particular thing at appropriate time.

(5) Sabda naya: - Sabda naya defines that the synonymous words carry the same meaning provided they do not change gender, tense or case ending. Here the two synonymous words are having different meanings due to the difference in the above things. Example: - There was a river called Saraswati. This means that the river existed in past but it is exeunt today. The Saraswati River existed in those days when the author was existent at the same time simultaneously. Sabda naya differs by gender. Example: - "Nara" "Nari", "Mayur", "Mayuri". Nara and mayur are of masculine gender and nari and mayuri are feminine

gender. Man has different relation with different person. The words convey the difference in relation- Example: - Say uncle, nephew, father, son etc. The time phase is conveyed by different words. We use present tense when the action is taking place. We use past tense for action happened and we use future tense for the action anticipated to happen. We use singular word to convey the one thing and use plural to convey more than one thing. The verb expresses the particular type of relation to convey the particular association with the thing. Example: - "Rajnah prasadah"- king's palace.

One should note that the standpoint which is useful and appropriate at a particular time should be principle adopted at the time and on the occasion.

(6) Samabhirudha naya: - Samabhirudha naya refers to the etymological meaning of a word and emphasizes that every word has some different meaning in accordance with its root. This standpoint shows that each one word has one separate meaning. This naya throws light on differences amongst synonymous words. In case of sabda naya the gender, tense and case had the same meaning. Here in case of Samabhirudha naya, it has separate meaning. Here the particular aspect becomes more prominent. As we mentioned earlier that it is etymological matter. Example: - The word 'Raja", "Nrup","Bhup", all carries different meaning.

(7) Evambhuta naya: - Of the various aspects and gradations in the manifestation of a thing, only one is contemplated by the root of a term, and it is this aspect that is the legitimate meaning of a term in the current usage. Example:- Raja is called "raja" when he is ascending the throne with royal cloths and accessories in the royal court. Only at a time when the person is performing some act than only he will be called by particular word. Example:- A person will be called teacher when he is teaching and not at other time.

Thus, these nayas take note of different possibilities of analytic thought processes with reference to varied aspects and distinctions of the object or of reality. All above seven categories of naya can have NAYABHASA-fallacy. It is a fallacies, when naya taken as absolute and entire.

Nikshepa

The four varieties of NIKSHEPA are leading to different view point. When we try to determine meaning of a word, we look at the WORD from four different points of views.

These four nikshepas are (1) Nama (Name) (2) Picture (staphana) (3) potentiality (Dravya) and (4) Bhava.

The first three are applicable to Dravyartika naya and Forth one is of Paryayrtika naya. We do not go into details of them.

Important aspects of naya

Dravyarthika naya is from the point of view of substance. It is in its pure form, only concerned with the simple statement "It is". The Ultimate reality is without division, limitation or attribute of any kind, single and whole. This is general, universal principle can only be mentioned in "IT IS". Rest of the things deal with limited aspect of reality and have some element of difference, division, part or attribute. These statements are not exclusive belong to Dravyarthika, but belongs to the province of Dravyartika and paryayrtika naya.

Only one statement, which deals with ultimate particularization beyond which there is no possibility of further particularization falls under the preview of paryayrtika naya. This naya is from the point of view of modification or condition.

Both of them diverse from each other can certainly give a partially true idea of that entity. However, in singleness any one cannot give whole truth. When this two naya with harmony of each other and gives own view without trying to refute, assertion or the view of other naya than both are right in their view. This way they give partial but true view of an entity without refuting the opposite. If however, they consider themselves as supplementary of each other, they are right in their viewpoints.

These two nayas should not encroach upon the province of other naya and should not refute in other naya view. The naya will give wrong meaning on wrong application. You use the word which is appropriate for vyavahar naya replace sangraha naya then there will be no difference between "Mother" and "Wife" for example. You use the word which is appropriate for sabda naya replace in naigama naya than the ascetic is with cloths only and not in spiritual term for example.

Samabhirudha naya has own meaning for each word. Sabda naya is having different meaning in synonymous words when they differ in gender, case-ending or tense. The origination of word is in root. The word is connected with some activity. Look at the word "Yoddha" means warrior. As per Samabhirudha naya, Warrior is known as warrior throughout the life. As per Evambhuta naya, he is warrior only when he is fighting in the war. Same way "Pujari" means one who worships. As per Evambhuta naya, when he performs the worship at that time "Pujari" only. As per Samabhirudha naya, he is pujari for life time. In Evambhuta naya, the word is fit till its actual action is present in thing. According to Evambhuta naya all the words are action words and derived from verbal root.

The subject matter of naigama-naya is generic and specific. Sangraha – naya is the existence alone. The vyavahar naya is the division of existence. Rjusutra naya is subtle than vyavahar naya. Sabda naya is subtler than Rjusutra naya. Samabhirudha-naya is subtler than sabda naya and evambhuta-naya is subtler than samabhirudha-naya. Every succeeding naya is more limited in extent than every preceding naya. Rjusutra-naya accepts only present so the subject matter is specific. Like this you can make out number of distinctions in all seven nayas.

Literary application of naya

The difference or division of an object, with some sort, than it becomes Paryayrthika naya from Dravyarthika naya. This difference can be of two types. They are (1) Difference depending ON words and (2) Difference NOT depending on words.

Vyanjan Paryaya

When division super imposed in sense of TIME and SPACE on object than numerable differences will appear. These differences described in words, it known as VYANJAN PARYAYA.

Artha Paryaya

Now a point comes where there is no possibility to make further sub division or differences of object than this known as ARTHA PARYAYA.

The object is subject to Artha paryaya. Vyanjan paryaya is in sense of time aspects –past, present, future and space.

The Vyanjan paryaya is "Nameable characteristic", artha paryaya in "Un -nameable characteristics". The thing in so far as it is called by a name is similar to all the things called by the same name, while in so far as it is a UNIQUE thing, it is un-nameable.

If we desire to say that one part of thing exists then it is said, "IT EXISTS".

If we desire to say that one part of thing does not exist then it is said, "IT DOES NOT EXIST".

If we desire to describe a thing simultaneously from the standpoint of its own particularization of another thing then it baffles the description and said to be "INDESCRIBABLE".

If we desire to describe a thing, partly exist and from one point of view and does not exist from another point of view than it is said, "IT EXIST" and "NOT EXIST".

If we desire to say that one part of thing exists and another part exist and does not exist at the same time, the thing is said to be "EXISTING" and "INDESCRIBABLE".

If we desire to say that one part of a certain thing does not exist and another part does and does not exist at the same time, the thing said to be "NOT EXISTING" and "INDESCRIBABLE".

If one part of thing does and does not exist and another does and does not exist at the same time – the thing said to be "EXISTING", "NOT EXISTING" and "INDESCRIBABLE".

All these seven modes of stating a thing are possible in Artha paryaya.

The divisible (SAVIKALPA) aspects of a thing as well as indivisible (NIRVIKALPA) aspects of a thing are possible only in VYANJAN PARYAYA.

In Vyanjan paryaya only (1) Affirmation (2) Negation and (3) Affirmation and Negation of a quality, one by one is possible.

8.7   Importance Of Anekantvada.

"To day, we think of the world as a "GLOBAL VILLAGE" in the sense of inter-racial co-existence. Anekantvada outlook is not only good for our day-to-day life, but it also has a great intellectual appeal. Post modernism and its related theory of post structuralism widely used in literary criticism are of very recent origin. Post modernism suggests that every field of ideas is a field of conducting forces. All facts and events are subject to multiple interpretations. Thus, the attitude of Anekantvada could work at the starting point of eliminating or, at least, reducing religious, social, political, family conflicts, which often culminated in intolerance at all levels-national and even international".[197] When you are thinking of the development of humanity, people welfare and or world welfare than anekantvada is the only centre of it. An anekantvada can remove poverty of people; can give justice to poorer among poor, minorities and different caste and creed. Today, world needs the equality, humanity of co-existence and world welfare, which can be achieved by way of anekantvada. Anekantvada is the only medium for solving individual, social problems, difference of opinion and it gives the solid and impartial judgment. In anekantvada one cannot say that my view point is correct. This will be an ekantvada. Anekant is the word, which is negative like Ahimsa as Non-absolutism. Anekantvada does not allow any inconclusive, non-day–to–day affairs.

Anekantvada is an important tool in modern management. Earlier the trade and industries were working on operational research of U.K. and U.S.A. Earlier it was highly centralized. As more and more people are participating in trade and industries, new thought was require. There is a lot of change in office working of news and media and advertising and transport and banking and all other sectors due to computerization.

---

[197]   Editor: - Tara Sethia, Ahimsha, Anekant and Jainism, Essay of Kamla Jain, page no.113 to 121.

Therefore, decision-making is very important aspect. Now you have to decentralize and give power to down the line of management. The decision theory is working on rational choice where as the consumer is working on actual choice. This is a big difference. We have to develop such a thing, which can combine both the things in business.

Anekantvada is the foundation of all possible functions and relations of all living and non-living. The living and non–living are the two different knowledge aspects of the same reality though they are indifferent from each other. Anekant means changing phenomena. Whatever known today may not be the same tomorrow and it will reveal new secret of reality. This replaces the existing function and interchanges the whole concept. We explore new dimension. Anekantvada is the principle of all activities of life and knowledge. A value system acknowledged by Anekantvada may be very helpful technique to overcome all the conflicting situations.

Anekantvada speaks of many sidedness of an object. My feeling is that the opponent will know your views and try to take benefit out of it or misuse it. As a result, there will be a series of problems including legal, which will continue lifelong in one's life. People do not take Anekantvada in true spirit and this will create problems at national as well as International level. Everyone will take such a view in to consideration which is beneficial to him.

The metaphysic aspect is apart but men should come out of any type of dogma and /or fanatical approach to life. It can significantly reduce the intellectual chaos and social and religious conflict in the present day life with the help of Anekantvada.

Anekantvada can bring peace in society. All will respect each other's view. When you respect others view then you are putting the other person on same level without looking in to caste, creed, religion, or position and his wealth. This will increase tolerance and understanding. When you understand each other views than the enmity will not be there. The rich or poor society applies an anekantvada then it will create the atmosphere of brotherhood and faith in each other.

Anekantvada will minimize the conflict and all religion will survive in harmony with peace. The criminal effect will come down due to anekantvada. The social fabric will have the patterns of good colours and designs due to moral and ethics.

Ekanta view is selfish and will not yield anything in any field, religious, social, political or economical, at individual or society level. Ekanta view is harmful to individual and society. It gives birth to dictator, anarchist, or fanatics. Ekanta view will not give truth but it gives adamant viewpoint. Therefore, in any case it is better to avoid such type of mental thinking and adopt Anekantvada in one's life.

8.8   Philosophy of Welfare in Anekantvada

The definition itself shows the way for the welfare. First the person's mind must be positive. This will help to create way for new thing, resolves critical issues, iron out the differences and most important is positive attitude to do this.

Second thing is examination. Here the parties come into agreement to examine difficult issues. This will be like a joining of hands to think in right manner and direction. Examination is after the acceptance of proposal. Here the examination from all possible points of view proposed. When the proposal accepted, it is a joint confidence to look in to it. All the possible points may be positive, negative, opposite, additive and subordinate nature. The result may be anything. Both the parties are allowed to accept or reject any thing. This may result in agreement or disagreement. This will bring in the clarity of thoughts in mind. This will bring the people together on one platform. The effects will result in the union of agreed and disagreed people. The creative atmospheres will be aired. The people are bound to think from others point of view and give them new look. New ideas and new horizon will be created. This will be something like silver lining in the clouds.

When it is said, test everything from different points of view means person should open up his mind. Person should try to think as many possibilities as of a thing. The result will be something like VIBGYOR-rainbow. There may be number of possibilities. This will be an APEKASAVDA-expectation.

The person has limited knowledge. His intelligence is sky high, even though it will be limited in light of knowledge. Man's wisdom has limit. The person may not be able to know all the possibilities of a thing. The person does not possess infinite knowledge.

Person has to look at the thing not from one point of view but many points of view. Here the contradictory properties are most important. The affirmation and negation resides in a thing together. They exist in the thing. This is the beauty of ANEKANTVADA.

The person thinks many possibilities of a proposal. It is understood that person has to develop various thoughts. These thought development is a way to speculation about proposal. Thus Anekantvada is speculative method of looking at a thing. This will open number of avenues to think in number of manners. When person wants to express this, he cannot say in positive or negative manner. It is quite possible that the one side will be stronger than other one. The person should use the word "SYAT". Syat means probable. People are using this term in different manner such as "Possible", "May be". There can be in all seven possibilities to express the thing. This will be in connection of material, nature, place and time.

Anekantvada is applicable in following ways.

A) Macro economics level

B) Micro economic level

Macro economical level one can consider the U.N.O. and its' activities.

Micro level economics one can consider the country, state, family and individual human.

Macroeconomic level

The wise and foresighted people signed a charter after the Second World War in the year 1945. The charter is known as united nation organization. As on to day 192 countries are member of this organization. U.N.O. has democratic working system. U.N.O. is working on many fronts with many good objectives.

All countries in the world should work in harmony and there should be possible balance in each and every aspect.

U.N.O. is divided in six main sections. They are (1) trusteeship council (2) Security Council (3) general assembly (4) economic and social council (5) international court of justice (6) secretariat. These six main divisions have subsidiary bodies, functional commission, specialized agencies and departments and offices. U.N.O. has branches at Geneva and Huge.

Economics and social council has functional commissions and regional commissions. Under this council, specialized committee like UNICEF, ILO, FAO, UNESCO, WHO, World Bank and IMF are working.

It can be said that U.N.O. is substance and many objectives are its qualities and many working fronts are its modes.

Micro economic level

In micro economic, anekantvada can apply at all level. We can think in terms (1) Country (2) State (3) Society (4) Individual.

Let us think of a project for country and state. In this project, we are looking for the possibilities of 1) increase in literacy rate (%), 2) school dropout rate (%), 3) gross enrolment rate in school (%) and 4) money spending on education (% of GDP). The empirical data will be collected. The period can be four to five years. You have to select the state and in state, districts. The selected pocket will be surveyed. The method of collecting data will be by way of questioner. The collected data will be analyzed, tabulated. By using various statistical methods, one can finally arrive at desire result. On this result country and state can decide the increase in spending, to take preventive measure for school dropout and pursue the parents to send girl child to school and not to send the boy student to work and earn for family. You can tell the parents that education is better investment. The policy decision can be made on these bases. This is anekantvada.

The country and state applying the policy of delegation of power from top level to grass root level. The power delegated in the chain to the last person. This makes the function smooth, efficient. Anekantvada is present here in the form of infinite modes.

In the family, the head of family has various relationships with the family members. He is a father of his children, husband of his wife, son of his father, uncle of his nice, nephew and cousins. This way he is multifunctional person. The same person may be chairperson of co-operative society, member of state planning commission, president of community council and trustee of a charitable hospital. This is the form of anekantvada where more than one function is fulfilled by the same person.

Anekantvada is to understand the others' view. Anekantvada is to examine the statement from all the sides and from all the point of views. Individual has to work in society, in harmony. This will help him to keep the tradition of society healthy and to uplift the moral level of human in society. Society will be tolerant and understanding. In short Anekantvada is useful in many ways. This will bring welfare to human.

9 Dr.Amartya Sen's ideas on Poverty and Famine, an essay on Entitlement and Deprivation

9.1 Poverty and Famine

The population growth is directly related to poverty. The birth rate is more in poor people. It is not good from overall economic point of view. The opposite of this is correct; more children bring in more income to sustain the family at individual level. The population growth created problems for food, clothes and housing and as a nation for her resources in general and many more things in particular. The fate element is the main cause for poverty in India and other countries. People have lucrative ideas about fortune. People are eager to know about their future. The attractive future makes man ideal and put him in day dreaming. The fate element comes in prominence in the bad time. The work culture habit hampers as a result. Poverty can be due to less political freedom, exploitation and ignorance. Dr. Amartya Sen has different view for poverty in welfare economics.

Definition of Poverty

"The study of the causes of poverty, Alfred Marshall observed at the turn of century, is the study of causes of degradation of a large part of mankind." "The vast number of people both in town and country (U.K.)", he noted, "had insufficient food, clothing and houseroom; they were overworked and under taught, weary and careworn, without quiet and without leisure. The chance of their succour, he concluded gave to economic studies, their chief and their highest interest." [198]

---

[198]   Prof.J.K.Galbraith, The affluent Society, Page No.244

The causes of poverty

Prof. J. K. Galbraith- "WE now attribute the poverty of nations and to which we relate our remedies

- The people are poor because they prefer it that way.
- The country is naturally poor.
- The country is poor because it has been kept in a state of colonial oppression.
- Poverty is the consequence of class exploitation.
- Poverty is caused by insufficient capital.
- Over population is the cause of poverty.
- Poverty caused by incompetent economic policy.
- Poverty is caused by ignorance." [199]
- "Poverty ceased to be a general case and become special case."

Professor J.K. Galbraith defined poverty in two broad categories "(1) Cash poverty (2) Insular poverty. [200]

Cash poverty

This poverty is in every community and in rural and urban area. The poor farm family with the junk-foiled yard and dirty children playing in the bare dirt or it is the grey black hovel besides the railroad tracks. Or it is the basement dwelling in the alley. [201]

Some qualities particularly to the individual or family involved –mental deficiency, bad health, inability to adopt to the discipline of industrial life, uncontrollable procreation, alcohol, discrimination involving a limited minority, some educational handicap unrelated to community shortcoming, or perhaps a combination of several these handicaps-has kept these individuals from participating in the general well-being.

Insular Poverty

"This manifests itself as an "ISLAND" of poverty. In the island, everyone or nearly everyone is poor. It is not easy to explain matters by individual inadequacy. We may make individuals down as intrinsically deficient in

---

[199]   ibid, page no.245.
[200]   ibid, page no 245.
[201]   ibid, page no. 246.

social performance; it is not proper or even wise so to characterize an entire community. The people of the island have been frustrated by some factor common to their environment. Most modern poverty is insular poverty and islands are the rural and urban slums. The most certain thing about this poverty is that is not remedied by a general advance in income. Cash poverty is not remedied because the specific individual inadequacy precludes employment and participation in the general advance. Insular poverty is not directly alleviated because the advance does not remove the specific frustrations of environment to which the people of these islands are subject. This is not to say that it is without effect. If there are jobs outside the ghetto or away from the rural slum, those who are qualified, and not otherwise constrained, can take them and escape. If there is no such job, none can escape." [202]

The person is consuming the things in his day-to-day life. This consumption reflects in his life style. The life style is high in case of rich and low in case of poor. A poor defined in terms of comparison of consumption and shortfall in consumption.

Nobody wants to be poor. Philosophy of Lord Mahavir also does not advocate the poverty. Lord Mahavir advocated the glory of work with certain golden rules to be followed.

9.2   Entitlements and ownership

Starvation is the property of some people, not having food and not enough food to eat. There are many reasons for this and not enough food to eat is one of them. Food supply is commodity and man has relationship. Here the ownership comes in picture. The crux of the problem is ownership. The other meaning of ownership can be entitlements. This entitlement is generally applicable to poverty and particularly to famine. Entitlements can be of various types and they are connected with some rules. In market economy, entitlements can be transferred from one kind to another kind. They are 1) trade base entitlement 2) production base entitlement 3) own-labour base entitlement 4) inheritance entitlement. The above entitlements are of simple and complex nature depending upon type of transaction.

---

[202]   ibid, page no.247.

There is a line of demarcation about entitlements. Socialist economy may not permit, ownership, may not allow hiring another person for work where as capitalist economy will agree the right of ownership, allow hiring person for production and making union to accept long working hour. Both economies are against bonded or slave labour which was custom earlier in plantation and colonial rule.

Exchange entitlement has benefits two ways. Either it is the result of trade in first instance and production as second instance. This can be the result of both also. Now the bundle of entitlement is not having enough food exchange amount than it will be a starvation. We can identify such bundles-entitlement sets. The person can have set of entitlement by way of employment, sale of his assets, production with his own labour and require raw material and its cost. The enough earning to buy food by way of ownership and exchange will save him from starvation. The starvation can result in to high price of food grains, low remuneration in wages or decline in price of own goods.

Now we have to think about the modes of production. One possibility is he may be owner of land; second possibility is he may be a crop sharing partner and third one is land less labourer. This will have impact of remuneration and will have definite effect in abnormal situation-say calamity in agriculture-flood or cyclone. In such position the share crop partner as well as land less labourer will be in trouble- less income and then starvation. The artisan class will be more sufferers.

The government can extend the help by way of social security and related various programmed. This can be termed as 'relief', 'benefits', 'pension' etc. Social securities are in developed countries with a view to that person cannot give service till death. So after some age limit, he will be compensated by way of some relief through government. This system is in Britain and America as well as other developed countries. In case of socialist country, government gives guarantee for number of days employment. Recently the government of India has started employment guarantee scheme for able villagers in some districts of country for hundred days. This requires enough fund to run the scheme and mediator should be HONEST.

General perception is starvation is due to over population. The empirical data shows that except Africa, the food production has match or on higher side than population growth. Starvation is not the cause of food production but the food buying capacity of a person. After food production, food distribution comes in picture. The rich and poor will have definite difference in food buying capacity. As per statistics, one out of eight people is suffering from starvation. This is due to his inability to by the food and not the availability of food grain. The economists and bureaucrats have usually analyzed the starvation and famine problem in terms of food availability and not thought about the food buying capacity of person. Dr.Amartya Sen has gone deep enough and found out the "Entitlement approach" as a remedy of the problem.

9.3   Requirement of concept of poverty

Now we have to define the poverty. It can be by way of either consumption norm or below poverty line definition. The poverty is in relation to only poor, only non-poor or both. The point is the effect of poverty is important question. The poor will be affected in his well-being and rich will not. This has definite relation with non-poor. One has to study the causes of poverty and reach to the bottom of question. Here we have to think of well-being of entire nation. One can think the problem of poverty on this line and has to make aggregation of poor. In tradition, poverty is defined by number of poor in total population in the form of ratio. Total population number will be divided by number of poor in the population. This is known as "Head count measure'. There are two defects in this. First thing, the income of poor will be reduced than it will not reflect as become poorer without affecting the lot of rich people. Second thing, the income transfer from poor to rich in poor class but below poverty line will not reflect any where. Here we have to find out the total number of poor in population known as identification and make sets of such people at all level in poverty. This leads us to the different approaches in the literature.

The Biological Approach

Dr.Amartya Sen says SEEBOHM ROWNTREE defines the poor family that "If their total earnings are insufficient to obtain the minimum necessities for the maintenance of merely physical efficiency". [203] The author is talking about the physical efficiency. Here the work efficiency or survival is given the utmost importance.

---

[203]   Amartya Sen, Poverty and famine Page 11

This definition is short for physical condition, geographical location and work habit. It is difficult to decide nutrition standard. The biological needs may differ from the above in three ways. First, it is the body structure, work habit and climate. Labourer wants more food compared to mental worker. In labourers, unskilled and heavy load carrying people need more food compared to skilled worker. Generally the food consumption is more in cold countries than in hot countries due to energy requirements. Man will require more food compared to woman. This may be a social norm also. Ladies are generally eating after the male persons finished their meal or dinner. Ladies consume the residual part of food and sometimes they let go some food items which are less in their meal or dinner.

People survive with less nutritional food and on improvement of supply of nutrient; people in Japan, America and Europe have improved their physical appearance. The nutritional requirement depends upon item of food person choose. The minimum nutritional requirement may not give correct picture. The nutritional requirement is more in case of pregnant woman than ordinary woman. This is not possible due to different groups and regions and culture.

One may try to find out minimum cost for nutritional food which is not possible due to the habits of people. You fix your budget for food than also it will not serve the purpose because of availability of food, price variation. The portion of income spent on food is important. In food budget, the other related thing like packing, transport and retailer margin have to take in to account. In highly developed countries; the packing cost is nearly 40% of the food price and transportation cost and retailer margin are there. Second thing, due to health consciousness the date "Best before use" makes lot of wastage and it creates a hole in the food budget of a person. U.K. People spend nearly 1000 crores pound as food waste. Out of this nearly 60% food items are untouched. Individual family is spending nearly £420 pound per year and in case of family with children, it is about £610 pound per year. U.S.A. is spending much more than this. This is due to bigger quantity packaging and marketing strategy of food producing and distributing companies for high turnover and high profit. The law of country and social customs do not allow them to use surplus food for distribution to poor people. This goes as waste and it is clear misuse of food grain items. The cost of food items are more due to the best quality and its' import from various destinations of the world. Poor is sufferer at the cost of rich.

It is important to know that how the income is earned. The human nature is important factor here. Some people are by nature idle. Some believe in fortune and do not put enough labour to earn. Some people are satisfied with minimum income. The family is having sustainable income as a result some member of family will not work or work for fewer days in a month. Culture of community say- Rich people will not work to earn. Certain artisan's class will work to earn but for them the sufficient number of days for earning is a question mark due to limited work availability. All above factors will decide the level of income and in turn poverty line.

We cannot have general nutritional standard of a country. The discussion regarding poverty and nutritional standard are to some extent vague. We should go with the assumption that person is getting nutritional food bundle or not apart from his income. One can collect information by way of sample survey. As soon as we accept nutritional standard, we can move to convert it into poverty line income. Function of malnutrition in poverty is on low level now a day.

The inequality approach

You transfer some income from rich to poor. This will help to reduce poverty. Important point is we have to identify the poor in the group or community. This is something like inequality. This is another approach to poverty. MILLER and RUBY have forcefully represented inequality approach as under. "Casting the issues of poverty in terms of stratification leads to regarding poverty as an issue of inequality. In this approach, we move away from efforts to measure poverty line with pseudo scientific accuracy. Instead, we should look at the nature and size of the differences between the 20 or 10 per cent and the rest of the society. Our concern becomes one of narrowing the differences between those at the bottom and the better-off in each stratification dimension." [204] Inequality and poverty are different. The transfer of income from rich to middle class will not reflect in below poverty line calculation. General income decline will result in starvation and malnutrition. Rich was unwilling to give up their enjoyment, they have. The poor were in favour of great equality.

Prof. J.K Galbraith-"The concern for inequality and deprivation had vitality only as long as the many suffered with a few had much. It did not survive as

---

[204]   ibid, page no, 14.

a decisive political issue in a time, when the many had much, even though others had much more. It is our misfortune that when inequality declined as an issue, the state not left clean. A residual and in some ways rather more hopeless problem remained." [205]

The concept of "Relative deprivation"

The concept of "Relative deprivation" is important in the light of poverty. This is a sociological aspect. It understood socially that poor is deprived in relative term. PETER TOWNSEND says "conditions" are the better form to judge poverty in relative deprivation condition. We have to find out the relative items. Here two important relative items require to be examined, (1) Feeling (2) Conditions. [206]

Feeling of poverty is subjective term. One person, who has made up his mind to live life in the income whatever he is earning. Other person feels that the present income earning is not sufficient for him looking to the higher life style of others. Person would like to imitate his immediate higher income person and tried to capture that standard. Person is more cared about customs, activities and comparison of diet. The person who is unable to fulfil his will feel deprivation. The feeling is a mental stage. It is very difficult to compare one person with another person. You cannot set a standard of poverty for such people. Therefore, feeling and conditions are interrelated. Again, the comparison of individual in a group is very difficult in case of poverty.

A value judgement

Now a day moral has come forward in favour of elimination of poverty. It is a subjective view to look at poverty. Some agreed, some may not agree. Dr. Amartya Sen is against this thinking with opinion that to describe poverty is one thing and to eradicate poverty is another thing. Here the philosophical aspect comes in. ERIC HOBSBAWN puts it this way. "It is always defined according to the conventions of the society in which it occurs". [207] The poverty is not a value judgement. Convictions are a most important and influential wisdom rules in the society. People follow the long traditions and the advice of their ancestor.

---

[205] Prof. J.K. Galbraith, The affluent Society, Page No.250

[206] Amartya Sen, poverty and famine page no, 15-16.

[207] ibid, page no.17.

Before two hundred years, Adam Smith had given importance for some standard of living. It may be necessary linen shirt in present day but it was not necessary in the times of Greeks and Romans. Morally one is required to follow certain minimum thing as per society norms. Same view was expressed by Karl Marx in relation to labourer for their standard of living. He was in favour of minimum means of subsistence.

A policy definition

There is another way to measure the poverty. There are certain given standards. Regarding standard one can ask, whether it is a public policy or mere a guide line. It agreed that balancing of community capabilities and desires. It is doubt that political governing party is responsible to put into practice the decided policy for poverty elimination. Here many points are important to check like, who rules, what type of governing system and influencing people in organization and source of power. These things vary as per the government policy. Professor Duesenberry has stated explicitly that "Ours is a society in which one of the principle social goals is a higher standard of living." [208] The author had made the thing clear. He suggested the higher standard of living.

Low-income earning people has to satisfy with physical survival and higher income society can think of better. Prof. J.K Galbraith said "Beyond doubt wealth is the relentless enemy of understanding. The poor man has always a precise view of his problem and its remedy; he has not enough and he needs more. The rich man can assume or imagine a much greater variety of ills and he will be correspondingly less certain of their remedy. Also until he learns to live with his wealth, he will have a well-observed tendency to put it to the wrong purposes or otherwise to make himself foolish." [209] Now the standard is for policy recommendation than also there are problems. Oil reach country Kuwait and its' citizen will not find difficult to support his family members or War devastated country may lower his standard for definition of deprivation. Adam Smith's notion of minimum means of subsistence is applicable everywhere.

---

[208] Prof.J.K.Galbraith, The affluent Society, Page No.128
[209] ibid, Page No.1

Standards and aggregation

We have to look into intercommunity comparison. The extent of deprivation in community and comparison in two communities by given standard for forecasting the difference for second community compared to one. Now we have to make aggregation to identify the deprivation level by some method in which we incorporate different people. Here arbitration may take place.

We have seen earlier that lots of question comes up in case of standard. When we talk about the standard, there are two difficulties. One is common standard and second is comparison. It is very difficult to make a common standard due to various aspects of poverty. Again, the set standard arrived at with great difficulty than also the social conditions are so fluid, it may not be applicable after some time. It is difficult to compare with two communities through the standard. There can be lot of different things in two communities. Comparison in between two community with given standard is a inter community problem. It is difficult to compare two societies also.

Now we have to make aggregation to identify the deprivation level by some method in which we incorporate different people. Here arbitration may take place. When we think of aggregation, we have to combine the deprivation of different people into one indicator. Now it is difficult to see that how conversion accepted. Conversion is most difficult. One can take help of arbitration. The arbitration will be on higher scale. This will affect aggregation. The conversion, arbitration are most difficult things in aggregate. This way the term poverty is most ambiguous.

Here we have to bring in ethics. The ambiguity will come into existence. Therefore standard and aggregation also will not help us to measure starvation and poverty in society. Overall one has to accept deprivation in absolute and relative term. Poverty and inequality are related but not different in their own place.

9.4 Poverty Identification And Aggregation

The measurement of poverty is clearly depending on two things (1) Identification of poor (2) Aggregation in terms of measurement of poverty.

Commodities and characteristics

First we have to decide the method for identification of poor. The basic need of people is to be decided. The non-fulfilment of basic need is the test of poverty. The basic need can be defined in two ways (1) By way of commodity (2) By way of characteristics. Commodities can be food item such as wheat or rice. Characteristics are the qualities of commodity - say Protein and fat, fibre, vitamins and minerals. In case of characteristics, it is difficult to transform it into one commodity. Any one commodity is not sufficient to obtain required quantity of protein, fat, fibre and vitamins, minerals. We have to take commodity and its characteristics. Again, some commodities are food nature, some are of shelter nature, and the third one may be any type of commodities. It is prescribed in both the vector for this reason.

Therefore, the energy criteria, in other words "Calories" are the appropriate item to measure the poverty. There are various types of commodity. They may have different characteristics. It is a matter of reason we should put them under heading of 'Basic'. An interesting point is we can have many source of 'protein'. Now a community may be using one commodity say RICE, to fulfil their requirement in terms of characteristics. The calories from rice should be considered. This is little difficult.

The Direct method versus the Income method

We have to identify poor in society. First of all, one has to consider the "Basic need". This basic need can be found out in two ways.

(1) Direct method (2) Income method

    (1) Direct method: - we check the set of people. We take in to account their consumption. The basic need is defined. We check the consumption. It was found that some unsatisfied basic needs are there. Here the requirement of people is an important factor. This will give direct answer about shortfall. We do not take into account the income factor. We do not consider the consumption pattern. Consumption pattern may be accurate or may not. Here the person, who fast, will be considered as 'POOR' even though he may be rich. The fast may be due to some health problem, religious purposes or just a desire not to eat. This gives a wrong answer.

Direct method gives an idea about the short fall in conventional basic needs with constrain of community preference.

(2) Income Method: - Income method suggests two things (a) Actual consumption (b) persons' ability to full fill his minimum need. Income method is more analytical. We take into account the total basic need and convert it into monetary term. The monetary unit will tell us about the short fall in basic need requirement. One has to find out who is falling short in income to satisfy his basic needs. Here the monetary position is important. The difference will lead us to understand 'poverty'. The difference in income may be due to the person's ability. The reason of poverty is the inability of a person to meet the minimum basic need. Hicks prefer Income method in welfare economics of real income comparisons.[210]

In income method we go for minimum expenses as cost method. We take rice. There are different varieties of rice and different approach for taste. There is vast difference in 'TASTE' factor of urban and rural population. The taste can give us an idea about the cost, which is very necessary to measure poverty. This taste factor gives the idea about price and consumption habits. The taste may differ from community to community. When you go for cost and minimizing the cost on food items then the test of that food may not palatable. When you measure poverty in between two communities then distinctly you have to consider the need in term of characteristics and need in terms of commodities. In that case comparison in between inter community will give better result. This comparison will give idea about price as well as consumption habit.

Now direct method is easy but some information one can have by way of income only. Income method gives idea of actual consumption in monetary term. Say an ascetic is observing fast on expensive bed will be a case of direct method as poor. Direct method does not take into account the economical condition of a person or wealth. In case of income method, ascetic will be in a position to have full nutritive food. Income method will give different judgment under different conditions, for different community.

---

[210]   Hicks-1958-'The measurement of Real Income 'Oxford Economics paper no. 10, and Amartya Sen, poverty and famine page no, 27 footnote.

The income method is superior than direct method, in a sense that it gives picture of shortfall in income. The negative point of income method is; it is against uniform poverty line. You cannot have a uniform poverty line for all by which you can decide the poor. In deciding poverty line, there can be a different income groups and different location points for income. This will be a mixture of many things. The poverty picture will not be clear. This will distort the reality. In extreme cases, say famine, it will differ and results into non-healthiness due to the change of diet and that too of inferior type. People have to consume whatever is available and the quality of food may not be up to the mark.

Family size and equivalent adults

Until now, we have thought in terms of individual. One has to take into account the family. Family gives an idea of consumption behaviour. One has to convert individual income into family income by some method. Again, family size is important. In poverty elimination formula and social security system, family is converted into 'equivalent number of adult'. The simple method is to divide family income by number of members. This does not give benefit to large scale family. Children requirements will be different than adult. The old and sick people requirements will be different from adults. The pregnant women requirements are different than child or old age person. This may result in to uneven distribution in family. If you take in to account, nutritional standard for family than also some problems remains unsolved.

There is another approach. One should calculate how much extra income is required for well-being of a family. Here the well-being standard will be equal for large and small family.

The third approach is one should examine the actual consumption of families of different size and their behaviour. This is the step in the direction of welfare of family. Find out the fractional amount spent on food and compare it with other family. After doing this, still the problem of weighting is there. Consider equal weight for each house holder OR consider equal weight for each individual OR consider equal weight for family of equivalent number of adults.

It is actual consumption behaviour and this behaviour will indicate the welfare aspect in family. The welfare is in measurement of suffering of each member in the family. This may be laborious job. It is difficult to compare data of one family to another family.

It is difficult to prove by way of empirical investigation in equivalent adult method. There are number of questions arises such as workload, gender, nutritional requirements, different age etc. The extra income approach for well being of family and larger family are same. Well-being stand is useful one. One can use here empirical data and prove it.

Poverty gap and relative deprivation

As we have brought the income in picture, it is interesting to know the "INCOME GAP" of poverty and relative deprivation.

The definition of Income gap is the shortfall of personal income than the poverty line income, is his "Income gap". Now person A is below poverty line income. Person B is slightly less than, but below poverty line income, of person A. Here B is poorer than A. Therefore absolute and relative term is necessary even after taking in to account the set of minimum need.

Now if we transfer some income from person A to person B than person A will increase his absolute shortfall and person B, who is receiver, will reduce his absolute short fall. There will be number of people in between A and B in the range of transfer of income. This is in terms of diminishing marginal utility of income. A is greater looser in terms of utility and B is lower looser in terms of utility. There is no cardinal welfare scale to measure this. Does it mean than overall poverty of community, is increased? The answer is yes. This proves in spite of defining need and income gap, the relative and absolute deprivation will be there. Aggregation exercise of absolute deprivation has supplemented by relative deprivation. We have to examine the standard measures of poverty.

Critique of standard measure

We examine the head count theory. It is very simple that head count measure is symbolizing as "H". If Q is number of people identified as poor as per earlier discussion- poverty line income-and N is the total number of population in community. Therefore $H = Q/n$. Eminent economist and organization like U.N.O used this formula in quantitative study to measure poverty.

There is another popular measure known as "POVERTY GAP". Here all poor, who are below poverty line of community, are taken together. The short fall is in average income of all poor from poverty line. The poverty measurement is shown in percentage. We will say it 'I' income gap ratio. The income transfer to each other amongst poor within poverty line than it is not giving any effect to the measurement. This is a drawback and damaging factor in analysis.

In case of H, head count theory, it is sensitive to that particular society but does not consider the poor below poverty line. Now some income from poor person transferred to rich person, who is above poverty line then the transfer of income will not reflect as increase in poverty. Even if you transfer some income of rich person to poor person and rich person is not coming below poverty line; at the same time the poor person who receives income from rich person will not cross the poverty line. Here Head count theory is not use full. This effect is not reflecting in Head count theory in terms of number. Any way it will not reflect in poverty measurement. Head count theory for poverty is popular in economics.

The combination of head count and income gap will help or not is to be seen. Here a person below poverty line transfer a unit of income to another person who is richer but below poverty line than, it will not reflect in any poverty measurement theories. This does not reflect in aggregate poverty OR relative deprivation. If we assume that "ALL POOR" are having the same income than it will work. This will help to clarify the position of poverty line and relative deprivation. This will help in solving the problem of distribution amongst poor. WE say it "P" as poverty measure.

Axiomatic deprivation of a poverty measure and variants

Utilitarian concept can be used here. We have to take into account individual income. We say individual income then it will be in absolute term. We are lacking in "Relative term". The relative deprivation is as "R" and "I" is as ordering of all poor in decreasing order of income. In this case, greater the rank value, more persons are in category of relative deprivation. One can derive from above that weight on person's income shortfall increase with his rank value $R(i)$. Say $R(i) = 12$. This is twelfth worst person in all poor. If more than one person having same income will be ranked in arbitrary order. Poverty measure is indifferent for the choice of arbitrary order. As per Runciman and Townsend –"The greater the rank value, the more the person is deprived in terms of relative deprivation with respect to others in the same category." [211] The poorest poor will be last person in queue. This we say as "Q". The person near to "Q" is more deprived than person near "I" Here the distance will be equal between two people. This satisfies the Borda's rank ordering system. The combination of H and I is also satisfied here.

We impose the H & I axioms on poverty measure with weighted income gap. It will result into GINI effect. The formula is as under. P=H {I+ (i-I) G}. Where there is equal income of all poor than GINI co-efficient will be zero and P=HI. With the above assumption, poverty measure "P" increases with greater inequality of income below poverty line. This you can say that it is "Ranked Relative Deprivation". Many people use this method to measure poverty in a big way. As Poverty measure has unique advantage in measuring poverty, the variants are giving different interpretations, which are useful. This is pluralism. This is important to take into consideration the absolute and relative deprivation in measurement of poverty.

Prof. J. K. Galbraith-"We will be rich but never quite rich enough to spare anything much for the poor-including our own. We shall not present a very enchanting picture to the world or even to ourselves." [212]

9.5 Starvation And Famine

Famine, time contrast and group contrast

There are many things, which emerge out of poverty. Starvation is one of them. Starvation is the main act of poverty. Famine suggests starvation but starvation is not famine. Starvation can exist in normal condition. Starvation is defined as less food for consumption due to poverty. Starvation in famine is cause of no entitlement for purchasing the food. Poverty is in term of income. Poverty means relative deprivation. There will be no starvation in the society but poverty very well exists there. Therefore, starvation and poverty has sine connection. All above terms are interrelated to each other in general as well in absolute term.

---

[211]   Amartya Sen, poverty and famine page no, 35.
[212]   Prof.J.K.Galbraith, The affluent Society, Page No.271

Starvation is normal in many parts of the world. One has to distinguish between the starvation due to poverty and starvation due to famine. In violent famine good number of people died. History has account from 1 B.C. to till to day of famine. In famine thousands of people die.

The three main reasons of starvation is precisely the matter of examination. The analysis of starvation reasoning has three meaning. They are higher and higher in degree for one another as a result of starvation.

(1) Lowness of the typical level of food consumption,

(2) Declining trend of food consumption and

(3) Collapse of the level of food consumption.

Empirically it proves that in India food production was on rise in spite of drought, which was moderate and less frequent. In Japan, during the two ruler period one can say that the food consumption was not stable in the time of famine where as in stable condition people consume less but regularly. It is a fact that food availability is on rise at world level but acute starvation is very often.

The appropriate definition of famine is as under.

"An extreme and protracted shortage of food resulting in widespread and persistent hunger, evidenced by loss of body weight and emaciation and increase in death rate caused either by starvation or disease resulting from the weakened condition of the population", JOHNSON (1973) [213] Famine can take place even the regular food consumption is on decline. Famine can be widespread with acute starvation.

"Famine is an economic and social phenomenon characterized by the wide spread lack of food resources which, in the absence of outside aid, leads to death of those affected". (UNRISED, 1975) [214] There is a historical record of famine of various countries at different time from 500 B.C. to 2005 A.D. There were famines in Kashmir in 918 AD, in China 1333-37, In India 1770 and Ireland 1845-51. The food crisis of 1972 is a global example of this time contrast. Colin Tudge describes the development in dramatic terms.

---

[213]   Amartya Sen, poverty and famine page no, 40 footnotes.
[214]   Ibid, page no. 40 and 40 footnotes.

"The 1960s brought good harvest by the third world's green revolution, based on American - developed dwarf strains of wheat and rice. The world's food problem was not shortage, apparently, but over-production, leading to low prices and agricultural depression. The US took land out of production, and in the early 1970s both U S and Canada ran down their grain stores. Then the bad weather of 1972 brought dismal harvests to the USSR, China, India, Australia and the Sehal countries south of Sahara. Russia bought massively in the world grain markets before others, including the U S, realized what was happening. By Mid-1974 there was only enough grain left in store to feed the world's population for three –and - a – half weeks; terrifying brinkmanship." [215]

In India, in 1344-45 A.D. than King - Mohammad Bin Tughlak was unable to obtain household necessities as he had a famine relief programme. He had opened the famine relief programmes including relief in tax remittance, distribution of cash and opening relief centres and distribution of cooked food. As per Alemgir, Dutch famine in 1944 was very widespread.[216] In case of famine condition, there will be wide spread starvation but this will not affect different groups, as they have different command over foods. In case of inter group distribution, the different group may have unequal share in over all shortage. Famine can be widespread.

9.6   The Entitlement Approach

Endowment and exchange

The starvation and famine are related to ability to command of food. The command of food leads to entitlement. The legal meaning is to have command of food by way of production, trade, heritage, and own labour entitlements. Starvation is two-sided coin. One side is, Person is unable to command food and other side is person is not using his ability to procure food to avoid starvation. You can not include looting and no change in food habit in entitlement. The entitlement approach is for bundle of commodities and having command over food is one of them. Starvation means not enough food in his entitlement bundle.

---

[215]   Ibid, page no.42.
[216]   Ibid, page no.43

In directed economy, a person will be assigned bundles of good. Person can have two advantages, exchange of trade and production in private economy. You can say 1) An endowment bundle 2) exchange entitlement. Here a person has liberty to exchange his commodity bundle for different set of alternative. There can be number of combinations. His endowment is exchanged for a bundle of goods, which includes food. Starvation is the result of not enough food in that bundle of goods.

A person can have his endowment in terms of land, own labour and other resources. One can produce a bundle of goods by using land, or by sealing his labour or from earned wage can buy different commodity bundle. There are number of possibilities in endowment bundle. The exchange entitlement depends on the legal, political, social and economical characteristics. This exchange entitlement will depends on many things including social security and taxation. The exchange is in terms of cost; therefore, it is a "BUDGET SET". Production entitlement depends on many opportunities. It is in the form of legal as entrepreneur and as social conventions for migrant family. Social security provision is also a part of budget set.

Starvation and entitlement failure

The person affected for starvation due to (1) Endowment collapses and (2) Shift in exchange entitlement. Endowment collapse will happen to a certain group in society. This will happen with rural flocks due to sale of cattle or annihilation of land. Your asset is not affected but due to change in your exchange entitlement, the value will decrease and there will be a starvation.

Limitations of entitlement approach

Entitlement approach has number of limitation. Entitlement is not well defined. Property rights are vague set. In case of empirical study one has to compromise on data. Here shift in ingredients is to study. The big shift may give decisive result in entitlement failure. The legal structure and violation of rights are also a cause of failure in entitlement approach. The loot is violation of legal right and this is a defect to entitlement approach in famine. During 1943 Bengal famine, people were died due to starvation because they were not having legal endowment. Sometimes a particular community is having a habit of consuming certain type of food grain only. As a result, the actual food consumption may fall below the entitlement.

Starvation is different from famine. In famine, more deaths accrued due to epidemic. This includes the death due to population movement, breakdown of sanitary facilities.

Direct and trade entitlement failures

Person is having commodity to sell or consume. This commodity is not produced but his own labour power. This is only the means of his survival. Some time a person can be a producer of agriculture commodity, Say rice. Here we have assumed simple model. This may not be workable in industrial economy or analysis of famine in developed countries. Now, in case of starvation, the commodity, may or may not be produced by person. Here we discuss the direct and trade entitlement failures. Commodity is produced less for his own consumption or he can get less due to exchange. It will effect on his direct entitlement and trade entitlement. The direct entitlement and trade entitlement will affect in case of production is meant for consumption as well as exchange. The Ethiopian shepherd eats the animal product and sale the animal to buy food grain. Same way a Bengali fisherman consumes the fish catch and sale some fish to get high calories food grain.

9.7 Entitlements and Deprivation

Food and entitlements, the poor, world food availability

Famine is not the cause of food availability decline. This approach shows us the relationship of food and famine. The FDA-Food availability decline-gives us less information regarding starvation. Starvation can be due to variety of reasons including food availability. Starvation can be point out in specific group on the ground of food consumption. The entitlement approach comes in picture. Here the why and what will give us the answer. Why will lead to entitlement, what will lead to inter group comparison. The entitlement approach has to be looked from economic, social, political and legal prospective.

A person's ability to command food depends upon his entitlement. This depends on what he has and exchange possibility. A barber has labour of his own and has to exchange for entitlement. Barber entitlement collapses due to no demand of his services. He can survive only on social security or another job. Here food availability has nothing to do. One more possibility is sharp change in price of his labour will bring him starvation due to decline in price of his labour. Here food availability has nothing to do. Thus the matter comes to the shortage of income I.e. entitlement approach. This proves the entitlement approach is the very affecting thing for his starvation and not the food. This gives us partial picture of starvation.

Food may be one of the variance. People died due to no income to buy food. This depends on what they can sale and at what price. Sometimes the income may be 'notional'. The peasant can consume food grains grown in his field. He has to exchange remaining/balance food grains, for other items. The above theory reflects man's ability to command commodity in general and food in particular.

The poor: A legitimate category?

An entitlement approach requires further discrimination in terms of poor in to less poor and more poor. We have to go to occupational groups of different ownership, which governs different entitlements and different entitlement relations. Different group in poverty will share in different way. Famine will not help to point out as poor or rich in different occupational groups. This will help us to evaluate the percentage of poverty of the nation. Assessment of poverty is all to gather different than the assessment of inequality. The severity of deprivation among the poor is worth discriminating. Here head count is not of much help. We have to go further in detail for 'poor'.

The head count gives an idea of the quality in poor. Here the people just below the poverty line should be taken in to account and not the deep poverty. The discrimination among poor gives us an idea about deprivation. This can be described in terms of intensity of poverty. There are evidences that general poverty will not help for right public policy. It leads to wrong policy choice.

World food availability and starvation

The FAD- Food availability decline- approach is for world food availability and world population. The fall of food availability has nothing to do with the intensity of hunger in the world. This is most general but the empirical data will indicate the food availability per head. If food availability goes on decline over a period, it will indicate the time for starvation to come. In fact, the food production and world population has never felt any shortage of food, but it is in balance. The entitlement approach will help us to find out starvation and famine without giving any hint about food production. The analysis will help to find out the venerability of food in particular country. It helps to know how the food aid affects to the domestic production and distribution, in the light of world food prices. The food balance sheet should add in to social accounting procedure. Apart from food production, the famine accrued due to deficit in entitlement. The entitlement relations depend on simple, complex, use of market mechanism, upon public policy; affected by Macro economic development and deal with local calamities. Again, these relations are influenced by speculation.

Prof. J .K .Galbraith- "To eliminate poverty efficiently, we must, indeed, invest more than proportionately in the CHILDREN of poor community. The high quality schools, strong health services, special provision for nutrition and recreation are most need to compensate for the very low investment which families are able to make in their own offspring. In case of poverty eradication, the limiting factor is not a lack of knowledge of what they can do. Over whelming, it is a shortage of money."[217] Government of India has put in to practice many things as listed above by Prof.J.K.Galbraith

Market and food movement

The dependence on market during famine was able to abolish the same by food movement. This was a political argument and supported by stalwarts. There was a famine in Gujarat In 1812. At that time, governor of Bombay prohibited the movement of food grain and left it to the fortune of market mechanism. [218] This was done on the ground of misinterpretation of economic thought. This was continued till the end of nineteenth century. The market mechanism failed. The Cuttak division commissioner RAVEN SHAW, during 1865-66 famine in the Orissa, blamed the traders not to bring enough food from other areas. The small group of traders can act in monopolistic way to hinder the movement of grain to famine area. [219]

Here The Adam Smith idea related to efficiency of market mechanism is important. It might not turn useful in the absence of entitlement and purchasing power of people.

---

[217] Prof.J.K.Galbraith, The affluent Society, page no.252
[218] Amartya Sen, Poverty and famine, page no.160
[219] Ibid, page no.160

It so happens that during famine, food exported from famine area. Say for example, the case of Wollo, Ethiopia, in 1973 and Bangladesh 1974, Irish famine in 1840 and China famine in 1910. It is clear from the above famines that the food grain exported to other part, even though the people were starving. [220]

In market mechanism, entitlement approach is stronger than food which will move in such direction irrespective of famine or non-famine condition. This phenomenon does not take in to account the NEED. Here the person with strong entitlements and less acute need will win.

Famine as failures of entitlement

Famine is an economic disaster than food shortage. Traditionally people say that it is food availability decline. We can have general observation about famine. This is the result of entitlement failure. The reasons are as under. This is a general approach to famine. Starvation in famine can be due to not change in food habit but refusal of entitlement transfer. The failures of different types of entitlements difference are the cause of famine. This will help to formulate the anticipation of famine relief plan and prevention of famine.

Second thing is famine can occur in boom and recession condition of food production. The famine condition at the time of recession of food production is due to contraction of output. In Boom time food production, one group may have benefited due to boom in output, but other groups may not have benefit. The boom time food output can help the farmer to sale surplus food at the market price.

Third one is the decline of food availability and direct entitlement of food should distinguish in famine time. Food availability defines the quantity where as entitlement is each food grower output and part there of as direct consumption for him. The former one is general, while latter one is connected to particular. Say for example farmer. If farmer's own crop failed then, he will starve and others will not, where as if his crop is good then he will do well and other will suffer at the time of famine.

The fourth one, the legal right is the most important in entitlement approach. The legal position is very important from the ownership,

---

[220]   Ibid, page no.161.

contract and exchange entitlement approach. The law is hurdle in between food availability and food entitlement. The person will be looser in case of contract and exchange entitlement. Only ownership will have help but again the price rise or availability will be a hurdle in using the entitlement. It can be a villain for death due to starvation

9.8 Philosophy of Welfare in poverty and famine

Dr. Amartya Sen had examined the poverty in detail starting from its root as ownership approach and at top entitlement approach. The poverty and starvation with famine, all are different aspects. Starvation is in relation of poverty and famine. In any case the victim is poor in all the three position. It is very important to have effective solution. Poverty and famine is unwanted thing in the society and it is moral responsibility of society to remove them.

The various definitions of poverty are given. Various patterns of comparison for groups of people or community are well analyzed. There are various theories put forward for the reason of poverty. Poverty can be seen from many angles. All the angles may be true in their own respect but it requires a total bird's eye view approach to have the proper solution of the problem. Famine had various approaches in the light of the prevailing circumstances depends upon places, culture and thinking of the people who manages the famine affairs.

The great Bengal famine was the victims of exchange entitlements. The Ethiopia famine was related to pastoral people and agriculture economy. Sehal famine was due to failure of food entitlements. Bangladesh famine was the result of boom of production but affected with market mechanism and uneven spread of food entitlements which made some people in luxury and others in starvation.

The recommendations of Dr. Amartya Sen are accepted by International Labour Organization, for world employment programme. The same salutation is accepted by most of the world country to eradicate the poverty and reduce starvation and apply preventive measure for famine. The most of the countries are putting the recommendation by their respective government in their budget to follow the various schemes to help the poor people to bring them up from poverty line and make them self sufficient to develop their capacity to have better entitlements. Many a time governments are interfering and applying quick method to control further damages and remedial measure applied for the problem. This is good for society to have welfare of a class of poor in their wellbeing. Society through politics can have good result by way of agency entitlement for poverty striking people.

The human nature is to apply rational thought, added with feelings and emotion and tendency to earn along with good health are affecting factor to the poverty reduction programme. This is a mixed bag of things and only economics cannot do the job. It requires the help of physiology, sociology, politics and medical science.

We have to look in to poverty of world in many different ways. The poverty of East Asian countries is due to lack of development. Myanmar is under Military junta and country is suffering. We do not have detail information. Aung San Sue Kyi is a democracy leader and she is under house arrest. The other Muslim country like Indonesia, sub Saharan countries of Africa is under strict religious practice and poverty cannot be measured in correct way. In India, poverty is in existence. This is due to political, economical and philosophical reasons. People are having variety of castes and creeds. State level culture is also effective at all level. The U.P. Orissa, Bengal more concern for religious matter and Bengal is a big cause of infiltration of Bangla Deshi at the same time it is ruled by Communist ideology. Maharashtra, Gujarat is highly industrially developed states and mixed population is the cause of economic growth. The poverty in these states may be negligible in term of definition of poverty. The Punjab, Hariyana and Andhra are very well advanced in agriculture and poverty may be in some pockets and in low caste population. This is due to high caste prominence and deprivation of economic opportunity.

In general, central government makes budgetary provision for number of programmes for low income level people and encourages the education, health, rural development, pure drinking water scheme and sanitation, road and electricity, communication and many more things. State government with the help of central budgetary allocation and their own resources implements the programme. The result is not percolating at the lowest level. Middle man and political agents takes the benefit of it. The dropout rate from school, migration of labour from one state to another state, mass killing of them in fear of losing employment by local people and no proper reforms for land allocation, less irrigation facility and uneven rain pattern makes the farmer run into heavy debt trap resulting in to commit suicide. The corruption at central and state level allows the prohibited pesticides to use.

The solution to tackle the poverty programme requires political courage at all level of governs and people's cooperation to have economic outlook. Indian governments have made lot of efforts to improve the standard of living and made changes in law in many areas. The Special economic zone policy has miss fired. The result of other countries is that it widens the gap between poor and rich. Poor has to put in much efforts to sustain themselves. The poverty is mental concept and it is related to the deep rooted culture in the society.

Lord Mahavir told that human is having different capacity in different fields. It is possible to discuss the equality in principle and as a chief subject but it is not possible at practical level. Philosophically, no one is inferior or superior but practically there is difference. There are ways to remove poverty (1) to control population growth (2) to improve the environment (3) to remove unemployment.

People believe in fortune. This is a big hurdle in the way of all types of remedies. Lord Mahavir believed in hard labour in present situation. Lord Mahavir interpreted the fortune as the cause for our labour. Government does not use the resources to remove poverty and to remove unemployment.

The powerful nation thinks that other less powerful country should accept their authority. Poverty had brought ill health, malnutrition and high birth rate. This is the result due to hoarding. The inner feelings of human are decreasing due to selfishness and outer ratio is changing in favour of rich. Economics had to bring in to the periphery of philosophy and thought, psychology and sociology to have better result and to create a new human generation. [221]

---

[221]   Acarya Mahapragnya, Mahavir ka Arthsastra, Page no.71 to 79.

10 the doctrine of Aparigraha, Effective tool in Jain Philosophy

10.1 Moral In Jain Philosophy

Moral made a part of religion by the Jain thinkers and ethic to club the idea of metaphysical and theological consideration. This is a link between human and cosmos. As per Jain religion, the soul is having fourfold feature.

(1) Anant Jnana-Infinite knowledge quality - knowledge

(2) Anant darsan-Infinite Darsan-vision quality -perception

(3) Anant charitrya-Infinite Character-conduct quality -bliss

(4) Anant Virya-Infinite strength quality -power

Generally religion is understood as merely a ritualistic thing. People do the ritual as a part of religion. Ritual is a convention. The tradition is in the family and society. In an ideal mental state, duty takes the form of habit and ethic changes into psychology. The body and mind are covered into these aspects. Habit and psychology are the clue for human behaviour. Human behaviour associated throughout one's life. Ethics is an important aspect of religion. In ethics, there is no difference in man's duty for himself as well as to the society.

Another important aspect of human is in moral sense. Person acts in his day-to-day life. This act is done after some thought. Person thinks of right and wrong. Person has to find out merit/demerit in his act. Adam Smith argued that our 'first perceptions' of right and wrong 'cannot be the object of reason, but of immediate sense and feeling.'[222] Person has to think scientifically for this. Person has to find out the working and method for implementation of moral in his life. As per the moral, it directs person to act in "OUGHT TO BE" sense. This is a very effective tool for our spiritual development. Jain religion has prescribed ten virtues to practice in day-to-day life.

(a) Uttam Kshma (b)Uttam Mardav (c)Uttam Arjva (d) Uttam Sauch (e) Uttam Sayama (f)Uttam Tapa (g)Uttam Tyaga (h) Uttam Akinchantv (i) Uttam Satya (j)Uttam Brahmacarya.

  (1) Uttam Kshma – forgiveness. Person should forgive the other person as a mark of respect. This is irrespective of age, caste and creed. This virtue brings the inner strength to a person and his mental power will become strong.

  (2) Uttam Mardav – humility. Person becomes humble. He will respect others view and will follow anekantvada in his life. Person will develop humbleness and set an example in society.

  (3) Uttam Arjva – straight forwardness. Here the person will be straightforward. He will behave with people in upright manner. Person will not apply any tricks or any foul play.

  (4) Uttam Satya – truthfulness. This virtue does not require any detail to be explained. It is a matter of experience. The day to day life with truth will make him fearless. This is universal.

  (5) Uttam Sauch – cleanliness. Person should be clean in his deed, behaviour. This is in physical sense as well as in psychological sense. Person should be crystal clear in his dealing.

  (6) Uttam Sayama – restrain. Person should apply as far as possible all types of control in his life. Person should do every deed with utmost precaution, not to harm and give any bad effect to other person.

  (7) Uttam Tapas – penance. As and when occasion arises, person will observe the penance of various types as per his capacity, prescribed

---

[222]   Amartya Sen, Argumentative Indian, page no. 279.

in the Jain religion. He will not do it for fame or prestige or to earn the money. Person will observe penance with a view to annihilate his karmas and make progress on the path of purification of soul.

(8) Uttam Tyaga – renunciation. Person will do this as per Jain religion to become from extrovert to introvert. He will leave the things gradually as prescribed by religion to make progress on the path of purification of soul.

(9) Uttam Akinchantv–indifference. Person will be indifferent for anything and everything. Person will not please or repent for anything. He will slowly give away control of the things to his family member and will not take part in decision making; he will not give consent to any decision of family. He will keep himself aloof from worldly activities. He will try to concentrate on his pure form of soul.

(10) Uttam Brahmacarya – control of sexual passion. Celibacy is a virtue. This helps person to concentrate on inner self. Celibacy gives physical and mental strength. Person observes the vow of celibacy as to restrict and satisfy his/her sexual urge with his wife or her husband in initial period of life. In no case anybody will keep extramarital relationship. Person will take vow of total celibacy after certain age.

This leads human to think worthiness of moral. There is a subjective and an objective connection. Once an act is object, which connected with human inner self-subject, becomes moral. Therefore, moral judgment is external as well as internal. The intuition of a person, hereditary character is the forces behind moral act. This moral act becomes a nature of man gradually. Human has restricted energy to apply in the subjective matters. The success of nerve energy results into good judgments. If this energy is unsuccessful, it will hinder the moral act. In extreme cases, it can turn into immoral act. A key to moral worth lies in the human mental states. Here the stamp of moral on act will react in self. This proves the functional relationship between active subject and external object. The strength of desire can be measured in terms of pleasure and pain. One can say that intensity of desire and nature of man will decide the moral value of a man.

Charvak and materialism

CHARVAK-Indian philosopher was most probably contemporary of lord Mahavir. Charvak was teacher of systematic atheistic materialism. He had put the doctrine of pleasure into practice in his life very well. He thought that one should enjoy the life fully. He suggested his followers to incur debt and drink GHEE (clarified butter) means live life happily. HAPPINESS IS SUPREME. Human should not worry for next day. Nobody is beyond the range of death. There is nothing after death. Death itself is liberation. He did not believe in rebirth theory. There is nothing like SOUL. Consciousness is the result of fragmentation of four eternal elements. The body is the only visible and cause of existence due to four eternal elements. Whatever is beyond the experience of the senses is false and is non-existent. Whatever sensed is real. This happiness is momentary.[223]

This cannot be a goal of life. Person cannot say that he wants to eliminate pain from his life permanently by this theory. The utilitarian believes in increase of pleasure. They do take into account conduct. Conduct is part of life. They say that objective feeling of sensuous pleasure is not a standard of moral. Jonathan Glover, an oxford philosopher, argues in his recent and enormously interesting "Moral history of the twentieth century" that We must not only reflect on what has happened in the last century, but also 'need to look hard and clearly at some monsters inside us' and to consider ways and means of 'caging and taming them'.[224]

Pillars for character building

It is a fact that moral judgments depend upon the essential nature of man. Aristotle said, morally good act is doing well. He meant that activity should be as such that it leads to higher excellence. Again, to achieve this is a most difficult task. According to STOIC- rational nature of man is a moral of man. Persons' immediate right or wrong sense is his moral sense. Here intuition is at work. An intuition is lacking rational thought. It does not take in to account past experience. It is spontaneous. This does not suggest that all people are actually living moral life. Moral living requires continuous and perfect conception of the fundamental character of a human nature, throughout the life of man.

---

[223] Haribhadra, book:- Sad-darsana samuccya, translated by K. Satchidananda, ch.7, page no. 101 to 108.

[224] Amartya Sen, Argumentative Indian, page no.273.

A person should be pure in his day-to-day activities. He should not weight less, give less, show one thing and give another thing and grab some one's money, property or anything. This is a vow in Jain religion known as Acauryavarta (non-stealing).

There are two important points before HUMAN.

(1) Control of senses.

(2) Satisfaction by senses

You find these things in old economics. It is noted in the history that Chanakya advised king to have control on senses and sex, anger, greed, deceit, pride and jealousy. This is a combination of physical and mental position of a king. In present days person does not think in terms of MORAL. Person is unable to have at least a one thing in his control. He says he will tackle moral problem at later stage.

In early historic period, the act had only one value and that was a religious value. In the name of religion various good and bad acts were performed in the society. The preachers of religion were taking shelter in the name of religion. The immoral act done by way of religion was acceptable in the society. Very recently, the act separated as religion or moral. This act of moral is conducive to man's immediate ultimate welfare. The ultimate welfare is the emancipation of soul as per Jain religion. Lord Mahavir achieved the emancipation of soul. Lord Mahavir show the way to his followers for emancipation of soul. Jain believes that practicing the moral in life and achieving higher and higher grade, one can transform oneself as Siddha. Now this evolution will set an example and it will guide, advice and give encouragement to others. Siddha is nothing but above everything and has attributes of divinity. Thus moral conduct is the ladder of success for liberation of soul. Man is permanently free from pleasure and pain.

10.2 Definition of Aparigraha (Non-possession)

Moral is connected with wealth accumulation. Parigraha-attachment is the nature of every living being. The industrialization and consumerism, urbanization are the fruits of it. Now these things are the golden route to accumulate wealth which is the mother of parigraha. Parigraha is the cause of all problems. It takes away peace, encourages doing all sorts of wrong things and makes man devil. It is the root cause in terms of finance and creates all types of imbalances in society. The special economic zone idea has created lots of trouble in many countries and especially in India.

Definition of possession is taking interest in worldly things and establishing ownership by person. The opposite of this is non-possession. Yoga is act done by way of body, speech and mind as per Jain philosophy. The act done with acute passion is known as pramatta yoga. The possession will cover persons' intelligence and for him entire world is in his possession. Person will establish his right of "MINENESS" everywhere. Person has desire of ownership. This possession factor is the strongest when compared to effect of any astrological planet. Raga or the feeling of possession and as such, has the consciousness of his activities applied towards the attainment of desirable objects as well as a feeling of pleasure, arising from the attainment thereof.[225]

The MOHANIYA-DELUDING karma is responsible for giving wrong information and to act in possessive way. The darsan and charitra mohaniya are the chief element in this. The Antray karma does not give the benefit to the person for which he is entitled. One's Antray karma comes into existence by interfering with another person's exercising his power of Labh-benefit, Dana-donation, Bhog-consumption, Upabhoga-re use of items and Virya-vigour, [226] Person should have the sense of non-possession by way of physical and mental order. Person should not accumulate possessions and power beyond his bare minimum requirement. This is the spirit of non-possessiveness. Person can have that much possession which fulfils his basic needs as an individual. This very fact leads person to think of possessiveness. Possession means person deny and deprive others right to possess which other person requires. The best advice is person should give up his sense of 'mineness'.

Possession of material things will bring unlimited anxiety, surrender to immoral activities, to do injustice and take shelter in falsehood. The loss of material things will result into pain, no peace and bad thoughts. There are eighteen types of sins described in Jain philosophy. The possession is at number five in the list. Possession increases person's passion and wishes. One poet described, body requires maximum 500 grams food

---

[225] Hari Satya Bhattacharya, Jain Moral and Doctrine, page no.25
[226] Ibid, page no.38-39.

whereas person has unlimited desire. The illusion of possession makes man dis-satisfied and has no trust in others. As a result, he prepares to commit sins-wrong doing. Possession instigate person to act for theft, killing, untruthful conversation, makes him cruel and to do all sorts of bad-immoral things.

Aristotle said at one place that Money should only acquire in order to provide the means for exercise of the capabilities and not wasted for non-monetary and non-acquisitive goals.

Lord Mahavir had shown the way to welfare in economics. Lord Mahavir suggested limits in each and every thing. The limit of MONEY gives you PEACE and HAPPINESS. Here, a human remains in the centre and money around him.

Types of possessions

Jain philosophy described the attachment of two types (1) Out ward possession (2) Inward possession (Psychic). The Jain religion is the first religion to consider and marked difference of psychological aspect. The psychological aspect is BHAV aspect and body aspect is DRAVYA aspect in Jain religion.

Outward possessiveness is of nine types (a) Land – residential, agricultural, and industrial. (b) Instruments- all types (c) silver – in quantity (d) gold – in quantity (e) Money – in any form cash, Fixed deposit, traveller cheques and bank balance (f) Food grains – own consumption and storage. (g) DUPAD – two legs human – slave – servant- messenger in office, driver-attendant etc. (H) CHAUPAD – four legs- animals, in modern age car, aeroplane (I) Kuviya –luxury and household items,

The outward possessiveness is the cause of mental unrest. The unlimited desire for any of the above things will make human immoral and unethical. This will make human illogical in thought and will act badly. The limit will give him strength to act sensibly. The feeling of non attachment will become stronger and stronger.

Inward – psychic possessiveness are of fourteen types. (a)Anger (b) Ego (c) Deceit (d) greed (e) Laughter (f) passion for sex (g) Non – passion for sex (h) Danger (I) Sorrow (j) Dugancha – strong psychological dislike (K) Female gender (l) Male gender (m) eunuch gender (n) Mithyathva – wrong belief.

They are fourteen in number as stated above. The limit of them will be real taste of persons' conviction and measurement of his inner strength. The temptation will drag person down from his earlier firm position. Person has to resist it and come out with more strength and determination to follow the vow faithfully.

10.3 Vow philosophy of lord Mahavir

Lord Mahavir thought of VRATA-VOW SOCIETY. Vrata-vow means to refrain through manas-mind, speech and body. Here refrains means to do away from the evil activities and to do the positive activities. When you do the above things, only then, you are vrati-observer of vrata. Sadhu-Ascetic has to observe the TOTAL renunciation and Shravaka-laity has to observe partial renunciation. Lord Mahavir gave many rules for ascetics and house holders. These rules were given from philosophical point of view for welfare of human in his ultimate benefit. Person has to combine materialistic thoughts with spirituality. Historian Arnold Toyambi said-man cannot live only on food or only on faith. Human required both. Lord Mahavir was realist. Lord Mahavir realized the difference in materialistic life and spiritual life. Materialistic life will give temporary happiness and spiritual life will give eternal happiness. Materialistic life will ultimately result into unhappiness. This will be a cause of pain and suffering. Lord Mahavir told it was a wrong path. Lord Mahavir connected subject with object, self to cosmos. Lord Mahavir suggested the path of emancipation as ultimate goal of person.

Jain vow for ascetics and householder

Human wants to get rid of pain and misery. In other words, Human wants emancipation. The way to get emancipation in Jain religion is to follow three moral steps, Samyag Jnana-right knowledge, Samyag darsan-right faith and Samyag charitra-right character.

Samyag charitra – Right character based on Ethics and moral for ascetics and householders. This moulded in the form of conduct. The ascetics and householders are required to observe good conduct in their lives. Jain thinker knew that man and woman is having difference in intellect and firmness of will. Women are kind hearted. Women cannot be as cruel as men.

There are in all twelve vows. These vows divided into three broad categories. First five are MAHA- big for ascetics and ANU-small for householders. Anu vrata-vow means compare to ascetic at minor scale. Three are gunvratas-multiplicative vows and four are siksa vratas-disciplinary vows. This is a foundation of character building. Apart from main twelve vows there are other subsidiary disciplines different for ascetics and different for householders to get emancipation. We can say, technically charitra-character is the nearest condition of emancipation.

The ascetics are supposed to follow the first five vows without any atichar-transgression. The ascetics are without any worldly possessiveness. They are not allowed to have transgression for these five vows. The ascetics are allowed transgression only in extra ordinary and unavoidable circumstances with the permission of head of guccha with due Prayascitta-penalty. Householders have no or small penalty for transgression for these five vows. Ascetics are putting their efforts to achieve SAMVAR-stoppage of new karmas and NIRJARA-the shedding of existing karmas. Their goal is Nirvana-Moksa, emancipation of soul. The ascetic, who lives on the ideal of non-possessiveness, will be benefited by annihilation of all his karmas. Ascetics are to observe twelve vratas and three kinds of guptis, five kinds of Samiti, ten kinds of dharma-virtue and twelve Bhavnas, twenty two types of parishajaya and five types of charitrya-(character).

Twelve bhavnas are as follows.*

(1) Anitya Bhavna   (2) Asarana Bhavna (3) Samvar Bhavna (4) Ekatva Bhavna (5) Anyatva Bhavna (6) Asuchi Bhavna (7) Asrava Bhavna (8) Samvara Bhavna (9) Nirjara Bhavna (10) Lok Bhavna (11) Bodhi-Durlabha Bhavna (12) Dharma Bhavna

* Detail is given in chapter on Karma.

Also twenty-two kind of Parisaha-jaya-subdue of suffering and five kinds of charitra-conduct. Apart from this, ascetics are supposed to observe twelve types of internal and external penance and last two categories of meditations from prescribed four categories of meditations.

First five vows are as follows (1) Pranatipataviramana (non–violence) (2) Mrsavadaviramana (truthfulness) (3) Adattadanaviramana (non–stealing) (4) Maithunaviramana (sexual contacts) (5) Parigrahaparimanaviramana (non-possession). Non–possession comes in first classification of five vows. It is important for ascetics.

Householders have to observe above five vratas on minor scale. He had to observe three guna vratas and four siksa vratas. Three guna vratas-multiplicative vows are as follows. (6) Digparimana-To limit the use of direction i.e. east, west, north and south, upward, down ward and slant direction. (7) Bhogopabhogaparimana-To limit once and repetitive use of items. (8) Anarthadandavirmana-To limit punishment without purpose to soul.

In seventh vrata, the other part of vow is for householder. A householder is to observe the voluntary limits on daily basis and lifelong basis. The following items consumption limit is to cultivate the habit as a part of non-possessiveness. They are following (1) one time consumption of food and liquid things. (2) The limit of several time usable items-say cloths (3) Personal usage items such as Towel, napkin and such things. (4) Limit to personal use item such as toothpaste and tooth brush (5) Limit to use the hair wash-Shampoo- items for gents and ladies (6) Limit to use the oil for body massage (7) Limit of the item used for body beautification such as powder, scent, hair oil, cosmetics (8) Limit of consumption of water for clothe washing and bath (9) Limit the number of garments to be used in specific period say-one year (10) Limit to use of sandal wood powder, paste and any other material for bath (11) Limit to use of flowers in any way-worship, garland, personal adoration for ladies etc (12) Limit to use of ornaments of all types Gold, silver, diamond, platinum and jewel studded items (13) To limit the use of air purifying item to be burnt, in modern time- spray (14) To limit the use of sweet and sweetmeats (15) To limit the use of number of grains out of twenty four types (16) To limit the use of number of pulses on daily basis as well as during lifetime (17) To limit the use of oil, curd, butter, butterfat, milk, jeggery, sugar and things like that on day to day basis as well as during the life time (18) To limit the use of vegetables in number on daily basis as well as during lifetime (19) To limit the use of all types of fruits on daily basis as well as during lifetime (20) To limit the number of items to be consume in meal and supper (21) To limit the usage of mouth freshener (22) To limit the consumption of drinking water during the day (23) To limit the use of vehicles (24) To limit the number of shoe pairs (25) To limit the items for use of furniture (26) To limit the items to eat and drink. This list is old one. This was supposed to be effective in Lord Mahavir's time. One has to take in to consideration the present situation and make changes accordingly.

A householder advised not to deal, to perform or to act in any way for fifteen types of trade and industries prescribed in seventh vrata. These fifteen types of trades and industries are supposed to give you heaviest karmic matter, which will drag you in cycle of birth and death. Lord Mahavir put here the purity of income as top most priority in trade and industries.

Four siksa vratas-disciplinary vows (9) Samayika-The control of mind, body and speech for limited time (10) Desavakasikavrata–to practice the limit of usages of items for twenty-four hours and act as an ascetic (11) Posadhavrata -not to eat for twenty four hours and act as an ascetic (12) Athithisamvibhagvrata-desire to offer the water and food and any other required items to ascetics (13) Samlekhana-fast unto death.

Apart from above twelve vows, householder has to observe eleven pratimas - (1) Darsan 2) Vrata 3) Samayika 4) Prosadhopavasa 5) Schitta tyag-to leave the use of living things 6) Ratri bhojan tyag- not to eat after sunset 7) Celibacy 8) Aarambh tyag 9) Parigraha tyag 10) Anumati tyag 11) Uddista tyag and six aavasyaka-daily duties. Householder is to meditate upon four virtues such as (1) Maitri-friendship (2) Pramoda-delighted by seeing an advance person on the path of liberation (3) Karunya-compassion for others (4) Madhyasthaya-tolerance. The different Acarya have given different list for the above items looking to the present social conditions and interpretation of agamas.

One has to examine carefully the twelve vows to have good idea about Jain moral sense. Vow is practice or act. This practice is done about its nature and with intelligent decision. This practice is a positive act. When you say positive act, it means that you have to refrain from negative activities. One has to act continuously in positive ways.

Jain philosophy shows the three danger which comes in a way of moral (1) Maya salya–deceitful turn of mind. (2) Mithya salya–wrong belief (3) Ninda salya–a secret desire to get pleasure in present and future birth. The moral act should not be deceiving for one-self as well as for others. One has to make self-analysis. One has to keep in view the non-worldly possessiveness and be away from it. One should contemplate about this birth as transit and has to develop the sense of VAIRAGYA–the spirit of renunciation. One should follow the TEN dharmas–religious steps–prescribed earlier. One has to have a voluntary limit of the outwardly things. One specifies the limit of land, buildings, shop, factories, for one self. One limits ones' tangible and non-tangible assets for one self. One has limit of male and female servants, drivers, messengers, security guards etc. for one self. One limits the number of animals for agriculture or such other things and vehicles and other things. One limits the household things like T.V., fridge, washing machine, music system computers, decorative items, costly carpets, furniture for one self. Person should control his desires. The result of desire control will be as follows.[227]

(1) There is no poverty, but at the same time no luxurious life.

(2) Money is the instrument for need. Money is for man and man not for money.

(3) Person will fulfil his need with a view not to harm others.

(4) Person should decide limit of income.

(5) Person should think that money is useful. Person should be indifferent to excess money.

(6) Person should accept that virtue of money is to give satisfaction.

(7) You should develop a capacity to use money for good purpose.

Person does not require wealth to do certain things.[228]

(1) Accumulation of wealth is not necessary for the fulfilment of some human choices. In fact, individual and society make many choices that require no wealth at all.

(2) A society does not have to be rich to be able to afford democracy.

(3) A family does not have to be wealthy to respect the right of each member.

(4) A nation does not have to be affluent to treat women and men equally.

---

[227] Acarya Mahapragnya, Mahavir ka Arthsastra, Page no.111.
[228] Ibid, page no.196-197.

(5) Valuable social and cultural traditions can be-and are-maintained at all levels of income. The richness of a culture can be largely independent of the people's wealth.

(6) Human may want wealth, but at the same time, his quest for knowledge, long and healthy life, participate freely in community, clean environment and peace of mind, job, home and society.

(7) Wealth maximization and human development have definite co-relation. This will result into break down of too many societies.

(8) Many countries have high G.N.P. per capita BUT low human development indicators and Vis-a-Vis.

(9) Countries at similar level of G.N.P. per capita may have vastly different human development indicators depending on the use they have made of their national income.

10.4 Social And Economical Importance

Social and economical importance of spirit of non – possession

There are principles of ethics for universal. Aparigraha-Non-possession is also one of the ethics of Jaina religion. The ethics is not limited to some ascetic code of conduct or rule of scriptures. Lord Mahavir defined the 'greed' in UTTRADHYAYANA SUTRA as follows. "Where there is inner desire for material gain and possession of worldly objects of enjoyment, there is greed."[229]

According to UTTRADHYAYANA SUTRA," the root of all mental and physical suffering is the desire for worldly enjoyments".[230]

What person possess and consumes, gives him happiness. There is a link with accumulation and our restlessness. This thing is a hurdle in the way of our spiritual progress. Therefore Lord Mahavir told to apply discrimination of wants. Lord Mahavir told that one which is harmful to our body, mind and feeling should be avoided. Lord Mahavir told to control imaginary

---

[229] Edited: - Dhiraj Muni, Uttradhyayn Sutra, ch.8, stanza no.17, page no.45, free render.

[230] Ibid, ch.6, stanza no.6, page no.35, free render

need. Lord Mahavir gave golden equation. Limit of money =peace and happiness. [231]

In case of possession, it is unimportant but our mental attitude gives importance to possession is dangerous. This mental attitude is the real hurdle in our wish to give away attachment. Simplicity is a virtue. One should put simplicity in to practice. This should become a natural habit to be with oneself as being. When one follows simplicity faithfully than material abundance will lose both, its spirit and attraction.

Person violates the vow of Aparigraha by accepting and holding what is not needed by him. What one possesses in surplus has to go to those who need them badly. The principle of continence is significant in maintaining the morals in society.

Man's ego is short lived selfishness. Ego is limited to this life only. When you are selfish, you are open to temptation. Selfishness and temptation has harmed us like anything. Temptation had abolished our wish of self-sacrifice. Selfishness had abolished our motto of service to needy persons.

Ambition: - Economists say you increase your desire. This will give development and progress. Lord Mahavir put opposite of this-"LESS DESIRE".[232] The ambitious person will indulge in all types of unlawful activities. The person becomes lavish in his life style. The animal cruelty is for perfume, fur making and medicines. He will carry out all sorts of wrong things. He will go to the extent of killing. He will wage a war. There is a way to come out of this. Person should try to limit his ambition.

Minimum Desire: - Desire is like sky, limitless. The person lives with limited desire. This will give effect in all spheres of his life to start with capital. The capital will not be concentrated at one place. Gandhi was in favour of decentralization. The decentralized thing will come in to existence than the human will act with trusteeship idea.[233] The distribution of capital in society will bring evenness. Minimum desire will help to solve the ecological problem. The air, water will be less polluted. The forest will give rain and more pure air. It will have all round effect. This minimum desire person will walk with moral, fearful nature and more or

---

[231] Acarya Mahapragnya, Mahavir ka Arthsastra, page no.25.
[232] Ibid, page no.35.
[233] Ibid, page no.35.

less straightforward. The person will live the life with religious thought.

Formula of Limit: - Lord Mahavir gave formula of limit. Lord Mahavir put an idea of purity of means in earning and limits of personal consumption.[234] Lord Mahavir gave a list of items of consumption, which should be limited. Lord Mahavir gave the list of items of daily consumption also. Lord Mahavir advocated the limit of means of transport, jewellery, money and houses. This should be followed throughout the life. He suggested fourteen items for observance of limit in daily consumption. One should decide voluntarily how much to consume of each item daily. For example, Person decides to eat one grain, than either wheat or rice. Person limits the consumption of vegetables, fruits in the same way. Person can limit the use of water for bath, washing clothes and other things. This will help person as well as society. The list of items need not be fourteen but one can increase them as per his wish.

The best thing about Aparigraha-non-possession is, it is realistic, it is practical, and it is a rational principle. Aparigraha-Non-possession has a solid foundation in our social system. Lord Mahavir was great philosopher.

10.5 Welfare Philosophy of spirit of non-possession.

Thoughts of economists:-

One can define economy as follows. Person should manage his resources in such a way that, he can get maximum satisfaction out of it. Economist thought that more production is the cure for poverty. There is a social imbalance. One should take care of downtrodden and masses rather than a few selective people. Economist should not neglect entitlement of person like health, education and capability development. The negligence of these is equal to deprivation.

There is an advertisement slogan. "Neighbours envy owners pride". It is equally correct that one man's consumption is his neighbour wish. "Development" - "Progress" – "Growth" is some of the concepts of most modern economy. It is true but without human thought it is useless. Economist should think in moral way.

---

[234]   Ibid, page no. 39.

Change as law of nature

It is a law of nature to have constant change. The new becomes old and old becomes new. Human wants new things every day. The variety is necessary. This has resulted in the name of fashion. The fashion is wasteful expenditure. It creates ripple in class of people who cannot afford it. This will result into social unrest and it can go up to the any extent in relation to crime. One has to accept this as social unrest and outcome of economic growth. Waste is not acceptable in the name of economic growth. Waste or exhaust is the result of consumption. Here person's self-interest is of prime importance and social welfare becomes a secondary thing. One can say that economic progress is at the cost of social welfare progress.

Consumption

Consumption is necessary. The consumption has three stages. In first stages, you are curious to get thing. In second stage, after consumption you require to repeat the action. In third stage, it is impossible to get rid of consumption. This will form a habit. These three things make person to do anything. He will fulfil his wish of consumption at any cost. This gives birth of all types of activities like cheating and corruption, killing. Moral and human values do not come in the way.[235] The target is to fulfil unlimited desires, unlimited expectations and unlimited consumption. Look at the other side of the coin. The limited desire, expectation and consumption will make man happy. He gets his primary need easily. Person will not go to the extent of killing; cheating and corruption will bite his conscious. Religion is known best for the simplicity, contentment and self-control. The same has become a prey to philosophy of consumerism. The corruption at all level is the result of consumerism. The strong hold of religion is eroded.

Social evils

It is in the interest of human and for his future to limit his number of possessions. This will save waste full use of material. The possessed item should be of long lasting nature and to maintain them is important. As consequences of this, the total stock of material will last for longer period for the present population and for future generation. The limit of population growth, at any level, say national or global, will be like to see a star in the sky on sunny day. The population growth has to be minimized.

---

[235]   Ibid, page no.29.

Unlimited consumption is the symbol of modern culture. Unlimited consumption has given a mark effect on health, mind and conscious. Lord Mahavir studied human behaviour. Lord Mahavir suggested two types of desire (1) Minimum desire (2) No-Desire human. [236] Minimum desire people will create effect in all fields. Desire conquered person has no desire. He will be an ascetic. He has no activities and he will not start trade or industry.

Inequality:-

We have accepted inequality. This became a reality. We think that we cannot do anything for this evil. Inequality in limited sense is product meant for affluent people of society for few and same way employment for few in society. Here we deprive the larger employment opportunity. Social welfare economics is not in favour of this. The concept of human welfare pushed in to corner. It seems that economics has nothing to do with social service and social work-"welfare". Welfare being satisfaction, happiness - These words require today.

10.6 Environment And Spirit Of Non – Possession

Our ethics is to preserve the environment. The ecological balance is a prime thing of today's world. The two types of people are cruel to our environmental assets (1) A well to do people for their greed. (2) A penniless people due to their needs. This cruelty has become a burning issue. 'ICCHAPARIMANA'-limited desire is the only human solution for Non–possession. The voluntary control of wishes is the only remedy and it is voluntary socialism.

Consumerism is the cause of physical environmental degradation and social environmental too. Physical environment decrease day-by-day and social environment is scare. The sustainable development will protect the environment. This is the need of a day. Lord Mahavir had prescribed certain voluntary rules for environment for ascetics and house holders. Lord Mahavir has suggested making minimum use of water, air only for respiration for ascetics and for other purposes to householder. Fire, earth and plant usage totally prohibited to ascetics and with limit to householders.

---

[236]   Ibid, page no.51.

Ascetics are not doing any worldly activities and they do not have any thing which can create physical possessiveness to them. They should free from their mental possessiveness too such as praise, fame, to be known as scholar, known as knower of scriptures, known as great penance recorder. These are their mental possessiveness. They are not free from physical possessiveness such as to create a charitable trust and under the name of trust to build the temple and library, research centre, to start a school to teach old agamic language etc. Lord Mahavir gave three negative criteria for production. (1) You should not produce war machines (2) You should not assemble, collect, store war machine (3) You should not teach art or give education which increases sin and killing.[237] This includes the technology transfer. This is an effective tool to day for terrorism.

Lord Mahavir had given a list of trade and industries, which are very prohibitive for householders. The householders are not to act upon it. They are fifteen in numbers. (1) Smithy – small and big industry related to fire is prohibited (2) not to cut forest and trade of wood. (3) Cart, chariot, ship, motorcar etc. to manufacture and to trade is prohibitive (4) not to retain cart, horse, rickshaw, taxi, and to earn out of them by way of rent. (5) To excavate the earth for the purpose to build the dam, well, tank and large reservoir is prohibitive (6) not to trade in teeth, bone, horn, nail of animals (7) not to trade in sealing wax, colour, and wax made out of beehives or other insects (8) Not to trade in smooth hair of cows, which used in temple. (9) Not to trade in wine, meat, honey, butter, fat etc (10) Not to trade in poison, opium, insecticide and pesticide (11) Not to trade in machinery for sesame, groundnut, other oil seeds for oil producing, cotton for removing cottonseed and sugarcane to manufacture jaggery and sugar (12) Not to mutilate the bodies of human, animal and to create mark by making use of fire on body of human and animal, To make horse and ox from male to neutral gender (13) Not to put on fire in the field, forest and mountain (14) Not to empty the well, large reservoir, large portion of river (15) Not to maintain slave – male or female, animal and wild animal for earning for self maintenance.

These fifteen types of trade, business and industries will give you a heavy NIKACHIT type karma. This karma, one has to experience it. You cannot escape. Over and above, the householder has to observe the self-imposed voluntary limit for so many things in number of ways through

---

[237]   Ibid, page no.34.

out of the life. All twelve vows have transgression and you are supposed to observe vows and not to repeat mistake. You are supposed to perform PRATIKARAMAN- to come back from sins which were committed earlier. The practice of vratas will give you strength and will uplift your soul towards the emancipation. As human life is precious, like animal and plant life are also valuable. They should be preserved and protected. All outrageous usage is prohibitive such as limitless exploitation of natural foundation of life, ruthless destruction of the biosphere, and militarization of the cosmos. We are responsible to future generation for misuse of earth, cosmos, water, environment and air. The population is dependent on preservation of all these things. We must create harmony with nature.

Lord Mahavir era was of normal life. The people were very simple and religious minded. The main activities were agriculture and trade. The system of kingship and his administration was simple. The present day things might not exist in those days. The types of social, political and economical development may not be there. This reflects in the list of trade and industry, which were in primitive stage. The analysis of list of trade and industry shows that great care was taken for NATURE and its growth and preservation. The analysis further shows that the voluntary and minimum use to preserve the natural assets for present generation as well as for future generation. The all five element of NATURE, animal from one sense to five sense and human are in the centre. We have to take great care for not to harm or to kill them. The day-to-day menu of diet and activities mirrored the way of life of those people in those days. Lord Mahavir preached the above thing by way of ethics and moral. We should pay great homage to lord Mahavir by saying that HE WAS THE GREATEST ENVIRONMANTLIST OF HIS AGE.

Wishes V/s Requirements

Lord Mahavir said the wishes are infinite as limitless sky. Wish list is never ending. As per economy the demand is more than supply. One who has resources can fulfil his requirements. Demand is limited in comparison to requirements. Requirements are limited in comparison to wishes. Wishes are natural where as requirements are decided as per geographical condition, social custom, physical need, circumstances and religious sentiments. A requirement of poor person is limited. Rich has very big list. One who has decided to live with religious thought will have balance in his requirements. Lord Mahavir told that due to benefit, greed increases. As per Marshal-economist, the requirements and wishes of man are of numerous types. One desire is satisfied then another desire crops up. This is the law of progress. This is requirement but one has to look into the other side of it. Human will have pleasure and pain. This will affect his mental balance. In the light of this, it is necessary to limit the requirements. Religion thinks in terms of internal development and economics thinks in terms of external development. Therefore one has to apply the conscious limit of wish and requirement. It will be something like this.

Things	Use of the thing	not use of thing.
1) Necessary	you get little happiness.	You become sad.
2) Comfort	you get little more happiness.	Sadness will be less.
3) Luxury	you get much more happiness.	You will not become sad.

Man lives in social condition therefore he cannot totally leave the things but definitely he can apply the limit in his needs and requirements. Economics expressed in a sense of consumption. Consumption may be useful or may not be useful.

Impotence of Moral

Economics do not think in terms of human welfare. Moral laws are giving the ideals in life. Person, who breaks the moral laws, feels guilty. One, who follows the moral law, makes progress in spirituality. Honesty, straight forwardness is counted for efficiency. These are the moral things and economics had to take into account these things. At the same time economics also impress the moral laws. Therefore the control of desire is the ultimate solution. [238] The non possession is useful tool at every movement in the life. I think it is in the interest of mankind to follow the sense of control in life and have happiness.

---

[238] Ibid, page no.100 to 111.

11 CONCLUSION

Dr. Amartya Sen's thought of philosophy in economics

All though the comparative account of welfare economics of ancient thoughts of Jaina religion with the present day thinking of Dr.Amartya Sen, one can see a philosophical linking. Like Jaina religion, Dr.Amartya Sen also strives to go to the roots of the thoughts. Dr.Amartya Sen believes that the truth will take us to the roots of the cause and gives us better understanding. This is also applicable for development and welfare economics. This thought has no "normative" stamped but it becomes "Objective". In this approach Dr.Amartya Sen is truth conscious. In this quest, Dr.Amartya Sen presents the evaluation in Economic as thought. It is the magic of Dr.Amartya Sen to put philosophy on practical drawing board and practical thing incorporated into philosophy. Dr.Amartya Sen's approach is both subjective as well as objective. When Dr.Amartya Sen thinks about subject, he does not forget the object and vice-versa. Dr.Amartya Sen brings here the "OUGHT TO BE" point in economics. This is a real aspect of the living life too.

A lot of changes have taken place in economics after awakening of Europe and search of North America and other countries. The East was developed much earlier than these countries and knowledge spread from BHARAT to China in East and European countries through Arab countries in Middle East. Spain, France and England made race to conquer the other kingdom in other part of the world. England was winner in the race and established their kingdom. They pushed their education system along with science and economics. In this way, they made revolution in industry and applied the economics laws. They forget the MAN. Alford Marshal was an economist, who wrote and care for common man. The welfare thought got off from there to Dr.Amartya Sen in present day.

Within three hundred years, lot of changes has taken place. The capitalist Economy did not work in many areas. As a result, the socialist system and dictatorial system came into existence. The exploitation was the main theme. The labour supremacy was a popular thought for some time. Mixed

Economy of agriculture and industries came in lime light. This also does not prove successful in the field of economics. Again the capitalist economy was favoured with the idea of WELFARE in it. Any activity in economics is related to HUMAN. Therefore welfare of man which was forgotten had brought in by Dr.Amartya Sen through Philosophical route.

Welfare as Major point

The Moral practices of human and ethical way of social understanding are the ingredients of welfare of human. Dr.Amartya Sen was more impressed by Kautilaya's "Arthsastra"-an Indian economist of fourth century B.C. Kautilaya blended the economics and moral in the form of king's duty for the welfare of public. The thought of welfare economics came to the mind of Dr.Amartya Sen from the situation of high standard of living and lop sided richness of North America and Europe. Many countries of the Asia, Africa along with South America were reeling under poverty, illiteracy, poor health and malnutrition. Dr.Amartya Sen picked up the idea of Aristotle, "wealth is necessary to live the life but not beyond certain limit." Welfare in a philosophical term has accommodated in economics. Recently Justice and fairness is the criteria in welfare economics. It is a blend of economics, sociology, politics, and philosophy and psychology. The point of capability of human and its development by state is good mixture of human and state.

Dr.Amartya Sen gave another criteria that when all or majority of people are thinking the policy measure about the happiness of poorest person, in such case they will forgo individual happiness in interest of poorest person. This is useful in distribution of national income. This type of thinking helps us to depart from the problem of conflict and problem of assessment in society. Democracy gives right to people to form the forum and ask government about its working by way of opposition, using electronic and press media with effective use of the right of freedom of speech and right to information. The political will and understanding is most important to increase the welfare of people in democratic process.

Dr. Amartya Sen tried to find out the answer for welfare of man from the present economics. He took the help of epistemology and philosophy.

He started thinking on Socrates line. He had abstract idea of "what ought to be" and tried to find the answer. Ought to be is an institutional type approach. The economics was standing on scientific base. Dr. Amartya Sen converted it in to rational of social and philosophical event. Ought to be should be the heart of economics for welfare. Dr. Amartya Sen brought the ethics and moral via theory of justice and fairness. The Rawls theory of justice and fairness may work in certain area.

Dr. Amartya Sen is of the opinion that in politics, tolerance is important element for equality and justice. Social circumstances are far more important for political justice. Political considerations are important for justice and fairness. Unity will be costly affairs in politics. Dr. Amartya Sen approves the "PARETO OPTIMAL" for individual. Welfare economics is to increase the welfare of public. The philosophy in welfare economics by way of collective choice reflects in the caution that the personal choice may be wrong, as it is guided by mental position and social, economical situation. Dr. Amartya Sen believes that the choice association with internal behaviour of person is not enough for logical conclusion.

Maximization of personal interest is logical. At the same time the other than personal interest maximization is also not logical, is not correct. Dr. Amartya Sen combines the selfishness and non-selfishness and it gives a specific area in choice function. Person can sacrifice his little self interest in benefit of larger people say- society. This is a new thought in economics. Dr. Amartya Sen raised the question of public choice and collective choice. Collective choice is the reflection of public choice. The collective choice concept had dead end in terms of Kenneth Arrows "Impossibility theorem". Dr. Amartya Sen gave solution that unless and until you do not provide information; it will remain as it is. The information is most important in welfare economics.

The sum of utility can be considered as the degree of social welfare. The social choice is based on more information regarding individual attitude and social alternatives. The economist had firm view that human, with keeping in view the economic situation, individual is taking the decision rationally. Dr.Amartya Sen surprised over such a situation. In case of individual, it is a mistake that the person will always act rational.

The rational fool is the best example of it. According to Dr.Amartya Sen, human is making the preference and not final choice. This choice is not necessarily reflect his welfare.

The moral and right attitude cultivated in individual, will influence the collective social scale in course of time. "Pure" system of collective choice is well known but limited with impurities. The "impure" elements may be more practical and useful to institution. Dr.Amartya Sen knew that social development is necessary with freedom as development. Therefore Dr.Amartya Sen give emphasis on education, medical help and entitlement, to remove poverty from society, with the globalization of the economy of the country. The public policy of democratic government is extremely important for welfare of public. The considerable significance stays in human nature for philanthropy, sacrifice and donation. A thing of sacred or beautiful is valued in market terms. The theory of market mechanism has no place for love, respect, pity, beauty, compassion for nature or human.

Dr.Amartya Sen believes in equality of men and women and wrote on many problems for women; to start with mal-nutrition, dignity in family, independent economic development of women, missing women and equal opportunity for them in society. The atrocity on women and sub human condition of women in many places of world is the matter of disrespect for women of the world.

Dr.Amartya Sen said that every individual is not that selfish who do not think about the other person's welfare. Human is happy with the object in mind for other's happiness. This is the philosophy which is the inbuilt part of every human and Indian culture. This is important quality of human being. The Indian culture says "when you are hungry and eat that is the 'nature', when you are not hungry though eat, it is 'defect' and when you are hungry and the hungry guest comes, you give your food to your guest to eat, is the 'culture'."

Dr.Amartya Sen has given a new definition of development. The new definition is the full use of capability of a person. The capability depends on the entitlements. The capability is the sums total of natural, social, political, anthropological, cultural, and legal and other matters in human. The Human is in centre. The price and market mechanism proved wrong in case of entitlements. Entitlements are available to a person by way of legal, hereditary, ownership, exchange and own labour cum partnership. This requires the support of society. The democratic government working should be run by majority and in total interest of welfare of people. Liberty is personal aspect and freedom is social aspect. The income and resources are linked to freedom ultimately. Equality requires freedom to chose anything In terms of optional or selection way. Poverty is a black spot on the character of any nation.

Dr. Amartya Sen talk about truth and consciousness. The eastern philosophy is expressive in terms of truth, peace, consciousness, coexistence and distinction between body and soul. The people of east are not blind runner behind materialistic life. They have noble virtue of tolerance, mercy, co-operation, love and selfless service to fellow human. This type of thinking and working coincide in their day to day life. There is less space for zealous, cheating, hurt feeling and ego. The western philosophers have brought out these noble virtues in their writing in past and in present. The exploitation, false statement as cunning factor, along with too much importance to body is some of the prime points in every culture. The human nature is as such that it gets changed from good to bad and bad to good. The eastern philosopher are thinking not only in terms of human on the earth but had linked themselves with cosmos and thought for welfare of universe. They make no distinction in terms of human and animal or human and other elements in the universe. The concept in economic is for the life spans i.e. one day life to hundred year life. Here the thought for after death does not count or life before birth is not considered. The only individual and its independent existence are considered. The animals and plants life are considered as dependant to human. The care, safety or health problems of animals and plants are not given any importance. The care, safety or health problems of animals and plants are considered only as for hobby and as a wealth of a person, family or nation.

Dr. Amartya Sen has discussed the main theme of welfare via philosophy in economics. It is difficult that to presume that the person will act in the same way. At the same time man is intelligent. Man will mixed many things and result may be opposite than desired. In such circumstances, the thought of Dr. Amartya Sen may not bring the desired result. Say the problem of poverty or capability development. The Famine is rare occasion but the starvation in term of mal nourishment and undernourishment much depends on government policy, administrative directive. The administrative machinery may work against the very aim and objectives, as the human has uncontrolled wish for wealth. It is good in policy but implementation of it is a tuff job. This requires a general consciousness about the fair intention of all and at all level.

Jain Religion and Human Welfare

In Sanskrit- religion means DHARMA. The word religion has very deep and broad meaning. The men can have self development on spirituality and to be successful in worldly affairs. Here religion regulates activity of man and evaluate him to have ultimate motto of selfless services. Religions of India are having clear distinction about soul and body. They talk about past birth and rebirth for future with a view to ultimately get out of cycle of birth and death. Other Semitic religion does not think in this term which is the prime difference.

Human being belongs to very selfish breed. The constituents of human are body and soul. Here human does not wish to recognize the two different aspects such as BODY and SOUL. One can say that body is a golden cage and soul is as parrot living in it. Parrot loves to fly free in sky but at the same time loves the golden cage to live in. Human entangles in karma-activity and dose all right and wrong things. He develops selfishness and collects all types of items in his list. The Anger, Ego, and cunning nature with pride become his permanent friends. The world does take note of SOUL. When soul left the body, the human is declared as dead. Indian philosophy has considered the SOUL and its uplift. The spiritual development depends on non-killing, truth, celibacy and non-stealing. These are universal principles. The final goal of soul is to get rid of the cycle of birth and death. Soul can have eternal peace. Here all the activities will come to rest.

According to Plato, an indestructible soul substance is inherently immortal[239]. Kant refers self to as the transcendental self[240].

---

[239]   S.Radhakrishnan,, An idealist view of man, page no.211
[240]   Ibid, page no.215

The philosophy of Lord Mahavir was accepted as a religion. It is a Jain religion. The definition of Jain is who has conquered the desire arising out of five senses and effects originate in of psychological region of human. Here man has to reduce his wants and make progress towards the non-possessiveness. Lord Mahavir was of the opinion that human should follow the morality and to save himself from deceit and take in to account the equality and many-sidedness of an object. This is to be experienced. Jain religion believes in "PARASPAROPAGRAHO JIVANAM"[241] interdependence of living beings. Jain religion believes in "LIVE AND LET LIVE" policy. We should take into account the effect of social and human destruction for environment. Jain religion believes in to remove disparity in any sense from the society and embraces every human being without distinctions of caste and creed, inferiority or superiority. This is real universal brotherhood. Jain religion thinks for the happiness of all.

In Jain religion, the welfare is for the people. Jain religion had two clear thoughts. One should accept house, world and follow religion. House holder is having welfare in material and spiritual term. House holder has to follow the vows to keep him in main stream of religion. Householder has to purify his mental condition and observe rules for physical and vocal act. House holder has to perform the duties with moral and ethics to make progress on the path of emancipation of his/her soul. House holder continues his journey in this birth and in coming births to get emancipation. Lord Mahavir got emancipation of his soul in 22nd life. House- holder and ascetics have to follow Ahimsa thoroughly in life. Both have to observe the rule of karma and to follow non-possessions partially for house holder and wholly for ascetic. Second step is to leave the worldly affairs and become ascetic. Ascetic has welfare in spiritual term. Live the life with intention of emancipation of soul. Soul is only the eternal substance.

The six types of living being killing is the greatest sin. This attracts heavy karmic matter result into bad effect. The killing is considered as a cause of having birth in infernal or animal states.

Jain religion is in favour of higher income, building of assets and capital. The individual decides limit and extra income is used for religious and social purposes. There are number of ways described under the heading of donation.

---

[241]   Commentary: - Pandit Sukhlalji on book Tattvarthasutradhigam of Umaswatiji, ch.5, stanza no.21, Sanskrit text page no.15

Jain philanthropic activities are open for all caste and creed in hospital sector, subsidized help for food, education etc. At the same time Jain religion prescribes the limit by way of observing vows. Jain philosophy has described certain prohibitions. The use of everything should be up to your own requirement is the right meaning of non-possessiveness. This helps to protect the environment and teaches every individual how to behave with nature, animal kingdom and all other suksma-no visible elements on this earth.

The four multiplicative vows are for psychological position. Soul is in check, for making all good and bad psychological acts and control on them. This keeps soul in process of purification and attains higher and higher stage in spirituality. Body is material which gets destroyed. The man should not engross in the body and its activities.

Soul is in check, for making all good and bad psychological acts and to control them. This keeps soul in process of purification and attains higher and higher stage in spirituality and ultimately the nirvana-liberation.

Lastly, the Householder wishes to have a peaceful death by leaving all material and mental desires by way of looking in to the soul and get engrossed into the soul known as Samlekhana vow. The soul is permanent and material is impermanent. The Moksa-emancipation will give freedom to soul from rebirth and makes soul free forever. The Soul gets keval jnana known as siddahood. This belief is the most important spiritual position in Jain religion.

In Jain religion the non-killing is the mother of all sources of religious principle and practices. The Karma is the working force behind the man and anekantvada is the position to bring the peace in society. The non-possessiveness is applicable to Jain community with certain restrictions. The better thought will be of the trusteeship. The superior thought of Lord Mahavir is to have voluntary control on desire, wish, consumption, possession with a thought in mind to spare something for fellow human.

Economics and religion are complementary

Welfare in economics is important at its own place and religious welfare of human is at its own place. Religion do take into account the day to day economic activities and guide to human about the right and wrong thing by way of moral and ethics. Religion shows the pitfall in the life and suggests travelling in the proper direction to achieve spirituality and to hear the voice of soul. Jain religion believes in the Moksa-emancipation of soul as last wish of human being. Economic welfare is important to eradicate the hunger, to forecast the famine, to adopt proper measure for prevention of famine, to develop the capability of human and give him the freedom. Here the freedom is defined as a free will, free approach and free to do the things for ones' own betterment. If man answers to his/her spiritual call then all problems will be solved. A change in the outlook of human is more urgent than the scientific and technological developments for revival of love and reverence for life.

Welfare economics and Jain religion, both are in favour of liberty for people. Economics gives liberty for development of capability of man. Religion gives liberty to choose the way of life. Welfare economics is in favour of justice for all in the distribution of national income, political and administrative transparency in working. Religion gives justice in terms of bad and good rules of moral and ethics. The transgression of vow is a matter of justice. Welfare economics is in favour of equality in terms of opportunity, employment, capability development, away from deprivation and women welfare in all respect. Dr. Amartya Sen has given an idea of BASAL equality. Religion always favours equality in terms of gender and religious practice. In Jain religion the women ascetics are considered as lower level than counterpart- male ascetics. They are not allowed to study some specific Agamas and have to bow down a newly male ascetic irrespective of age, knowledge and other things. In case of house holder there are some differences in case of male and female but as far as children are concerned, they get equal treatment for everything till their marriages. Ladies are voluntarily accepting low status as per tradition or customs but have full say in family and social affairs. In welfare economics, fraternity is in down trodden people and is given full support by political parties and government as minority. There are special programmes for health, employment and distribution of national help of various kinds. In Jain religion, all are equal as far as religious practices and benefits are concerned. Normally economics and religion does not make any compartment for human being.

Dr. Amartya Sen is the authority on the subject of welfare economics and Jain sacred books are without fault as it is the preaching of Lord Mahavir which is considered as "APTA VACHAN". The study is not to degrade one in the eyes of another but it gives a choice to human which one to accept.

The efforts for the achievement of goal may by easy or difficult. Again this is one's own choice and thinking. This does not prove the superiority or inferiority of one over another.

We have to accept certain basic things in this universe for Economics and Religion. Broadly they are as follows.

There is heterogeneity in the universe.

There are different religions.

The human psychology is complex.

The education of people differs.

When we examine anything in light of man, it will be difficult to have proper analysis and finding will be diverse and may be of opposite nature due to above factors.

As far as economics is concerned, welfare of man is on top priority. Looking to above basic things one can say that it is good as model and achievement as target but the psychology of man will give different result. Human psychology changes every movement and good will be bad and bad may be good or worst. The person on opposite side also reacts in the same manner. The uniformity is the most difficult aspects. Any ruling government in any country will not be able to put into practice the concept of well being in full fledge manner. One can recommend and emphasize as a concept and harp on the subject, time and again, as and when opportunity comes. There are hardly one or two countries in the world that have achieved full target of wellbeing. Again, in those countries person is known by number only. How far they can become a role model to world is a matter of concern.

Same situation is for religion. But one can recommend HUMAN RELIGION and insists on some basic things. The evaluation of man is meant for ultimate good for human race and it is important that it is fulfilled in all respects. I feel that everyone should be tolerant for each other. One should control the anger and greed. One should allow having development of one's' capability and having entitlement and freedom. The co-operative efforts of each person for each other should be the motto. Political interference should be minimal. Man should be aware of his aspiration and wellbeing. The combining effect will work, more or less, major extent and man will make progress in his life.

In this writing, the mistake and misunderstanding are mine. The brilliant readers will pardon me for my sort coming.

BIBLIOGRAPHY

❖ Ajit Kumar Sinha and Rajkumar Sen, Economics of Amartya Sen, Deep and Deep Publication, India 2003

❖ Alex Callinicon, Marxist Theory, Oxford University Press, Oxford1989

❖ Amartya Sen

- The Argumentative Indian, Penguin Books, London2005

- Choice, Welfare and Measurement, Oxford University press New Delhi

- Collective choice and Social welfare, Holden-Day inc., 1970

- Development as freedom, Oxford University Press, New Delhi2001

- Development thinking at the beginning of the 21st century, London school of economics and political science, 1997

- Inequality Re-examined, Russell Sage Foundation- New York 1992

- Level of Poverty - Policy and Change, World Bank, Washington, D.C. 1980

- On Ethics and Economics, Basil Back well, Oxford and New york1987

- Poverty and Famines, Oxford University press New Delhi, 1999 paper edition

- Rationality and freedom, The Belk nap Press of Harvard University press, Cambridge year 2002.

- Resource, Value and Development, Oxford university press, new delhi1985

❖ Amartya Sen and Bernard Williams, Utilitarianism and beyond, Cambridge University press1982

❖ .Andre Beteille, The idea of natural inequality and other essays, Oxford press, India1987 2nd Edition

❖ Arunvijayji Maharaj, Karma tani gati nyari - part 1 and 2, Shree Mahavir Research Foundation, Pune, 1999 3rd. Edition

❖ Bimal Krishna Matilal. Edited by Dalsukh Malvania and Nagin J. Shah, The central philosophy of Jainism (Anekantvada) L.D.Institute of Indology, Ahmedabad1981

❖ Christopher W. Gowans, Moral Disagreement- classic and contemporary reading, Routledge London2000, 1st edition

❖ Dalsukh Malvania, Sthananag sutra, Gujarat Vidhyapith, April 1955

❖ D.D.Raphael and A.L.Mocfic, The theory of moral sentiments, Clarendon press, oxford1976

❖ Dhiraj Muni, Uttraadhyayana Sutra (Gujarati,) Vitrag Prakashan, Mumbai2003

❖ Debraj Ray, Development Economics, Oxford University Press, 1998

❖ Devbhadra Acarya,Shri Parswnath charitra, Translated in Gujarati, Shree Jain Atmanand Sabha, Bhavnagar, Year 2005.

❖ Frank Hann and Martin Hollis, Philosophy and Economic theory, Oxford University Press, Oxford1979

❖ Hansvijayaji Muniraj Shri, mahavir charitra, Shri Jain Atmanand Sabha, Bhavnagar1938

❖ Hari Satya Bhattacharya, Jain Moral Doctrine, Jain Sahitya Vikas Mandal, Mumbai1976 1St. Edition

- I.M.D.Littel, A critique of welfare economics, Oxford university press New Delhi1956 2nd Edition

- Jagdishchandra Jain, Jain Agam Sahutya me Bharatiya Samaja, Chowkhamba Vidhabhavan Varanasi1965

- Jean Dreze and Dr.Amarty Sen, India, Economic development and social opportunity Oxford University press, new york1999

- Jin Vijayji Muni shri and Rashiklal C.Parikh, Sanmati Tarka. Shri Jain Shwetambar education board, Mumbai1939   1st edition

- J.K.Galbrailth,The Affluent Society, India Book co. New Delhi. 1976

- J.K.Galbrailth, Economic Development, Cambridge press1969

- John Rawls, A Theory of Justice, Oxford University press1973

- Joseph C. Pitt, Philosophy in Economics, Dordrecht, D.Reidel Publishing Co.   1981

- Kailash Chand Jain, Lord mahavir and His Time, Motilal Banarsidas Delhi 1991

- Kamla Jain, Aparigraha- the Human solution, Parswnath Vidyapitha ,Varansi 1998 1st Edition

- K.K. Dixit Jain Ontology L.D.Institute of Indology, Ahmedabad1971,1st Edition

- Kanak Nandiji Maharaja, Philosophical and scientific analysis of karma, Dharma Darshan Vigyan Sodh Prakashan1990 1st Edition

- Kantilal J. Gandhi and Jasvantlal S. Shah, Shri Bruhad Jain Thok Sangrah (Gujarati) Sudharma Prachar Mandal, Mumbai1988 2nd Edition

- Kenneth J. Arrow, Social choice and Individual value, John Wiley and sons, New York1951 1st edition

- Kenneth J.Arrow and Tibor Scituvsky, Introduction-Reading in Welfare Economics, George Allen and Unwin Ltd., 1969

❖ K.Satischandra Murti, Saddarshan samuchaya, Eastern Book Linkers, New Delhi1986 2nd Edition

❖ L.M.Singhvi, A tale of three cities, Cambridge University press,1996

❖ Mahapragnya Acarya, Mahavir ka Arthsastra, Adarsh Sahitya Sangh Prakashana1994

❖ Mishrimalji Maharaj, Upasakadasanga Sutra, Hindi, Shri Agam prakashan simiti, Bewar, 1980

❖ Nagin J.Shah, Jaina philosophy and religion, Jointly published by Motilal Banarsidas publishers pvt,ltd. And B.L.institute of indology, Delhi, Edition 2000

❖ Nagrajji Muni shri, Agam and Tripitak-Ek Anushilan Etihas Aur Parampara, Jain Swatambar Terapanthi Mahasabha,1969

❖ N.P.Jain, Ahimsa-The ultimate winner, Prakrit Bharati Academy, Jaipur, 2004 2nd Edition

❖ Nathmal Tatia, Studies in Jain Philosophy, Jain Cultural Research Society Banaras1951

❖ Ram Mohan Das and Nagin J.Shah, A stroll in Jainism, Kaveri Books, New Delhi2002

❖ R.M.Hare, Essays in ethical theory, Clarendon press, oxford1989

❖ R.N.Ghose and others, Economic Development and change-South Asia and third world, New Age international,1996

❖ Rashiklal Shantilal Mehta, Saptika Karma Granth, Atmashreya Charitable Trust,Mumbai Vikram Samvat 2056 1st Edition.

❖ S.Gopalan, Jainism as a metaphilosophy, Sri Satguru Publication- New Delhi, 1991

❖ S. Radhakrishnan, an Idealist view of life, Unwin Books, London, 1961

❖ S. Radhakrishnan, Indian Philosophy- Vol.1, Macmillan-New York, 1951

❖ S.Radhakrishnan and P.T.Raju, The concept of Man, George Allen and Unwin Ltd., 1960

❖ Sadhviji Ramgunashreeji, Written by Acarya Devendrasuriswar maharaj, edited Book: - Karma Granth - part 1 to 6, Sri Omkar Sahitya Nidhi, 1997 1st Edition

❖ Karma Vipak, Part 1, Publisher: - Jashwantpura swetambar Murtipujak Jainsangh, Jasvantpura, Year Vikram Samvat 2056.

❖ Sadhviji Ramgunashreeji, Written by Acarya Devendrasuriswar maharaj, edited, Book: - Pancham Karma Granth, Juna Desa Murtipujak sangh, 2002 1st Edition

❖ Sangave Vilas A., Facts of Jainology, Popular Prakashan Pvt.Ltd. New Delhi2001 1st Edition

❖ Satischandra Chatterjee and Dhirendramohan Datta, an Introduction to Indian Philosophy, University of Calcutta, 1984 8th Edition.

❖ Satkari Moorkerjee, The Jaina Philosophy of non-absolutism- a critical study of Anekantvada, Motilal Banarsidas, Delhi1978 2nd Edition

❖ Shreyansh vijayaji maharaj, Shri Parswnath charitra, Shree Bhavanipur Swetambar murti pujak sangh, Calcutta, 1985 2nd Edition

❖ Sukhlalji Pandit, Tattvarthsutra of vacaca Umasvati, L.D.Institute of Indology, Ahmedabad2000, 2nd edition

❖ Surendra Bothara Ahimsa-the science of peace Prakrit Bharati Academy, Jaipur2004

❖ Tara Sethia, Ahimsa,Anekant and Jainism, Motilal Banarsidas, Delhi2004

❖ Acharya Tulshi and complied by Muni Nathmal, Aairo, Jain Vishva Bharti, Ladanun1974   1st edition

❖ Yugbhusanvijayaji Ganivarya, Karmavada karnika, Gitrath Ganga, Ahmedbad2001 3rd Edition